D1499092

AN INTRODUCTION TO FORMAL PROGRAM VERIFICATION

Ali Mili
Laval University

VNR VAN NOSTRAND REINHOLD COMPANY
———————— *New York* ————————

Manufactured in the United States of America

Published by Van Nostrand Reinhold Company Inc.
135 West 50th Street
New York, New York 10020

Van Nostrand Reinhold Company Limited
Molly Millars Lane
Wokingham, Berkshire RG11 2PY, England

Van Nostrand Reinhold
480 Latrobe Street
Melbourne, Victoria 3000, Australia

Macmillan of Canada
Division of Gage Publishing Limited
164 Commander Boulevard
Agincourt, Ontario M1S 3C7, Canada

15 14 13 12 11 10 9 8 7 6 5 4 3 2 1

Library of Congress Cataloging in Publication Data

Mili, Ali.
   An introduction to formal program verification.

   Includes index.
   1. Computer programs—Verification.   I. Title.
QA76.6.M5217   1984   001.64′2   84-3528
ISBN 0-442-26322-8

To my first instructors,
Aicha and Taieb

Acknowledgments

Even though this book has only one name on its authors' list, many persons have contributed to the best parts of it and influenced its development in many favorable ways.

I am indebted to my students at Texas A&M University, McGill University and Laval University who have been the major motivation for writing this book and have contributed a great deal of positive feedback to its earlier versions. I am also indebted to my colleagues Dr Homer Carlisle (Texas A&M), Dr Marcel Dupras (Laval), Dr Donald Friesen (Texas A&M) and Dr William Hatcher (Laval), and my students Chung-Ping Chung (Texas A&M) and Donna Reese (Texas A&M) for reviewing earlier drafts of this book and commenting on them.

Dr David Gries (Cornell University) read an earlier draft of this book and provided me with a thorough and constructive evaluation of its form as well as its content; this evaluation has helped me a great deal in rethinking and rewriting the current version.

A course I took at the Eastern Institute in Computer Science in June 1982 on teaching programming has helped me shape some of the ideas presented in this book. I gratefully acknowledge the favorable influence of the instructors of the course, Dr Victor Basili (University of Maryland), Dr Nancy Martin (Wang Institute) and Dr Harlan Mills (IBM).

My colleague Dr Stephen Whitney (Mathematics Department, Laval University) and my student Jules Desharnais (Computer Science Department, Laval University) have read the entire manuscript many times over, checking it for English as well as mathematical content, and making numerous improvements. They have contributed a great deal to the readability of the book by simplifying many proofs and improving the English. It is my pleasure to acknowledge their help and thank them.

Madame Nicole Lacroix helped me type and edit this book on the equipment of Laval University. I wish to thank her for her kind cooperation.

Despite all the help I got, there may still be room for improvement: I will gratefully accept any suggestions, comments or constructive criticisms the reader may have on the book.

Preface

Programmer X is trying to write a computer program. He cannot explain precisely what function his program is computing or what function he wants it to compute, but he is writing it anyway. His outer loop tests for a variable b being non-zero ($b \neq 0$) but he cannot tell whether testing for b greater than zero ($b > 0$) would work as well for his purposes; in fact he is not quite sure ($b \neq 0$) is the right condition to test for (perhaps $b > 0$ is).

In the loop body of the outer loop is a **while** statement using a variable t; variable t is initialized before the outer loop, though the programmer suspects he could also initialize it in the loop body, before the inner **while** statement. The index i of the inner **while** statement is initialized to 2 but the programmer suspects that, in order to take into account boundary values, he must set it to 1 and change the loop condition and the loop body accordingly. Since he is not sure, he has chosen to try it as is on non-boundary values then eventually change it to make it work for boundary values.

Inside the inner loop is a statement $t := a/c$; variable c is supposed to be non-zero before execution of this statement, but the programmer cannot tell you why; using a **goto** statement he has made sure that whenever c is zero, the control jumps outside both loops and sends an error message. The test of the inner loop is ($i \leq n$), where n is the size of an array; the programmer suspects that, in order to take into account the boundary condition $n = 1$ he should test for ($i < n$) and move the incrementation $i := i + 1$ inside the loop body; realizing that by doing so he causes an array reference out of bounds, the programmer has fixed the problem by merely increasing the size of the array by 1.

Now the program behaves reasonably well for the test values that the programmer has submitted to it; but the programmer can convince nobody (not even himself, in fact) of the worth of his program.

The situation just described is typical of a programmer who lacks the background needed for a firm intellectual control of the programming process. This background is not gained through an extensive practical experience of programming (generally, programming experience is not thought of as being cumulative); rather it is gained through the formal study of the mathematical processes underlying the programming process. Before one can undertake this endeavor, one must come to terms with two simple premises we accept as facts:

— First, the premise that programs are mathematical objects about which assertions can be made and proven, and that programming is essentially a mathematical discipline. Indeed, computers do not behave randomly; rather, they behave in predictable, predefined ways. Advances in the semantic definition of programming languages afford us the means to capture the behavior of computers in ways that are both rigorous and usable.

— Second, the premise that it is through a consistent and disciplined use of the mathematics of programming that one can gain the necessary latitude to intellectually manage the programming process. Applying mathematical formalisms to every statement, for every functional aspect is neither practical nor necessary; it is however necessary to understand the precise mechanics of the programming process and the precise semantics of each statement one writes, and be ready to use this understanding.

In this book, I have tried to collect a number of program verification methods and present them, as much as possible, with a common set of assumptions, notations and concerns. These methods can be seen both as complementary and as alternatives. Because each deals with one aspect of program complexity, each is more appropriate than the others for a *specific* class of programs, and this in a manner depending on where the burden of the complexity lies within the program. From this standpoint they can be seen as alternatives. On the other hand, because they give different perspectives on programs and their executions, they can be seen as complementary.

Even though it is derived from course notes I have developed for a university course, this book is meant to be of interest both to university students and to practicing programmers. Having used manuscripts of this book to teach short courses to practicing programmers, I have been repeatedly surprised by the positive response of participants, who seem to find the material relevant to their concerns. Whatever the reader's background may be, the author hopes this book will help him shape (or reshape) his view of programming for the better.

ALI MILI

Introduction

This is an outgrowth of notes I have prepared for courses I have offered in formal program verification at Texas A&M University in College Station and later, concurrently at McGill University in Montreal and Laval University (francophone) in Quebec City. Even though it has some similarities with CS14—Software Design and Development—and CS20—Formal Methods in Programming Languages—in the ACM-recommended curriculum (see: Recommendations for Master's Level Programs in Computer Science, *CACM* 24(3), March 1981), this course was most often taught as a graduate level Special Topics Course. Its prerequisites are fairly modest: at least one semester of programming, using preferably a Pascal-like programming language; and a semester of discrete mathematics, as covered, e.g. by C L Liu's *Elements of Discrete Mathematics*.

This book is based on the content developed for a fifteen-week course. Hence many topics are not covered even though they are both intrinsically interesting and quite relevant to program verification. These are, e.g.: specifying and verifying properties of data structures; verifying parallel programs; specifying and verifying cyclic programs; modal and temporal logic; program transformations; dynamic logic; weakest preconditions and guarded commands. These are available in the literature and in advanced texts (see bibliographic references).

In contrast with some earlier works on the subject, this book favors using functions and relations rather than predicates to explain program correctness. Also, no effort is made in the book to show how powerful program verification is; i.e. we seldom prove the correctness of large programs. Rather, the book concentrates on showing what program verification *is*. This choice of priorities is motivated by practical concerns (to improve the readability of the book), and to some extent by its introductory nature.

The book is made up of five parts. Part I contains Chapters 1, 2 and 3 and lays the background for the remainder of the book. Chapter 1 provides some motivation for program verification and presents the global perspective of the book. Chapter 2 presents some elements of discrete mathematics. Because most of the material introduced is presumed known by the reader, more emphasis is placed on naming conventions and notational conventions than on the material itself. Chapter 3 presents elements of logical expression and logical reasoning.

Part II contains Chapters 4, 5 and 6 and presents the basic formulas of program correctness. Chapter 4 gives the mathematical definition of a specification, Chapter 5 gives the mathematical definition of a program and Chapter 6 deduces the formulas of correctness of a program with respect to a specification and introduces the symbolic execution method.

Part III contains Chapters 7 through 11 and presents inductive methods for the proof of programs. A program is a multi-dimensional entity, with many axes of complexity; each verification method is concerned with one particular axis. Chapter 7 proves the correctness of programs by induction on their control structure and Chapter 8 uses induction on their data structure. Chapter 9 proceeds by induction on the length of execution whereas Chapter 10 proceeds by induction on the trace of execution. Finally, Chapter 11 discusses the semantics of recursive programs for which two inductive proof methods are presented.

Part IV contains Chapter 12, 13 and 14 and addresses the logical conclusion of program verification: program design. Chapters 12, 13 and 14 present models of program design on the basis of (respectively): predicate decomposition, functional decomposition and relational decomposition. They differ solely by how they represent specifications.

Part V presents three appendices. Appendix A is a BNF description of the programming language adopted in this book: SM-Pascal (standing for simple Pascal). Appendix B and Appendix C give some results on while statements which are intended to give the reader some more insight into the richness of iteration.

Each chapter has its own bibliography and practice set of problems, which are an extension of the course material, and each chapter is divided into sections. Each section has its own set of exercises, which are applications of the course material. Problems and exercises are labelled depending on their difficulty: A is easy, B is medium and C is difficult. For some short chapters, a single set of exercises is given at the end of the chapter, along with the set of problems.

The words *he, his* and *him* are used to denote a person of either sex.

Notations

lub	least upper bound.
iff	if and only if.
wrt	with respect to.
:	belongs to.
$\subseteq$	is a subset of.
$\subset$	is a proper subset of.
$\neq$	is different from.
$\leqslant$	is less than or equal.
$\geqslant$	is greater than or equal.
S|t	the subset of S for which predicate t holds.
:A	the predicate true for elements of A and false for all others.
$\times$	cartesian product of sets.
$\times\times$	cartesian power of sets.
*	numerical product, or relative product of relations (context distinguishes).
**	numerical power, or relative power of relations (context distinguishes).
$\wedge$	logical conjunction ("and").
$\vee$	logical disjunction ("or").
$\sim$	logical negation ("not").
$\Rightarrow$	logical consequence ("implies").
$=$	logical equivalence ("is equivalent to").
$\forall$	for all.
$\exists$	there exists.
$\bullet$	composition of expressions.
ite	alternative expression.
it	conditional expression.
def	domain of definition of an expression.
$+$	binary: addition.

@	unary: transitive closure.
—	difference.
∪	union.
∩	intersection.
F	full relation.
I	identity relation.
Eq	equivalence class.
f^{-1}	inverse of f.
R^t	transpose of R.
L*(S)	lists on space S.
(i → j)	path from i to j.
[i → j]	path function.
PD	Predicate Decomposition.
FD	Functional Decomposition.
RD	Relational Decomposition.

Contents

Part I: Motivation and Background

> It is reasonable to hope that the relationship between Computation and Mathematical Logic will be as fruitful in the next century as that between Analysis and Physics in the last. The development of this relationship demands a concern for both applications and for mathematical elegance.
>
> *John McCarthy, 1963.*

Chapter 1 provides some motivation for the verification of programs and presents the perspective and tone of this book. Chapter 2 introduces some elements of discrete mathematics. Chapter 3 presents elements of logical expression (propositions, predicates) and reasoning (induction and deduction).

Chapter 1

Motivation and Perspective

The purpose of this chapter is to highlight the mathematical nature of programs then discuss the perspective of this book with respect to the use of mathematics in program verification.

1 On the Richness of Programs

In this section we use a simple example to show how potentially rich (complex) programs are. We consider the following two programs on integer variables a, b and p:

$$M = (\textbf{while } b \neq 0 \textbf{ do begin } p := p+a; \ b := b-1 \textbf{ end}).$$
$$M' = (\textbf{while } b > 0 \textbf{ do begin } p := p+a; \ b := b-1 \textbf{ end}).$$

We wish to discuss the following questions:

a) Prove that if $(a = a0 \ \wedge \ b = b0 \ \wedge \ p = 0 \ \wedge \ b0 \geqslant 0)$ before execution of M then M terminates and $p = a0*b0$ after.
b) Let a0, b0 and p0 be the values of variables a, b and p before execution of M. What are the values of a, b and p after execution of M?
c) Same question as (a), for program M'.
d) Same question as (b), for program M'.

Answers to these questions are briefly given below:

a) Claim: The assertion $(a0*b0 = p+a*b)$ holds after any number (including zero) of iterations.
   This claim can be proved by induction.
   Basis of induction: $a = a0 \ \wedge \ b = b0 \ \wedge \ p = 0 \ \wedge \ b0 \geqslant 0 \Rightarrow a0*b0 = p+a*b$.
   Induction step: $a0*b0 = p+a*b \Rightarrow (a0*b0 = p+a + a*(b-1))$. Because $b0 \geqslant 0$ and because b decreases by decrements of 1, M terminates in a state such that $b = 0$. This, in conjunction with the assertion above yields the result sought.

b) If b0$\geqslant$0 then the final values of a, b and p are

$$a = a0, \; b = 0, \; p = p0 + a0*b0$$

else the final values of a, b and p are undefined.

c) Claim: The assertion A = (a0*b0 = p+a*b $\wedge$ b$\geqslant$0) holds after any number (including zero) of iterations.
We prove this claim by induction:
Basis of induction: a = a0 $\wedge$ b = b0 $\wedge$ p = 0 $\wedge$ b0$\geqslant$0 $\Rightarrow$ a0*b0 = p+a*b $\wedge$ b$\geqslant$0.
Induction step: If A = (a0*b0 = p+a*b $\wedge$ b$\geqslant$0) holds at some iteration and one more iteration is needed (b>0) then A holds after the iteration (a0*b0 = p+a + a*(b−1) $\wedge$ b−1$\geqslant$0). Because b0$\geqslant$0 and b decreases at each step with a decrement of 1 the condition b>0 eventually becomes false and the program exits; the conjunction of the two conditions (a0*b0 = p+a*b $\wedge$ b$\geqslant$0) and (b$\leqslant$0) yields p = a0*b0.

d) If b0$\geqslant$0 then the final values of a, b and p are

$$a = a0, \; b = 0, \; p = p0 + a0*b0$$

else

$$a = a0, \; b = b0, \; p = p0.$$

One may draw two lessons from the discussions above:

— Even simple programs are hard to analyze: The discussions above are not as straightforward and simple as the shortness and simplicity of programs M and M′ may lead one to believe.
— Even simple changes to a program (b$\neq$0 vs. b>0) can cause a deep impact on its functional properties; hence the need for programmers to be aware of the significance of every single symbol they write in their program.

2   Programming as a Mathematical Discipline

Programs are potentially complex objects. How does one tackle their complexity? A cogent answer is given by Dijkstra ([1]):

As soon as programming emerges as a battle against unmastered complexity, it is quite natural that one turns to that mental discipline whose main purpose has been for centuries to apply effective structuring to otherwise unmastered complexity. That mental discipline is more or less familiar to all of us, it is called Mathematics. If we take the existence of the impressive body of Mathematics as the experimental evidence for the opinion that for the human mind the mathematical method is indeed the most effective way to come to grips with complexity, we have no choice any longer: We should reshape our field of programming in such a way that, the mathematician's methods become equally applicable to our programming problems, for there are no other means.

Mathematics (discrete mathematics, in particular) plays a dual role in the functional analysis of programs, by enabling us to firmly grasp all the richness of programs and to harness the complexity of programs by means of proper structuring.

The mastery of the Mathematics underlying the programming activity is a key to effective program development. It is the basis for the *intellectual control* of the programming process (notion due to Mills, [2]); this intellectual control is virtually the only source of confidence that a programmer is entitled to have in his program. No amount of testing can certify the correctness of a program because in general the number of possible test values is virtually infinite.

Of course, the mathematical validation criteria that we use to prove programs correct have intrinsic limitations. The basic incompleteness results (Halting Problem, Church's Thesis, ...) already tell us that no absolute validation criteria exist. But relative criteria do exist and some are quite effective. There is a strong analogy here with physical theories which can be absolutely refuted by counterexample but never absolutely validated through empirical confirmation (this did not prevent a relationship between mathematical analysis and physics to develop and be fruitful).

3 Perspective

In the following chapters, we shall discuss several aspects of the functional analysis of programs, along the various dimensions of complexity that a program presents. In doing so, we shall use mathematics to formalize the functional properties of programs, with an attempt to seek a proper balance between formality and intuition.

Through its wide range of program verification (analysis) methods, the book seeks to achieve the following goals:

— Present and discuss effective and reliable means to verify that a program is consistent with respect to the specification for which it was written.

— Shed light into the essence of automatic computations and the mathematical processes underlying the programming activity.
— Provide guidelines for the formal design of programs.

It is the second goal which is considered to be the most important one: It is both the most fundamental one—for it encompasses the others—and the most readily applicable one—for some theorems are so powerful that one cannot keep programming the same way after one has understood them. Fortunately, because of its logical nature, this understanding of programming scales up to programs of any size.

Bibliography

1: Dijkstra, E W. On a Methodology of Design. MC-25 Informatica Symposium, MC track 37. Mathematical Centrum, Amsterdam, 1971 pp 4.1-4.10.
2: Mills, H D. The Intellectual Control of Computers. Keynote address, The International Symposium on Current Issues of Requirements Engineering Environments. Kyoto, Japan, September 20-21 1982. Yutaka Ohno, editor. North-Holland, 1982.

Chapter 2

Mathematics for Programming

This chapter introduces some notions about sets, relations, functions and lists. Few results are novel. The main purpose is to introduce definitions and notational conventions which are to be used throughout the book. Because the tone of this chapter is not strictly formal, we may sometimes use objects (e.g. predicate) before they are formally defined; we rely, therefore, on the reader's background in discrete mathematics.

1 Sets

1.1 Preliminary Definitions

A *set* is a well-defined collection of distinct, identifiable objects, called the *elements* of the set. We say that s *belongs to* a set S, or that s *is a member of* set S iff s is an element of S. This is abbreviated by s:S. There is a specific reason for using the colon to represent the relation *is an element of:* In the programming language Pascal (to be used in this book), a variable declaration has the form *s:stype*, where *stype* is a Pascal data type, hence a set. The semantics of the statement *s:stype* is to declare that s belongs to set *stype*.

When the number of elements in a set is finite, we call that number the *cardinality* of the set. The cardinality of a set is a non-negative integer. There exists only one set with a cardinality of zero, the *empty set* (denoted {}).

When two sets S and T are such that any element of S is an element of T, we say that S is a *subset* of T (denoted $S \subseteq T$), or that T is a *superset* of S. If S is a subset of T and there exists an element of T which is not an element of S, we say that S is a *proper subset of* T (denoted $S \subset T$), or that T is a *proper superset* of S.

Two sets S and T are equal if and only if S is a subset of T and T is a subset of S.

1.2 Operations on Sets

The *union* of two sets S and T is the set of all elements which belong to S *or* to T (or both). It is denoted by $S \cup T$.

The *intersection* of two sets S and T is the set of all elements which belong to S *and* to T. It is denoted by S∩T.

The *difference* of set T from set S is the set of all elements which belong to S and do not belong to T. It is denoted by S−T.

The *cartesian product* of two sets S and T is the set of ordered pairs (u,v) such that u:S and v:T. It is denoted S×T.

If U = S×T, then S and T are said to be *cartesian components* of U.

The ith *cartesian power* of set S (denoted S× ×i, i⩾1) is the set of ordered i-tuples of elements of S.

The *power set* of set S (denoted **P**(S)) is the set of subsets of S.

A *partition* of set S is the definition of subsets S1, S2, ... Sk such that S1 ∪ S2∪ ... ∪Sk = S, and for any distinct integers i and j between 1 and k, Si∩ Sj = {}.

1.3 Defining Sets

A set can be defined in many ways. Finite sets can simply be defined by giving the list of their elements. For example, the set Traffic-lights is the set containing green, orange and red.

Countably infinite sets can be defined by induction. For example, the set ℕ of natural numbers can be defined by:

— 0 is an element of ℕ;
— If n is an element of ℕ then so is n+1.

A set can be defined as the subset of some previously defined set. For example, Evens is the subset of the set of integers, characterized by the relation

$$(i \text{ } \mathbf{div} \text{ } 2) * 2 = i.$$

A set can be defined as the *product* by some operation (union, intersection, difference, cartesian product, cartesian power or power set) on some previously defined sets. In particular, the cartesian product is often used to construct complex sets from simpler sets.

The elementary sets that we shall use throughout this book without formal definition are the following:

— **natural**, the set of natural numbers (including 0),
— **integer**, the set of integers,
— **real**, the set of real numbers,
— **char**, the set of alphabetic and numeric characters,
— **boolean**, the set of truth values, **true** and **false**.

1.4 Representing Sets

If S is a set whose only elements are a, b, c and d, we can represent S by

$$\{a,b,c,d\}.$$

If S is the set of elements of T which have the discriminating property p, we can represent S by

$$\{s\text{:}T\mid p(s)\}.$$

(read as: the set of elements s of T such that p(s) holds). If set T is implicit, we represent this merely as

$$\{s\mid p(s)\}.$$

If S is the cartesian product of T1 and T2, we can represent S by

$$T1\times T2.$$

REMARK 1. There exists a one-to-one correspondence between predicates (i.e. boolean valued functions) defined on set S and subsets of S. To the predicate p defined on S one can associate the subset $\{s\text{:}S\mid p(s)\}$. This subset shall be represented by $S\mid p$. On the other hand, to the subset T of S, one can associate the predicate p(s) defined by (s:T). This predicate shall be represented by (:T). We have, by definition, $(:(S\mid p))=p$ and $(S\mid(:T))=T$.

A more structured and more general representation of sets is given in section 3.5.

1.5 Operations and Expressions

The purpose of this section is to introduce some terminology regarding operators and expressions. The tone is essentially informal, if only because a formal treatment is beyond the scope of this book.

DEFINITION 1. Let A and B be two sets. An *external unary operator* from A to B is a symbol, say @, such that for any s in A, the sentence (@s) is a representation for an element s′ in B which can be computed from s. An *external binary operator* from A to B is a symbol, say @, such that for any s and s′ in A, the sentence (s@s′) is a representation for an element s″ of B which can be computed from s and s′. We use the generic term *external operator* to refer to an operator of either type.

An example of external unary operator from **integer** to **boolean** is (@s) = (s> 3). An example of external binary operator from **integer** to **boolean** is (s@s') = (s>s').

DEFINITION 2. An *internal unary operator* on set S is an external unary operator from S to S. An *internal binary operator* on S is an external binary operator from S to S. We use the generic term *internal operator* to refer to an operator of either type.

An example of an internal unary operator on **integer** is (@s) = (−s); an example of internal binary operator on **integer** is (s@s') = (s+s'). We use the generic term *unary operator* to refer to an internal unary operator or an external unary operator. We use the generic term *binary operator* to refer to an internal binary operator or an external binary operator. We use the generic term *operator* to refer to an operator of any kind defined above.

DEFINITION 3. Let A and B be two sets. The BNF description below gives the syntax of *external expressions* and *internal expressions*.
⟨external expression⟩:: =
    ⟨external unary operator⟩ ⟨internal expression⟩
    | ⟨internal expression⟩⟨external binary operator⟩ ⟨internal expression⟩
⟨internal expression⟩:: =
    ⟨internal unary operator⟩⟨internal expression⟩
    | ⟨internal expression⟩⟨internal binary operator⟩ ⟨internal expression⟩
    | ⟨element of A⟩

An example of internal expression on **integer** is −(s+s') * (s"−s); an example of external expression from **integer** to **boolean** is (s+3)>(s'−1).

DEFINITION 4. Let A be a set and s be the name of an element of A.

a) s is *free* in the (internal) expression s.
b) If s is *free* in the expressions E1 or E2 or both and @ is a binary operator then s is free in E1@E2.
c) If s is *free* in the expression E and @ is a unary operator then s is free in @E.
d) The *free* -dom of s can be established solely on the basis of criteria (a), (b) and (c).

Unless specified otherwise, all expressions considered henceforth are assumed to have at most one free variable.

DEFINITION 5. The *value* of an external expression, say E, from A to B, for an element s in A is the element of B (denoted E(s)) computed by replacing s for the free variable of E.

This definition generalizes trivially to internal expressions. The value of the external expression E from **integer** to **boolean** defined by (s<3) for element 4 is **false**.

DEFINITION 6. Let E be an external expression from A to B, or an internal expression on A. The *domain of definition* of expression E (denoted **def**(E)) is the set of elements s of A such that if s is substituted for the free variable of E, it is possible to compute E(s).

For example, the domain of definition of the internal expression E(s) = log(s) on **real** is {s:**real**| s>0}.

DEFINITION 7. Let E and E′ be internal expressions on S. The *composition* of E′ by E (denoted E′•E) is the internal expression on S obtained by substituting E for each occurrence of the free variable of E′ and letting the free variable of E be the free variable of the whole expression. The composition of two external expressions is defined in a similar fashion.

If E = (s+1) and E′ = s**2 are two internal expressions on **real** then E•E′ is the expression s**2 + 1 and E′•E is the expression (s+1)**2.

DEFINITION 8. Let E and E′ be two internal expressions on set S and p be a predicate on S. The *alternative expression* **ite**(p,E,E′) is the internal expression defined on S by: [**ite**(p,E,E′)] (s) = if p(s) then E(s) else E′(s).

This definition can be easily generalized to external expressions.

DEFINITION 9. Let E and E′ be two external expressions from A to B and from A to C respectively. The *cartesian product of expressions* E and E′ is the expression from A to B×C denoted (E,E′) and defined by

$$(E,E′)(s) = (E(s),E′(s)).$$

This definition generalizes easily to higher cartesian powers.

1.6 Finite Ordinals

Definition 10. A *finite ordinal* is the empty set or an interval of the set **natural** starting from zero, up to some natural number.

For example, {}, {0}, {0,1}, {0,1,2}, {0,1,2,3}, etc ... are all examples of finite ordinals. This notion was first introduced precisely to define the set **natural**; we use it here simply as a practical tool in our later definitions.

1.7 Exercises

1. [A] Determine whether each of the following statements holds.
   a) {}:{}.
   b) {}:{{}}.
   c) a:{a,{a},{{a}}}.
   d) {} ⊆ {{}}.
   e) {a,b}:{a,b,{{a,b}}}.

2. [A] Determine the cardinality of:
   a) {{a,b}}.
   b) {{s:**integer**| s>5 ∧ s<1}}.
   c) {{s:**integer**| **true**}}.
   d) {a,{a},{{a}}}.
   e) {a,b,{a}} ∪ {{a,b}}.

3. [A] Let S be a set of cardinality n. What is the cardinality of **P**(S)? Discuss the representation of set **P**(S) in a computer memory.

4. [B] Let E and E′ be internal expressions on set S. Determine **def**(E●E′) and **def**(E′●E).

2 Relations

2.1 Preliminary Definitions

An *external relation* (E-relation for short) R from set A to set B is a subset of the cartesian product A×B such that any s in A (resp. any s′ in B) appears at least once as the first element (resp. second element) of a pair in R.

If the pair (s,s′) belongs to E-relation R, we say that s is in relation R with s′. For the sake of being suggestive, we shall sometimes write the sentence (s,s′):R as s R s′.

The *domain* of E-relation R (denoted **dom**(R)) is set A; the *range* of E-relation R (denoted **rng**(R)) is set B.

2.2 Representing Relations

An E-relation R from A to B is a subset of A×B. Section 1.4 discussed the representation of cartesian products and subsets. If r is the predicate which characterizes the pairs (s,s′) belonging to the E-relation R, we write R as

$$\{(s,s'): A \times B \mid r(s,s')\}.$$

2.3 Operations on Relations

All set operations can be applied to E-relations, since E-relations are sets. If R and R' are E-relations from A to B, then so are R $\cup$ R', R $\cap$ R' and R $-$ R'. As for the cartesian product of R by R', it is not an E-relation from A to B, nor does it have a significant interpretation.

In contrast, the notion of *relative product* of two E-relations is very significant. It is defined as follows: Let R be an E-relation from A to B and R' be an E-relation from B to C; we define the relative product of R by R' to be the E-relation from A to C equal to

$\{(s,s''): A \times C \mid$ There exists s':B such that (s,s'):R and (s',s''):R'\}.

The relative product of R by R' is denoted by R*R'.

The *transpose* of E-relation R (denoted R^t) is the E-relation from B to A defined by

$\{(s,s'):B \times A \mid (s',s):R\}.$

It stems from this definition that **dom**(R^t)= **rng**(R) and **rng**(R^t)= **dom**(R).

2.4 Internal Relations

An *internal relation* (I-relation for short) on set S is an E-relation from some subset A of S to some subset B of S; the definitions of *domain* and *range* of I-relations extend naturally those of E-relations:

dom(R) = $\{s:S \mid$ there exists s' in S such that (s,s'):R\}
rng(R) = $\{s':S \mid$ there exists s in S such that (s,s'):R\}.

The notion of I-relation is as general as that of an E-relation; the distinction is introduced solely for the sake of convenience. An E-relation R from A to B can be viewed as an I-relation on A$\cup$B; on the other hand, an I-relation on S can be viewed as an E-relation from **dom**(R) to **rng**(R). When the context does not lead to confusion or when it is not necessary to be specific, we shall use the generic term *relation* to refer to an I-relation or an E-relation.

The I-relation F on set S defined by F=S$\times$S is called the *full relation*. Also, the I-relation I on set S defined by I=$\{(s,s')\mid s'=s\}$ is called the *identity relation*.

If R and R' are I-relations on set S, then so is the relative product R*R'. If R is an I-relation on set S, then we define the ith *relative power* of R (denoted R**i, i$\geqslant$0) by

if i=0 then $\{(s,s')\mid s=s' \wedge s:$**dom**(R)\}
else R**(i$-$1) * R.

It is left to the reader to verify that if $S = \{a,b,c\}$ and $R = \{(a,b), (b,c), (c,a)\}$ then

$$R^{**}0 = \{(a,a), (b,b), (c,c)\},$$
$$R^{**}1 = \{(a,b), (b,c), (c,a)\},$$
$$R^{**}2 = \{(a,c), (b,a), (c,b)\},$$
$$R^{**}3 = \{(a,a), (b,b), (c,c)\}.$$

One can check easily that the property $R^{**}1 = R$ holds for any I-relation R.

If R is an I-relation on S, then we define the *transitive closure* of R (denoted R^+) to be the I-relation on S equal to

$$R^{**}1 \cup R^{**}2 \cup R^{**}3 \cup \ldots.$$

It is left to the reader to verify that if $S = \{a,b,c\}$ and $R = \{(a,b), (b,c), (c,a)\}$, then R^+ equals F, the full relation on S.

An I-relation R on S is said to be *reflexive* if and only if for any s in S, (s,s):R (i.e. $I \subseteq R$).

An I-relation R on S is said to be *symmetric* if and only if for any (s,s') in F, (s,s'):R logically implies (s',s):R (i.e. $R \subseteq R^t$).

An I-relation R on S is said to be *antisymmetric* if and only if for any (s,s') in F, (s,s'):R and (s',s):R logically imply $s = s'$ (i.e. $R \cap R^t$ is a subset of $R^{**}0$).

An I-relation R on S is said to be *asymmetric* if and only if for any (s,s') in F, (s,s'):R logically implies ~((s',s):R) (i.e. $R \subseteq F - R^t$).

An I-relation R on S is said to be *transitive* if and only if for any s, s' and s" in S, (s,s'):R and (s',s"):R logically implies (s,s"):R (i.e. $R^{**}2 \subseteq R$).

An I-relation R on S is said to be *connected* if and only if for any two distinct elements s and s' of S, (s,s'):R or (s',s):R or both (i.e. $F - I \subseteq R \cup R^t$).

An I-relation R on S is said to be *strongly connected* if and only if for any two elements s and s' of S, (s,s'):R or (s',s):R or both (i.e. $F \subseteq R \cup R^t$).

An I-relation is said to be an *equivalence relation* if and only if it is reflexive, symmetric and transitive.

An I-relation is said to be a *partial ordering* if and only if it is antisymmetric and transitive. (Example: relation *is a subset of* on the set $S = \mathbf{P}(T)$, where T is a non-empty set).

An I-relation is said to be a *simple ordering* if and only if it is antisymmetric, transitive and strongly connected. (Example: relation $\leq$ on the set **integer**).

An I-relation is said to be a *strict partial ordering* if and only if it is asymmetric and transitive. (Example: relation *is a proper subset of* on the set $\mathbf{P}(T)$, where T is a non-empty set).

An I-relation is said to be a *strict simple ordering* if and only if it is asymmetric, transitive and connected. (Example: relation $<$ on the set **integer**).

Let R be a partial ordering on S and T be a subset of S. An element s of T is said to be *R-minimal* in T if and only if no element s' of T, distinct from s, is such that (s',s):R. An element s of T is said to be *R-first* in T if and only if for any s' in T distinct from s, (s,s'):R. An element s of S is said to be a *R-lower bound* of T if and only if for any s' in T, (s,s'):R.

An element s of T is said to be *R-maximal* in T iff it is R^t-minimal in T. An element s of T is said to be *R-last* in T iff it is R^t-first in T. An element s of S is said to be an *R-upper bound* of T if and only if it is a R^t-lower bound of T.

Let R be a partial ordering on set S. Let s and s' be two elements of S and T be the set {s,s'}. We define R-ub(T) to be the set of all R-upper bounds of T and R-lb(T) to be the set of all R-lower bounds of T. The R-first element of R-ub(T), if it exists, is called the *R-least upper bound* of s and s' (abbreviated R-lub(s,s')). The R-last element of R-lb(T), if it exists, is said to be the *R-greatest lower bound* of s and s' (abbreviated R-glb(s,s')). If any two elements s and s' of S have a R-least upper bound and a R-greatest lower bound, we say that R is a *lattice* on S.

Let R be a strict partial ordering on set S. We say that R is a *well-founded* relation if and only if any non-empty subset T of S has a R-minimal element. We say, equivalently, that S is *well-founded* by relation R. See problem 2 for an alternative definition of well-founded relations. When a well-founded relation is such that any non-empty subset T of S has a unique R-minimal element, we say that it is a *well-ordering*.

Let R be an equivalence relation on set S and let s be some element of S. The *equivalence class of* element s *modulo* relation R is the subset of S (denoted **Eq**(s)) equal to:

$$\{s':S \mid (s,s'):R\}.$$

For any equivalence relation R on S, the equivalence classes of S modulo R define a partition of S.

2.5 Exercises

1. [A] Which of the above properties are possessed by the following I-relations on S = {a,b,c,d}?
   a) R = {}.
   b) R = {(a,a),(b,b),(c,c)}.
   c) R = {(a,a),(a,b),(b,a),(b,b),(c,c),(d,d)}.
   d) R = {(a,b),(b,c)}.
   e) R = {(a,b),(b,c),(c,d)}.

2. [B] Can a relation be:
   a) Reflexive and asymmetric?
   b) Antisymmetric and asymmetric?

   c) Transitive and antisymmetric but not reflexive?
   d) Symmetric and antisymmetric?
   e) Symmetric and asymmetric?
   Justify your claim in each case.

3. [A] Give an example of a relation which is:
   a) Reflexive.
   b) Symmetric.
   c) Antisymmetric.
   d) Asymmetric.
   e) Transitive.

4. [B] Give an example of a set S and a relation R on S such that
   a) R is a lattice on S.
   b) R is not a lattice on S.
   c) R is a well-founded relation on S.
   d) R is not a well-ordering on S.
   e) R is a strict partial ordering but not a well-ordering.

5. [B] Let R be a relation on set S.
   a) Show that R^+ is transitive.
   b) Show that $R \cup R^t$ is symmetric.
   c) If R is reflexive and transitive, show that $R \cup R^t$ is an equivalence relation.
   d) Show that if R is an equivalence relation, then so is $R**2$.
   e) Let R be a relation such that for any (s,s') and (s,s'') in R, (s',s'') is in R. Show that if R is reflexive then it is an equivalence relation.

6. [A] Let R be an equivalence relation on S, and let E1, E2, ... En be the equivalence classes of S modulo R.
   a) What can be said about the union of E1, E2, ... En?
   b) What can be said about **dom**(R) and **rng**(R)?
   c) Let (s,s') be an element of R. What can be said about **Eq**(s) $\cap$ **Eq**(s')?
   d) Let (s,s') be an element of F $-$ R. What can be said about **Eq**(s) $\cap$ **Eq**(s')?
   e) Conclude by summarizing the results of (a) through (d).

7. [B] Find the R-first (if any), R-minimal (if any) and the R-greatest lower bound (if any) of set T in set S ordered with R.
   a) $S =$ **real**; $T = \{s \mid 0 \leqslant s < 1\}$; $R = \{(s,s') \mid s < s'\}$.
   b) $S =$ **real**; $T = \{s \mid 0 < s \leqslant 1\}$; $R = \{(s,s') \mid s < s'\}$.
   c) $S = \{a,b,c\}$; $T = \{a,b\}$; $R = \{(a,b)\}$.
   d) $S = \{a,b,c\}$; $T = \{a,b\}$; $R = \{(a,c)\}$.
   e) $S = \{a,b,c\}$; $T = \{a,b\}$; $R = \{\}$.

3 Functions

3.1 Preliminary Definitions

An *E-function* (external function) f from set A to set B is an E-relation from A to B such that for any s in A, (s,s'):f and (s,s''):f logically implies $s' = s''$.

A *predicate* on set S is an E-function from set S to **boolean**.

An *I-function* (internal function) on S is a function from some subset A of S to some subset B of S. Set S is said to be the *space* of function f. Just as we did for I-relations, we will talk about the *domain* and the *range* of I-functions.

We will use the generic term of *function* to refer to a E-function or a I-function.

3.2 Properties of functions

An I-function f is said to be *invertible* if and only if its transpose f^t is a function. f^t is then called the *inverse* of f and is denoted f^{-1}. We have

$$f * f^{-1} = \{(s,s')|\ s=s' \land s:\textbf{dom}(f)\}$$
$$= f**0, \text{ and}$$
$$f^{-1} * f = \{(s,s')|\ s=s' \land s:\textbf{rng}(f)\}.$$
$$= (f^{-1})**0.$$

See exercise 12 for a discussion of the properties of I-functions and their inverses.

3.3 Defining and Representing Functions

A function being a relation, one can represent it just like a relation, namely as $\{(s,s')|\ p(s,s')\}$. This representation is unsatisfactory because it hides one essential property of functions: that for any s in the domain of a function f, there exists a unique s' in the range of f such that (s,s') belongs to f. We shall devise two distinct notations for a function, depending on whether we are dealing with an E-function or an I-function.

Representing E-functions. A natural way to represent an E-function from A to B is to use an external expression from A to B, say E, such that

$$(s,s'):f \text{ if and only if } s' = E(s).$$

Let S be the set of integers between 1 and 5. The E-function from S to **boolean** equal to $\{(1,\textbf{false}), (2,\textbf{false}), (3,\textbf{true}), (4,\textbf{true}), (5,\textbf{true})\}$ is represented by the expression from S to **boolean** equal to $s>2$.

Representing I-functions. Let f be the I-function on **integer** equal to $\{(0,1), (1,2), (2,3), (3,4), (4,5)\}$. We notice that for any element (s,s') in f, $s'=s+1$. The expression E defined by $E(s)=s+1$ is not sufficient to represent function f since it does not carry the information that the domain of f is $\{0,1,2,3,4\}$.

Hence, the representation of an I-function f on S must be done in terms of two objects:

— A predicate p on S which characterizes the domain of f; i.e. such that S|p = **dom**(f). This predicate is called the *p-domain* of function f (stands for predicate domain).
— An internal expression E on S such that for any (s,s') in f, s' = E(s).

Function f is then represented by [p,E]. We say that [p,E] is the *pE-formula* of I-function f.

As an example, function {(0,0), (1,12), (2,60), (3,180)} is represented by [0⩽s⩽3, s**4 + 11* s**2]. Note that this function can also be represented by [0⩽s⩽3, 6*s**3 + 6*s]. This shows that the same function can have more than one expression. Nevertheless, we may sometimes talk about *the* expression of a function, because we are not interested in the form of an expression as much as we are interested in the value that it returns for any given value of its free variable.

REMARK 2. Any I-function has a pE-formula; a dual question to address is whether, for any predicate p on S and internal expression E on S, [p,E] defines a function. It does so if and only if S|p is a subset of **def**(E).

REMARK 3. Notational Convention: For a given function f = [p,E], the following are equivalent propositions:

— (s,s'):f.
— s' = f(s).
— p(s) ∧ s' = E(s).

Let E be an internal expression on S. The function f = [:**def**(E),E] is called the *implicit function defined by* expression E. Many other functions can have E for an expression; they are all subsets of f.

3.4 Operations on Functions

We shall concentrate on I-functions, leaving to the reader the derivation of similar formulas for E-functions.

Union. Even though the union of two relations is a relation, the union of two functions is not necessarily a function. For example, on set S = {a,b,c,d}, the union of functions {(a,b), (b,c)} and {(a,c), (d,c)} is not a function, only a relation. We shall, in the following, discuss when the union of two functions is a function, and eventually, what its formula is. Let S be a set and f and f' two I-functions on S represented respectively by [p,E] and [p',E'].

PROPOSITION 1. The union of I-functions [p,E] and [p',E'] is a function if and only if, for any s in $S|p \cap S|p'$, $E(s) = E'(s)$.

Assuming that the condition above is met by two functions f and f', we shall give the formula of $f \cup f'$. The p-domain of $f \cup f'$ is the logical disjunction of p and p', denoted $p \vee p'$. The expression of $f \cup f'$ is **ite**(p,E,E').

PROPOSITION 2.

$$[p,E] \cup [p',E'] = [p \vee p', \textbf{ite}(p,E,E')].$$

Note: If [p,E] and [p',E'] meet the condition expressed in Proposition 1, then **ite**(p,E,E') and **ite**(p',E',E) are interchangeable in the formula of Proposition 2, i.e. they give the same value for any variable in $S|(p \vee p')$.

Intersection. The intersection of two I-functions [p,E] and [p',E'] is a function. Its p-domain is $q(s) = (p(s) \wedge p'(s) \wedge E(s) = E'(s))$. Its expression is E (or E').

PROPOSITION 3.

$$[p,E] \cap [p',E'] = [p(s) \wedge p'(s) \wedge E(s) = E'(s), \ E].$$

Difference. The difference of two functions [p,E] and [p',E'] is a function. Its p-domain is $q(s) = ((p(s) \wedge {\sim}p'(s)) \vee (p(s) \wedge E(s) \neq E'(s)))$. Its expression is E.

PROPOSITION 4.

$$[p,E] - [p',E'] = [p \wedge {\sim}p', E] \cup [p(s) \wedge E(s) \neq E'(s), E],$$

where ~ denotes the logical negation.

Relative Product. The operation of relative product of relations can be specialized to functions. The relative product of two functions is a function. Its p-domain is defined by: $q(s) = (p(s) \wedge p'(E(s)))$. This formula indicates that in order for s to be in the domain of [p,E]*[p',E'], s must be in the domain of [p,E] (i.e. p(s)) and the image of s by [p,E] must be in the domain of [p',E'] (i.e. p'(E(s))). The expression of the relative product is E'●E, where "●"

denotes the composition of expressions introduced in section 1.5. Note that the expressions are evaluated in the reverse order of the relative product of the functions.

PROPOSITION 5.

$$[p,E] * [p',E'] = [p \wedge p' \bullet E, \quad E' \bullet E].$$

Restriction. Let [p,E] be a function and let q be a predicate on S.

DEFINITION 11. The *restriction* of function [p,E] to predicate q is the function [p $\wedge$ q,E].

The proposition below shows that function restriction is a particular case of function relative product.

PROPOSITION 6.

$$[p \wedge q,E] = [q,s] * [p,E],$$

where s is a variable in S, standing for the identity expression.

For the sake of notational convenience, we take the following conventions regarding the precedence of functional operations:

— The relative power is parsed before the relative product; hence, e.g. f*g**i is to be parsed as f*(g**i).
— The relative product is parsed before any set operation; hence, e.g. f $\cup$ g*h is to be parsed as f $\cup$ (g*h).
— Any function operation is parsed before application to arguments; hence, e.g. f $\cup$ g(s) is to be parsed as (f $\cup$ g)(s).

3.5 Spaces, States and Variables

Function theory affords us a convenient notation for representing sets. The subject of this section is to introduce and discuss this notation, which will be adopted throughout the book. Let S be the set {(r,i,c): **real** $\times$ **integer** $\times$ **char** | i $\geqslant$ r}. We wish to represent it in a Pascal-like form. A Pascal data type declaration of the form

$\langle$type-name$\rangle$ = $\langle$type-description$\rangle$

is but the definition of a set (described by ⟨type-description⟩) and the binding of a name to it (given by ⟨type-name⟩). The Pascal data type of **record** is particularly suitable for representing sets as cartesian products of other sets. For example, the declaration

$$
\begin{aligned}
\text{T} = \ &\textbf{record} \\
&\text{r: } \textbf{real}; \\
&\text{i: } \textbf{integer}; \\
&\text{c: } \textbf{char} \\
\textbf{end}&
\end{aligned}
$$

defines the set **real** × **integer** × **char** and binds the name T to it. The **record** structure allows us to represent cartesian products but not subsets. In order to overcome this weakness, we introduce the structure of **set**, whose syntax is

$$
\begin{aligned}
&\textbf{set} \\
&\textbf{crt} \quad \langle \text{variable-declaration} \rangle; \\
&\textbf{sub} \quad \langle \text{predicate-declaration} \rangle \\
&\textbf{end}.
\end{aligned}
$$

Then S can be defined by the following statement.

$$
\begin{aligned}
\text{S} = \ &\textbf{set} \\
&\textbf{crt} \\
&\quad \text{r: } \textbf{real}; \\
&\quad \text{i: } \textbf{integer}; \\
&\quad \text{c: } \textbf{char}; \\
&\textbf{sub} \\
&\quad \text{i} \geqslant \text{r} \\
&\textbf{end}.
\end{aligned}
$$

The semantic value of this statement is two-fold:

— First, it defines S to be $\{(r,i,c): \textbf{real} \times \textbf{integer} \times \textbf{char} \mid i \geqslant r\}$.
— Second, it defines
  – r to be the E-function from S to **real** which to every element (u,v,w) of S associates u.
  – i to be the E-function from S to **integer** which to every element (u,v,w) of S associates v.
  – c to be the E-function from S to **char** which, to every element (u,v,w) of S associates w.

Functions r, i and c are said to be the *elementary functions* of set S, or the *projecting functions* of set S. The attribute *elementary* refers to the fact that any function defined on S is expressed in terms of these functions; the attribute *projecting* refers to the fact that these functions project set S onto its components in the cartesian product. The keyword **crt** stands for *cartesian product*. It refers to the cartesian product defined by the list of variable declarations. The keyword **sub** stands for *subset*. It refers to the predicate defining a subset of the cartesian product.

If s = (3.14, 5, z) is some element of S, then we have:

$$r(s) = 3.14;$$
$$i(s) = 5;$$
$$c(s) = z.$$

The appropriateness of the syntax and semantics associated with the structure of **set** will be made clear as this structure is used throughout the book (see also exercises 13 and 14). The sets used are often subsets of cartesian products of predefined sets. Note that the Pascal construct of **array** enables us to conveniently represent cartesian powers.

Whenever the predicate of a set declaration is **true**, we may omit it, and describe the set following the syntax given below:

> **set**
> ⟨variable declarations⟩
> **end**.

3.6 Exercises

1. [A] For each expression E on **real**, determine the set **def**(E).
   a) E(s) = log(log(s)).
   b) E(s) = log(s−1).
   c) E(s) = Sqrt(log(s−1)).
   d) E(s) = 1/log(s+1).
   e) E(s) = 1/Arcsin(s).

2. [A] Indicate whether the following are functions:
   a) [**true**, Sqrt(s+4)], on set **real**.
   b) [s > −7, Sqrt(s+4)], on set **real**.
   c) [s ≥ −4, Sqrt(s+4)], on set **real**.
   d) [s ≥ 4, Sqrt(s+4)], on set **real**.
   e) [**false**, Sqrt(s+4)], on set **real**.

3. [A] List all the elements of the I-function on **integer** whose pE-formula is [0 ≤ s ≤ 3, s**4 + 11*s**2] and all the elements of the I-function on **integer** whose pE-formula is [0 ≤ s ≤ 3, 6*s**3 + 6*s]. Conclude.

4. [A] Let E be the internal expression on **real** defined by $E(s) = $ Sqrt(log(s**2 − 1)). Determine the implicit function defined by E.

5. [A] Let E be the internal expression defined on **real** by $E(s) = $ Sqrt(s+2). Let f be the I-function on **real** whose pE-formula is [s≥2,E]. Which of these assertions hold?
   a) (0,Sqrt(2)):f.
   b) Sqrt(2) = f(0).
   c) Sqrt(2) = E(0).
   d) 2 = E(2).
   e) 2 = f(2).

6. [B] Let S be {0,1,2,3,4,5,6} and let f be {(0,0), (1,2), (2,4), (3,6)}. Compute f * f^t and f^t * f giving the pE-formula of each. Compare with f**0 and f^t**0.

7. [B] Is the union of the two I-functions on **real**, [s≥0,2*s] and [s≤0,−2*s], a function? If it is, give its pE-formula.

8. [B] Is the intersection of the two I-functions on **integer**, [s≥0,s] and [s>0, 2*s−1] non-empty? Give its pE-formula.

9. [B] Let f and f′ be the I-functions on **integer** defined as follows: f = [s≥−1,−s] and f′ = [s≤1,−s]. Compute f * f′ and f′ * f. Conclude.

10. [B] Let f be the I-function on **real** defined by [s≥0,s**2−4*s+4]. Is f invertible? Let f′ be the I-function on **real** whose pE-formula is [s≥2, s]. Is f′ * f invertible? If it is, give the pE-formula of its inverse.

11. [B] Let S be the set {1,2,3,4,5,6,7} and let f and f′ be the I-functions on S {(1,2), (2,3), (3,4), (4,5)} and {(4,1), (5,2), (6,3), (7,4)}, respectively.
   a) Compute f * f′.
   b) Compute f′ * f.
   c) Find the pE-formulas of f and f′.
   d) Apply the equations of relative product to determine the pE-formulas of f * f′ and f′ * f.
   e) Compare (d) with (a) and (b).

12. [B] Let S be the set {1,2,3,4,5,6,7}, and let f be the I-function on S equal to {(1,2), (2,4), (3,6)}.
   a) Prove that f is invertible and compute its inverse.
   b) Let g be the inverse of f. Compute f * g;
   c) Compute g * f.
   d) Let f be an invertible I-function on set S; give general formulas for f * f^{-1} and f^{-1} * f in terms of the pE-representation of I-functions.
   e) Let R be an I-relation on set S; give general formulas for R * R^t and R^t * R.

13. [B] Let S be the set defined by

$$S = \quad \textbf{set}$$
crt
$$a, b, p: \textbf{integer};$$

sub

b⩾0

end.

a) Compute a(3,5,1), b(7,3,5) and p(0,5,0).
b) Let f be the I-function on S defined by [b(s)>0, (a(s),b(s)−1,p(s)+a(s))].
   Compute b(f(7,3,5)) and p(f(7,3,5)).
c) Let F be the I-function defined on S by [**true**,(a(s),0,p(s)+a(s)*b(s))]. Prove
   that F(f(7,0,3)) = F(7,0,3).
d) Prove that b(f(s))<b(s); prove that b(F(s))⩽b(s).
e) Let r be the function equal to f * f. Give the pE-formula of r. Compute
   p(r(7,3,5)).

14. [B] Let Circle-1 be the set defined by

Circle-1 = **set**

crt

x, y: **real**;

sub

x**2 + y**2 ⩽1

end.

a) Give examples of elements of this set.
b) Describe the E-function dist-O from Circle-1 to the **real** interval {s| 0⩽s⩽1}
   which associates to each element of Circle-1 its distance to the center of the
   circle. Comment on the appropriateness of calling functions x and y the elementary functions of set Circle-1.
c) Let *point* be an element of Circle-1. What is the significance of x(point) and
   y(point)? Comment on the appropriateness of calling functions x and y the
   projecting functions of set Circle-1.
d) Let sym-O be the I-function on Circle-1 which to each element of Circle-1
   associates its symmetrical image with respect to the center of the circle. Using
   the function dist-O, express that function sym-O does not affect the distance
   to the center.
e) Let sym-x be the I-function on Circle-1 which to each element of Circle-1
   associates its symmetrical image with respect to the x-axis. Express that function sym-x does not affect the x coordinate.

4 Lists

4.1 Preliminary Definitions

DEFINITION 12. A *list* on set S is a function from a finite ordinal to S.

S is said to be the *space* of the list. The set of lists on space S shall be denoted
by L*(S). The *length* of list s (denoted **lng**(s)) is the cardinality of its ordinal.
In particular, if the ordinal of list s is {} then **lng**(s) = 0.

4.2 Defining and Representing Lists

Let s be a list whose ordinal is $\{0, 1, 2, 3, \ldots n\}$ and whose space is set S; because s is a function from its ordinal to S, one can represent it as $\{(0,s0),$ $(1,s1),\ (2,s2),\ (3,s3),\ \ldots\ (n,sn)\}$, or in any other practical way available to represent functions (see section 3.3). Because of the natural ordering that exists in the ordinal, one can abbreviate the representation of function s to (s0, s1, s2, s3, ... sn); this representation is identical to that of an element of $S \times \times (n+1)$: Indeed an element of $S \times \times (n+1)$ can be understood as a function from ordinal $\{0,1,2,3, \ldots n\}$ to S.

4.3 Operations on lists

Operations on lists can be divided into three classes: *decomposition, composition* and *rearrangements*. Decomposition operators are: *car* and *cdr*. Composition operators are: *cons* and *cont*. Rearrangement operators are: *sort* and *rvs*.

car: Applied to a non-empty list s, function **car** returns the first element of s. For example,

$$\mathbf{car}((a,b,c,d,e)) = a.$$

If we are given a list s of length 1 and want to access the element that this list contains, we compute **car**(s).

cdr: Applied to a non-empty list s, function **cdr** returns the list obtained from s by deleting **car**(s). For example,

$$\mathbf{cdr}((a,b,c,d,e)) = (b,c,d,e).$$

cons: Function **cons** has two arguments: an element and a list. It returns the list whose head is the element a and whose tail is the list s given as arguments. For example,

$$\mathbf{cons}(a,(b,c,d,e)) = (a,b,c,d,e).$$

cont: Function **cont** has two arguments, two lists; **cont**(s,s') is the list made up of the ordered elements of s followed by the ordered elements of s'. For example,

$$\mathbf{cont}((a,b),(c,d,e)) = (a,b,c,d,e).$$

sort. If the space of list s is simply ordered by a relation, say $\leqslant$, then **sort**(s) is defined as the list obtained from s by rearranging the elements of s in *increasing* order. For example,

$$\mathbf{sort}((b,d,c,e,a)) = (a,b,c,d,e),$$

assuming that a $\leqslant b \leqslant c \leqslant d \leqslant e$.

rvs. When applied to a list s, function **rvs** returns the list obtained from s by writing its elements in reverse order. It is denoted **rvs**(s). For example,

$$\mathbf{rvs}((a,b,c,d,e)) = (e,d,c,b,a).$$

The functions above have some properties that we shall briefly give here without proof.

— For any element a and list s, **car(cons**(a,s)) = a and **cdr(cons**(a,s)) = s.
— For any non-empty list s, **cons(car**(s),**cdr**(s)) = s.
— For any list s whose space is simply ordered, **sort**(s) = **sort(sort**(s)) and **sort**(s) = **sort(rvs**(s)).
— For any list s **rvs(rvs**(s)) = s.

For the sake of ease of representation, we shall introduce an additional function, called *append* and denoted by **app**; this function has two arguments, a list and an element, and returns the list made up of all the elements of the list argument followed by the element argument. Hence, for example,

$$\mathbf{app}((a,b,c,d),e) = (a,b,c,d,e).$$

In general, **app**(s,a) = **rvs(cons**(a,**rvs**(s))); function **app** is convenient for representing the behavior of **write** statements in Pascal.

4.4 Exercises

1. [A] Let s be the list (e,x,e,r,c,i,s,e,s). Compute (if defined):
   a) **sort**(s).
   b) **rvs**(s).
   c) **cdr**(s).
   d) **cont(rvs(cdr**(s)),**car**(s)).
   e) **sort(rvs**(s)).

2. [A] Determine the validity of the following assertions, where s and s′ denote lists defined on a simply ordered space:
   a) **rvs**(s) = **rvs(rvs**(s)).
   b) **rvs(rvs**(s)) = s.

   c) **sort(sort(s')) = s'**.
   d) **sort(sort(s')) = sort(s')**.
   e) **rvs(s) = cont(rvs(cdr(s)),car(s))**.

3. [A] Same as 2:
   a) **sort(rvs(s)) = sort(s)**.
   b) **sort(rvs(s)) = rvs(s)**.
   c) **rvs(sort(s)) = rvs(s)**.
   d) **rvs(sort(s)) = sort(s)**.
   e) **cons(car(s),cdr(s)) = s**. (hint: try s = ()).

4. [A] Characterize s and s' such that the following conditions hold (one by one):
   a) **s = sort(s)**.
   b) **s = rvs(s)**.
   c) **sort(s) = sort(s')**.
   d) **rvs(sort(s)) = s**.
   e) **sort(rvs(s)) = s**.

5. [A] Same as 4:
   a) **car(s) = car(rvs(s))**.
   b) **car(s) = car(sort(s))**.
   c) **sort(cdr(s)) = cdr(sort(s))**.
   d) **sort(s) = sort(s')** and **sort(cdr(cdr(s))) = sort(cdr(cdr(s')))**.
   e) **cdr(sort(s)) = cdr(sort(s'))**.

5 Problems

1. [A] Give an example of two internal expressions on **integer**, say E1 and E2, such that the I-functions $[1 \leqslant x \leqslant 4, E1]$ and $[1 \leqslant x \leqslant 4, E2]$ are identical. List all the elements of this function.

2. [B] Let R be a strict partial ordering on set S. We say that (S,R) is a well-founded set (or, equivalently, that R is a well-founded relation on set S) if and only if any non-empty subset T of S has a R-minimal element. An alternative definition is: R is a well-founded relation on set S if and only if there is no infinite decreasing (in the sense of R) sequence in S. Prove the equivalence of the two definitions.

3. [B] Using the formula $R**2 \subseteq R$, prove that the transitive closure of a internal relation is transitive.

4. [B] Let f be the I-function on set S whose pE-formula is [p,E]; let q be a predicate on S such that S|q is a subset of S|p. We denote by I the internal expression I(s) = s.
   a) What is the pE-formula of rf = [q,I] * [p,E]?
   b) Is cf = rf ∪ [~p,I] a function? If so, give its pE-formula.
   c) Rewrite the expression defining cf using the notational convention **it**(q,E) = **ite**(q,E,I). Interpret the significance of **it** as a transformer of expressions.

5. [B] In this chapter, we pose that [p,E] is defined iff $S|p \subseteq \mathbf{def}(E)$. Then, [p,E] is equal to

$$\{(s,s')|\ p(s)\ \wedge\ s' = E(s)\}.$$

Alternatively, we could pose that [p,E] is defined for any pair (p,E) and that it is equal to

$$\{(s,s')|\ p(s)\ \wedge\ s:\mathbf{def}(E)\ \wedge\ s' = E(s)\}.$$

Discuss the characteristics of these two conventions with regard to conceptual elegance.

6. [B] Define formally the six functions introduced in section 4.3, using the definition of a list as a function from a finite ordinal to a set. On the basis of your definitions, verify the identities given at the end of section 4.3.

7. [B] Show that if A and B are I-relations on S then $\mathbf{dom}(A*B) \subseteq \mathbf{dom}(A)$. Deduce that $\mathbf{dom}(A^{|}) = \mathbf{dom}(A)$.

6 Bibliography

For more background on sets and relations, consult [4]: Chapters 1 and 3; [5]: Chapters 1, 2 and 3, and [2]: Chapter 1. Much of the set theoretic terminology used in this book is taken from [5]. For more information on ordinals, consult [5]. For a general presentation of mathematics for programming, consult [1].

Elements of function theory are given in [4]: Chapter 3 and [3]: Chapter 2.

Further discussions on lists can be found in [3] and [5].

1: Beckman, F S. Mathematical Foundations of Programming. Addison-Wesley, 1980.
2: Cohn, P M. Universal Algebra. Reidel, 1981.
3: Linger, R C, H D Mills and B I Witt. Structured Programming: Theory and Practice. Addison-Wesley, 1979.
4: Liu, C L. Elements of Discrete Mathematics. McGraw-Hill, 1977.
5: Suppes, P. Axiomatic Set Theory. Dover, 1972.

Chapter 3
Formal Logic: Languages and Methods

This chapter discusses formalizations of logical arguments. Sections 1 and 2 deal with expressing formal statements, and sections 3 and 4 deal with reasoning about them.

1 Propositional Logic

Propositions are declarative sentences such as "Houston is warm", "Montreal is cool". **True** and **false** are other examples of propositions. *Atomic Propositions* (or *atoms*) such as "snow is white" and "Montreal is cool" can be combined to form *compound propositions,* such as "snow is white and Montreal is cool". Atomic propositions will be abbreviated by identifiers.

1.1 The Syntax of Propositional Logic

Compound propositions can be built from atomic propositions using *logical connectives*. We are interested in five logical connectives: the *negation,* denoted ˜ (read: not), the *conjunction,* denoted ∧ (read: and), the *disjunction,* denoted ∨ (read: or), the *conditional,* denoted ⇒ (read: implies) and the *equivalence,* denoted = (read: equals).

DEFINITION 1. A *well-formed formula* (abbreviated: wff) of the propositional logic is defined as follows:

a) **True** and **false** are well-formed formulas.
b) An atom is a well-formed formula.
c) If w is a well-formed formula, then so are ˜w and (w).
d) If u and v are well-formed formulas then so are u ∧ v, u ∨ v, u⇒v and u = v.
e) All well-formed formulas are generated by rules a), b), c) and d) only.

The term *proposition* will be used to refer to a well-formed formula of propositional logic. In addition to logical connectives, we also use parentheses in order to describe the structure of well-formed formulas. Hence (a ∧ b) ∨ (c = b) is the disjunction of (a ∧ b) and (c = b).

1.2 The Semantics of Propositional Logic

DEFINITION 2. Let w be a well-formed formula with k atoms. The *space* of w is the k-th cartesian power of the set **boolean** (i.e. **boolean**$\times\times$k).

Let w be the well-formed formula $(a \wedge b) \vee (c = b)$, where a, b, and c are atoms. The space of w is defined as follows:

$$\text{space} = \textbf{set}$$
$$\text{a, b, c: } \textbf{boolean}$$
$$\textbf{end}.$$

We are abusing notation by using the same names to represent the atoms of w and the elementary functions of its space. The reader will find this notation natural and convenient.

DEFINITION 3. A *state* of a well-formed formula is an element of its space.

(**true, false, true**) and (**false, true, true**) are examples of states of the well-formed formula $(a \wedge b) \vee (c = b)$.

DEFINITION 4. Let w be a well-formed formula and s be one of its states. The *value* of w at state s (denoted by w(s)) is defined as follows:

a) If w is **true** then: w(s) = **true** (the first occurrence of **true** denotes a proposition whereas the second denotes an element of **boolean**; this slight ambiguity is tolerated for the sake of notational convenience).

b) If w is **false** then: w(s) = **false**.

c) If w is an atom, say a, then: w(s) = a(s) (the first occurrence of the name a refers to an atom, whereas the second occurrence refers to an elementary function of the space).

d) If w is the negation of a well-formed formula, say u, then: If the value of u is **false**, then w(s) = **true** otherwise w(s) = **false**.

e) If w is the conjunction of two well-formed formulas, say u and v, then: If the values of u and v at state s are both **true**, then w(s) = **true** otherwise w(s) = **false**.

f) If w is the disjunction of two well-formed formulas, say u and v, then: If the value of either of u or v is **true**, then w(s) = **true** otherwise w(s) = **false**.

g) If w is the conditional of two well-formed formulas, say u and v (i.e. w is u$\Rightarrow$v), then: If the values of u and v at state s are (respectively) **true** and **false**, then w(s) = **false** otherwise w(s) = **true**.

h) If w is the equivalence of two well-formed formulas, say u and v, then: If u and v have the same value at state s then w(s) = **true**, otherwise w(s) = **false**.

The table below summarizes the computational rules described in this definition.It is called a *truth table*. The two first columns show the possible values that the pair (u,v) may have. The remaining columns show, for each of these values, the value of ˜u, u∧v, u∨v, u⟹v and u=v respectively.

u	v	˜u	u∧v	u∨v	u⟹v	u=v
false	false	true	false	false	true	true
false	true	true	false	true	true	false
true	false	false	false	true	false	false
true	true	false	true	true	true	true

Given a well-formed formula w and a state s of w, one can derive the value of w at s; the value of w at s is an element of **boolean**; hence one can perceive a well-formed formula as a E-function from its space to **boolean**. This is why we denote the value of w at state s by w(s); the wff's **true** and **false** are constant functions.

It is left to the reader to verify that, if w is (a∧b)∨(c=b) then

$$w((\text{true},\text{false},\text{true})) = \text{false};$$
$$w((\text{true},\text{false},\text{false})) = \text{true}.$$

So far, we have relied solely on parentheses in order to describe how well-formed formulas are parsed. For the sake of simplifying notations, we shall introduce precedence rules among the connectives:

Logical Connective	Precedence Index
=	1
⟹	2
∨	3
∧	4
˜	5

Logical connectives with the highest precedence index are parsed first. Furthermore, when an operator occurs many consecutive times in a wff, the occurrences are parsed left to right. Hence, a∧b∨c=b is parsed as ((a∧b)∨c)= b; a∧b∨c∧b is parsed as (a∧b)∨(c∧b); a∧b∧˜c∨b is parsed as ((a∧ b)∧(˜c))∨b. The parsing of a well-formed formula indicates the order in which the evaluation is to take place: To find the value of a ∧ b ∧ ˜c ∨ b at some state s, one must compute the values of (a ∧ b) and (˜c), compute their conjunction ((a ∧ b) ∧ (˜c)) then compute the disjunction of ((a ∧ b) ∧ (˜c)) and b.

DEFINITION 5. A well-formed formula is said to be *valid* if and only if its value is **true** at all states; such a wff is called a *tautology*.

Tautologies are alternative representations for the constant well-formed formula **true**, just as "2+4" is an alternative representation for "6". If a is an atomic proposition then a ∨ ˜a, a⇒a and a = a are all tautologies.

DEFINITION 6. A well-formed formula is said to be *inconsistent* if and only if its value is **false** at all states; such a wff is called a *contradiction*.

Contradictions are alternative representations of the well-formed formula **false**; if a is an atomic proposition then a ∧ ˜a, a ∧ **false** and a = ˜a are all contradictions.

DEFINITION 7. Let u and v be two well-formed formulas; we say that v is a *logical consequence* of u if and only if (u⇒v) is a tautology.

For example, b is the logical consequence of (a⇒b) ∧ a; in order to prove this, one must prove that (a⇒b) ∧ a⇒b is a tautology; we abbreviate this well-formed formula by w and we determine its space.

$$S = \text{set}$$
$$\text{a, b: \textbf{boolean}}$$
$$\textbf{end}.$$

Let s be the state (**false, false**); by definition,

$$w(s) = (a(s) \Rightarrow b(s)) \land a(s) \Rightarrow b(s).$$

Now, a(s) = **false** and b(s) = **false**. Hence

$$w(s) = (\textbf{false} \Rightarrow \textbf{false}) \land \textbf{false} \Rightarrow \textbf{false}$$
$$= \textbf{true} \land \textbf{false} \Rightarrow \textbf{false}$$
$$= \textbf{false} \Rightarrow \textbf{false}$$
$$= \textbf{true}.$$

It is left to the reader to check that w((**false, true**)), w((**true, false**)) and w((**true, true**)) also equal **true**.

DEFINITION 8. Let u and v be two well-formed formulas; we say that u and v are *logically equivalent* if and only if u = v is a tautology.

It is left to the reader to verify that (˜a ∨ b) and (a⇒b), are logically equivalent wff's.

1.3 Equivalence and Substitution in Propositional Logic

By inspecting all the states of a well-formed formula, one can answer all the significant questions about it, such as whether it is a tautology, a contradiction or neither, or whether it is logically equivalent to some other well-formed formula, whether it logically implies some other well-formed formula. This technique is potentially cumbersome, because the number of states increases exponentially with the number of atomic propositions; furthermore, it is generally uninteresting because it gives no insight into the structure of the well-formed formulas involved. By contrast, the well-known technique we shall introduce in this section is elegant and suggestive.

THEOREM 1. Let u and u' be two well-formed formulas. Let w be a well-formed formula such that u is a sub-formula of it (i.e. w is obtained by composing u with some other wff's). Let w' be the wff obtained from w by substituting one (or more) occurrence(s) of u in w by u'. If u and u' are equivalent then so are w and w'.

In order to put this theorem into practice, we provide below a list of well-known equivalences (list due to D Gries, [4]).

1. **Commutative Laws**

$$\text{a- } (u \wedge v) = (v \wedge u).$$
$$\text{b- } (u \vee v) = (v \vee u).$$
$$\text{c- } (u = v) = (v = u).$$

2. **Associative Laws**

$$\text{a- } u \wedge (v \wedge w) = (u \wedge v) \wedge w.$$
$$\text{b- } u \vee (v \vee w) = (u \vee v) \vee w.$$

3. **Distributive Laws**

$$\text{a- } u \vee (v \wedge w) = (u \vee v) \wedge (u \vee w).$$
$$\text{b- } u \wedge (v \vee w) = (u \wedge v) \vee (u \wedge w).$$

4. **De Morgan's Laws**

$$\text{a- } (\tilde{}u \wedge v) = \tilde{}u \vee \tilde{}v.$$
$$\text{b- } (\tilde{}u \vee v) = \tilde{}u \wedge \tilde{}v.$$

5. **Law of Negation:** $\tilde{}\tilde{}u = u.$
6. **Law of Excluded Middle:** $u \vee \tilde{}u = $ **true.**
7. **Law of Contradiction:** $u \wedge \tilde{}u = $ **false.**
8. **Law of Implication:** $(u \Rightarrow v) = (\tilde{}u \vee v).$
9. **Law of Equality:** $(u = v) = ((u \Rightarrow v) \wedge (v \Rightarrow u)).$
10. **Laws of Or-simplification**

$$\text{a- } u \vee u = u.$$
$$\text{b- } u \vee \textbf{true} = \textbf{true}.$$
$$\text{c- } u \vee \textbf{false} = u.$$
$$\text{d- } u \vee (u \wedge v) = u.$$

11. **Laws of And-simplification**

$$\text{a- } u \wedge u = u.$$
$$\text{b- } u \wedge \textbf{true} = u.$$
$$\text{c- } u \wedge \textbf{false} = \textbf{false}.$$
$$\text{d- } u \wedge (u \vee v) = u.$$

12. **Law of Identity:** $u = u.$

EXAMPLE 1. Simplify the following well-formed formula, using Theorem 1 and the above Laws:

$$((u \wedge v) \vee (u \wedge \tilde{}v)) \wedge (u \vee (v \vee (v \wedge u))).$$

Using Law number:	we transform it into:
3(b)	$(u \wedge (v \vee \tilde{}v)) \wedge (u \vee (v \vee (v \wedge u)))$
6	$(u \wedge \textbf{true}) \wedge (u \vee (v \vee (v \wedge u)))$
11(b)	$u \wedge (u \vee (v \vee (v \wedge u)))$
10(d)	$u \wedge (u \vee v)$
11(d)	$u.$

1.4 Appendix: The Lattice of Propositional Logic

This section formalizes the intuitive notion of *strength* of a well-formed formula; it is natural, for example, to think of $u \wedge v$ as being stronger than v, or to think of u as being stronger than u ∨ v. Let W be the set of well-formed formulas of propositional logic.

DEFINITION 9. Let u and v be two well-formed formulas. We say that u is *stronger than* v (denoted u≫v) if and only if v is a logical consequence of u; the transpose of relation *stronger than* is relation *weaker than,* which is denoted by ≪.

The pairs (u,u∧v), (u∨v,u), (s>5,s>10), (1≤s≤3,s=3), (**true**,s=6) and (s=3,**false**) are all examples of elements of relation ≪, where u and v are well-formed formulas and s is an integer variable.

PROPOSITION 1. Relation ≪ is reflexive, antisymmetric and transitive.

The proof of this proposition is left to the reader. Because it is antisymmetric and transitive, relation ≪ is a partial ordering.

Note that the well-formed formula **true** is the ≪-first element of W, and that **false** is the ≪-last element of W.

PROPOSITION 2. The ≪-least upper bound of wff's u and v is u∧v.

Proof. The wff's u∧v⇒u and u∧v⇒v are both valid, which means that u∧v is an ≪-upper bound of u and v. Let w be another upper bound of u and v. We shall prove that u∧v≪w. We know that w⇒u and w⇒v are valid, hence (w⇒u)∧(w⇒v) is valid. We transform this wff using the substitution laws of section 1.3:

Law	expression
	(w⇒u)∧(w⇒v)
8	(˜w∨u)∧(˜w∨v)
3(a)	(˜w)∨u∧v
8	w⇒u∧v

Hence, by definition of relation ≪, u∧v≪w.
   Similarly, we can prove

PROPOSITION 3. The ≪-greatest lower bound of u and v is u∨v.

Therefore, in the set W ordered with relation ≪, any two elements have a least upper bound and a greatest lower bound. This makes (W,≪) a lattice.

1.5 Exercises

1. [A] Use parentheses in order to show how the following wff's are parsed:
   a) $u = u \Rightarrow v \Rightarrow w$.
   b) $u \wedge v = v \Rightarrow w \wedge \tilde{\ } u$.
   c) $u \wedge v \vee w \Rightarrow v$.
   d) $u \Rightarrow v = w$.
   e) $u \wedge v \Rightarrow v$.

2. [A] For each of the following wff's, determine the space and find a state for which the value of the wff is **true**.
   a) $u \Rightarrow v$.
   b) $(u \wedge v) \vee (\tilde{\ } u \vee \tilde{\ } v)$.
   c) $u \Rightarrow u \wedge v$.
   d) $(u \Rightarrow (v \Rightarrow w)) \Rightarrow v$.
   e) $((u \wedge v) \vee (u \wedge \tilde{\ } v)) \wedge (u \vee (v \vee (v \wedge u)))$.

3. [B] Verify that the following are tautologies of propositional logic:
   a) $(u \Rightarrow v) = (\tilde{\ } v \Rightarrow \tilde{\ } u)$.
   b) $(\textbf{true} \Rightarrow u) \Rightarrow u$.
      Conclude (using the rules of substitution) that $\tilde{\ } u$ is a logical conclusion of $(u \Rightarrow \textbf{false})$. Show that this is the rationale behind reasoning by *reductio ad absurdum*.

4. [B] Tell whether each of the following is a tautology, a contradiction or neither.
   a) $(u \wedge v) \vee \tilde{\ } v = u \vee \tilde{\ } v$.
   b) $(u \vee v) \wedge \tilde{\ } v = u \wedge \tilde{\ } v$.
   c) $((\tilde{\ } u \wedge v) \vee \tilde{\ } (u \vee v)) \wedge (\tilde{\ } u \vee (v \vee \tilde{\ } (v \Rightarrow u)))$.
   d) $(u \Rightarrow (v \Rightarrow w)) \wedge (u \wedge v \wedge \tilde{\ } w)$.
   e) $(u \Rightarrow v) \Rightarrow (u \Rightarrow w) \wedge (u \wedge v \wedge \tilde{\ } w)$.

5. [B] Show that set W (section 1.4) is not well-founded by relation $\ll$. Hint: give an example of an infinite sequence of wff's, u1, u2, u3, ... , such that the pair made up of any consecutive wff's is in relation $\ll$.

2 Predicate Logic

We consider the following sentence:

> If it rains then the sky is cloudy,
> and it rains;
> hence the sky is cloudy.

Substituting r for "it rains" and c for "the sky is cloudy", one finds that this sentence has the form

$$((r{\Rightarrow}c) \wedge r){\Rightarrow}c,$$

which is known to be a tautology in propositional logic (modus ponens rule).
Now we consider a slightly modified version of the same sentence:

> All rainy days are cloudy,
> and today is rainy;
> hence today is cloudy.

Even though this sentence is as valid as the first, propositional logic cannot
prove it so. Predicate logic attempts to probe more deeply into the structure of
sentences so as to recognize semantic relationships which are beyond the level
of propositions. In order to analyze the sentence above, one would define the
following predicates

> $r(s)$: day s is rainy,
> $c(s)$: day s is cloudy.

Then, one can write:

> For any s, $(r(s){\Rightarrow}c(s))$
> and r(today)
> hence c(today).

From the first clause one can deduce $(r(today){\Rightarrow}c(today))$; this in conjunction
with the second clause (r(today)) logically implies (c(today)), because in propositional logic c is the logical conclusion of r and $r{\Rightarrow}c$.

2.1 Predicate Logic: Syntax

A predicate on set S, as the reader will recall (section 3.1, Chapter 2), is a
function from set S to **boolean**. Complex predicates can be built from simpler
predicates by means of some syntactic rules that we wish to describe in this
section.

DEFINITION 10. If p is a predicate on set S, we say that S is the *space* of p.

DEFINITION 11. A *state* of a predicate is an element of its space.

DEFINITION 12. A *term* is defined as follows:

a) Each name of a state is a term.
b) If t1, t2, ... tn are terms and f is a function from $(S{\times}{\times}n)$—or a subset
   thereof—to S, then f(t1, t2, ... tn) is a term.

c) If t is a term then so is (t).
d) No string is a term unless it is generated by applications of (a), (b) or (c).

For notational convenience, terms will be written using functions whose range is some cartesian component of S, rather than S; this flexibility will allow us to use the elementary functions of set S to construct terms.

DEFINITION 13. An *atom* is defined as follows:

a) The symbols **true** and **false** are atoms.
b) If t1, t2, ... tn are terms and p is a predicate on $(S \times \times n)$ then p(t1, t2, ... tn) is an atom (the predicate of equality on S will be written in the usual way: t1 = t2, vs. = (t1,t2)).
c) If a is an atom then so is (a).
d) No string is an atom unless it is generated by applications of (a), (b) or (c).

Again, for notational convenience, we will use predicates whose arguments (t1, t2, ... tn) are not necessarily in S, but in some cartesian component of S.

DEFINITION 14. A *well-formed formula* (or wff) of predicate logic on set S is defined as follows:

a) An atom is a well-formed formula.
b) If w and w' are well-formed formulas then so are ~w, (w), w ∧ w', w ∨ w', w⟹w' and w = w'.
c) If w is a well-formed formula and s is the name of a state of w, then (∀s,w) and (∃s,w) are well-formed formulas.
d) No expression is a well-formed formula unless it can be generated by applications of (a), (b) or (c).

∀ reads: for all; it is called the *universal quantifier*. ∃ reads: there exists; it is called the *existential quantifier*.

EXAMPLE 2. Let S be the set defined as follows:

$$S = \textbf{set}$$
$$a, b, c: \textbf{real}$$
$$\textbf{end}.$$

(3.14, 2.18, 0.) and (1.01, −1.0, 3.19) are examples of states. Let s be an element of S. The following are terms:

t0: s;
t1: f(s), where f is [**true**,(a(s)+b(s),b(s),c(s))];
t2: f'(s), where f' is [a(s)>0, (log(a(s)),0,b(s))];
t3: f''(s), where f'' is [**true**,(b(s),c(s),a(s))].

The following are atoms:

a0: **false**;
a1: f(s)=(0.,0.,1.);
a2: f(s)=f''(s);
a3: f'(s)=s.

The following are well-formed formulas:

w0: (∃s, f'(s)=s);
w1: a2;
w2: (∀s, f(s)=f''(s));
w3: **true**.

2.2 Predicate Logic: Semantics

DEFINITION 15. Let s be a state name.

a) s is *free* in term s.
b) If s is *free* in terms t1, t2, ... tn and if f is a function from (S×Xn) or a subset thereof, to S or a cartesian component thereof, then s is *free* in f(t1, t2, ... tn).
c) If s is *free* in terms t1, t2, ... tn and p is a predicate on (S×Xn) then s is *free* in p(t1, t2, ... tn).
d) If s is *free* in a wff w then it is *free* in ~w, (w), (∃t,w) and (∀t,w), where t is a state distinct from s.
e) If s is *free* in w or w' then it is *free* in w∧w', w∨w', w⇒w' and w=w'.
f) No state is *free* unless it falls in one of the above categories.

We consider S= **real**; let s be an element of S; s is free in s, s+1, s>3, s= 3∧(∀s,s>t), (s⩾5) and (∃t, s=t); s is not free in (∃s, s>3).

DEFINITION 16. Let s be a state name.

a) State s is *bound* in the wff's (∃s,w) and (∀s,w), in which case we say that the *scope* of s is the symbol string between the parentheses.
b) If s is *bound* in w then it is bound in ~w, (w), (∃t,w) and (∀t,w), where t is a state name distinct from s.

c) If s is *bound* in w or w′, then it is *bound* in w ∧ w′, w ∨ w′, w⇒w′ and w = w′.

d) No state s is *bound* unless it falls in one of the above categories.

As an example, we consider the set S defined by

$$S = \text{set}$$
$$\text{a, b: } \textbf{real}$$
$$\textbf{end}.$$

State s is bound in the wff: ($\exists$s, a(s) = b(s) + 1); state t is not bound in the wff: ($\exists$s, a(s) < a(t) + b(t)).

DEFINITION 17. Let w be a well-formed formula of predicate logic on S. An *interpretation* of w is a function from the set of its free state names to S.

If some simple ordering is implicit among the free states, then one can simply define an interpretation of w as an element of $(S \times \times n)$, where n is the number of free states. In particular, if w is a well-formed formula with a unique free state, then an interpretation of w can be defined as a state of w. For example, {(s,(3.0,1.5)), (t,(5.1,2.4))} and {(s,(0.1,2.5)), (t,(4.0,1.6))} are interpretations of the well-formed formula w = (a(s) < a(t) + b(t)) on space S given above.

DEFINITION 18. Let w be a well-formed formula on space S, with n free states, $s_1, s_2, \ldots s_n$; the *value* of w at interpretation I is computed as follows:

a) The value of a term of w is computed by substituting each occurrence of s_k (k between 1 and n) by $I(s_k)$.

b) The value of atoms ˜a, a ∧ a′, a ∨ a′, a⇒a′ and a = a′ possibly appearing in w is computed from the values of a and a′ according to the evaluation rules of propositional logic.

c) The value of ($\forall$t,a) is **true** if and only if for any state t0 in S, the value of a at interpretation I ∪ {(t,t0)} is **true**.

d) The value of ($\exists$t,a) is **true** if and only if there exists a state t0 in S such that the value of a at interpretation I ∪ {(t,t0)} is **true**.

We consider the set S defined above and the well-formed formula w on S defined by $3 \leqslant b(s) \leqslant a(t)$; the value of w at interpretation {(s,(0.,4.)), (t,(6.,1.))} is **true**, whereas the value of w at interpretation {(s,(0.,0.)), (t,(0.,0.))} is **false**; also, if w′ is the well-formed formula ($\exists$t, $3 \leqslant b(t) \leqslant a(s)$), then the value of w′ at interpretation {(s,(0.,0.))} (or state (0.,0.)) is **false**, whereas the value of w′ at interpretation {(s,(5.,−1.))} is **true**; hence, the well-formed formula $w'' = (\exists s,(\exists t, 3 \leqslant b(t) \leqslant a(s)))$ has the value **true**, whereas the well-formed formula $v'' = (\forall s, (\exists t, 3 \leqslant b(t) \leqslant a(s)))$ has the value **false**.

Let w be a well-formed formula on space S and let n be the number of its free states, which we assume to be simply ordered; for any element (s1, s2, s3, ... sn) of $(S \times \times n)$, one can associate the value of w at interpretation (s1, s2, ... sn). For this reason, w can be perceived as a function from $(S \times \times n)$ to **boolean**, and its value for argument (s1, s2, .. sn) will be denoted w((s1, s2, .. sn)), or simply w(s1, s2, ... sn). In particular, if w has one free variable, it can be identified with a predicate on S.

DEFINITION 19. The wff w is said to be a *proper tautology* (P-tautology, for short) on space S if and only if the value of w at any interpretation is **true**.

The wff $w = (\exists t, a(t) = a(s) + b(s))$ defined on space S given above is a tautology; so is $(\forall s, (\exists t, a(t) = a(s) + b(s)))$.

DEFINITION 20. The wff w is said to be a *proper contradiction* (P-contradiction, for short) on S if and only if the value of w for any interpretation is **false**.

For example, the wff $w = (a(s) \leqslant b(t) \wedge a(s) > b(t))$ defined on space S given above is a contradiction.

In general, P-tautologies owe their validity to the specific definition of their space, their terms and their atoms. However, some well-formed formulas are valid regardless of their space, terms and atoms. These privileged tautologies will be called *universal tautologies,* or simply *tautologies* for short. Examples of universal tautologies are: **true**, $(\forall s, s = s)$, $(\forall s, (\forall s', s = s' \Rightarrow f(s) = f(s')))$, where f is some function defined on the space of the formula. We define *universal contradiction* in a similar way. Throughout this book, proper tautologies will be far more useful than universal tautologies.

2.3 Equivalence and Rules of Substitution

DEFINITION 21. Let w and w' be two wff's on the same space, with the same free states; w and w' are said to be *equivalent* if and only if they have the same value for any interpretation (or, equivalently, w = w' is a P-tautology).

On the space S given above, the two wff's $w = (\exists t, a(t) < 3) \wedge (\forall s, a(s) \leqslant b(s))$ and $w' = (\forall s, a(s) \leqslant b(s) \wedge (\exists t, a(t) < 3))$ are equivalent.

Theorem 1 given in section 1.3 regarding propositional logic can be generalized to predicate logic; before substituting u for u', one has to make sure that both u and u' are defined on the same space and that they have the same states

(i.e. same number of free states, with the same names). In order to put this
theorem into practice in the predicate logic, we provide below a list of well-
known equivalences.

1. **Generalizing De Morgan's Laws**
   a) $\tilde{\ }(\forall s, w) = (\exists s, \tilde{\ }w)$.
      This equivalence can be considered as an axiom; if the space is finite , it
      is simply a generalization of De Morgan's Law; if the space is infinite,
      this equivalence cannot be deduced from De Morgan's laws, but is,
      nevertheless, faithful to the semantics of the quantifiers $\forall$ and $\exists$.
   b) $\tilde{\ }(\exists s, w) = (\forall s, \tilde{\ }w)$.
      This stems from (a) and the law of negation of propositional logic.

2. **Distributing the Universal Quantifier**
   a) $(\forall s, w) \wedge (\forall s, w') = (\forall s, w \wedge w')$.
   b) $(\forall s, w) \wedge w' = (\forall s, w \wedge w')$, provided s is not free in w'.
   c) $(\forall s, w) \vee w' = (\forall s, w \vee w')$, provided s is not free in w'.
   d) $(\forall s, w) \wedge (\forall t, w') = (\forall s, (\forall t, w \wedge w'))$, provided s is not free in w' and t
      is not free in w.

3. **Distributing the Existential Quantifier**
   a) $(\exists s, w) \vee (\exists s, w') = (\exists s, w \vee w')$.
   b) $(\exists s, w) \vee w' = (\exists s, w \vee w')$, provided s is not free in w'.
   c) $(\exists s, w) \wedge w' = (\exists s, w \wedge w')$, provided s is not free in w'.
   d) $(\exists s, w) \wedge (\exists t, w') = (\exists s, (\exists t, w \wedge w'))$, provided s is not free in w' and t
      is not free in w.

In order to prove that a given wff w is a P-tautology, one can use these equa-
tions to show that $(\forall s, (\forall t, (\forall \ldots, w \ldots)))$, the so-called *universal closure* of
w, is equal to **true**, where s, t, ... are the free states of w.

EXAMPLE 3. Let w be the wff $(\forall s, \tilde{\ }u) \vee (\exists s, u)$;
   by law 1(a) and the law of negation, w is equivalent to

$$(\forall s, \tilde{\ }u) \vee \tilde{\ }(\forall, \tilde{\ }u);$$

by the law of excluded middle (propositional logic), w equals **true**.

2.4 Exercises

1. [A] Write the following using predicate logic; define the space and the free variables of each wff you write.
   a) Nobody under 13 is admitted unless accompanied by a relative over 18 years
      of age.

b) What is worth doing is worth doing well.

c) There is no $<$-minimal element in the set **integer**.

d) Among four arbitrary integers, either there are two whose difference is divisible by 4 or there are two whose sum is divisible by 4.

e) Among any m consecutive integers, there is one which is a multiple of m.

2. [B] Let S be the set

$$S = \textbf{set}$$
$$\textbf{crt}$$
$$\quad b: \textbf{boolean};$$
$$\quad r: \textbf{real};$$
$$\textbf{sub}$$
$$\quad b \Rightarrow (r > 0)$$
$$\textbf{end}.$$

a) Which of the following are elements of S: (**false**,0.), (**false**,1.), (**true**,0.), (**true**,1.)?

For each of the following wff's, determine

— its free states (give an example of interpretation).

— if it is a tautology on S; prove your claim.

— if it is a contradiction on S; prove your claim.

b) $(\exists t, b(t) \Rightarrow b(s) \land r(s) > r(t))$.

c) $(b(s) \land r(s) = 0)$.

d) $(f(s) = s)$, where f is the I-function on S whose pE-formula is $[\textbf{true}, (b(s) \land r(s) \geqslant 1, r(s) - 1)]$.

e) $(b(s) \land b(t) \Rightarrow r(t) \geqslant 0)$.

3. [B] Give three examples of interpretations for each of w, w' and w''; tell whether each is a tautology, a contradiction or neither.

a) Space, $S = \textbf{integer}$; $w = s + s' \leqslant t + t'$.

b) Space, $S' = \textbf{set}$
$$\quad a, b: \textbf{integer}$$
$$\textbf{end};$$
$$w' = a(s) + b(s) \leqslant a(t) + b(t).$$

c) Space, $S'' = \textbf{set}$
$$\quad a, b, c, d: \textbf{integer}$$
$$\textbf{end};$$
$$w'' = a(s) + b(s) \leqslant c(s) + d(s).$$

d) Highlight the relationships which exist between w, w' and w''.

e) Conclude on the latitude one has in deciding the space of a wff of predicate logic. Does one have the same latitude in propositional logic?

4. [A] The following are wff's on the set $S = \textbf{integer}$; determine their free and bound states.

a) $(\exists t, (\forall s, \sim divide(s,t)))$.

b) $(prime(t) = (\forall s, \sim divide(s,t)))$.

c) $p(s) \Rightarrow (\forall t, r(t) \lor (\exists u, q(s,t,z)))$.

   d) $(\forall s,(p(s)\Rightarrow(\exists t,r(t) \vee q(s,t,u))))$.
   e) $p(s) \wedge (\forall s,q(s,t,u))$.

3 Mathematical Induction

Mathematical induction is a method of proof which deduces the validity of a predicate p on *complex* elements of a set S from the validity of p on *simpler* elements. Among the seven program verification methods which are discussed in this book, six use mathematical induction. Mathematical induction is very useful in program verification because of the natural ways in which it tackles the many aspects of complexity of a computer program.

3.1 Simple Induction

Simple induction proves properties of the set **natural** or sets which are iso-morphic to it. It relies on the set having a strict simple ordering, whence its name. We shall briefly discuss two versions of simple induction: *stepwise induction* and *strong induction*.

3.1.1 Stepwise Induction

PROPOSITION 4. (Stepwise Induction Principle). Let p be a predicate on **natural**; if

   i) $p(0)$ is **true**, and
   ii) $p(n)\Rightarrow p(n+1)$ is a P-tautology on **natural**, then $p(n)$ is a P-tautology on **natural**.

Condition (i) is called the *basis of induction* and condition (ii) is called the *induction step*.

EXAMPLE 4. Prove that $0+1+2+ \ldots +n = n*(n+1)/2$; we abbreviate this predicate by the name $p(n)$.
Basis of induction: $p(0) = (0 = 0*(0+1)/2) =$ **true**.
Induction step: In order to prove that $(p(n)\Rightarrow p(n+1))$ is a P-tautology, we shall prove that $p(n+1)$ is a logical conclusion of $p(n)$; $p(n)$ is called the *induction hypothesis*.

$$p(n) \Rightarrow (0+1+2+ \ldots +n) = n*(n+1)/2$$
$$\Rightarrow (0+1+2+ \ldots +n)+(n+1) = n*(n+1)/2 + (n+1)$$
$$\Rightarrow (0+1+2+ \ldots + n+1) = (2*(n+1)+n*(n+1))/2$$

$$\Rightarrow (0+1+2+ \ldots + n+1) = (n+1)*((n+1)+1)/2$$
$$\Rightarrow p(n+1).$$

PROPOSITION 5. (Shifted Stepwise Induction Principle). Let a be an element of **integer** and let N[a] be the set of integers greater than or equal to a; let p be a predicate on N[a]; if

i) p(a) is **true**, and
ii) $(p(n)\Rightarrow p(n+1))$ is a P-tautology on N[a], then p(n) is a P-tautology on N[a].

EXAMPLE 5 (due to C L Liu, 1977). Prove that it is possible to make up postage of eight cents or more out of 3-cent stamps and 5-cent stamps.
We define predicate p on N[8] by $p(n) = (\exists k,(\exists k', n=3*k+5*k'))$, where k and k' are non-negative integers.
Basis of induction: $8 = 5+3$, hence p(8) is **true**;
Induction step: $p(n) = (\exists k,(\exists k', n=3*k+5*k'))$;
If $k'>0$ then $n+1 = 3*(k+2)+5*(k'-1)$,
otherwise $k\geqslant 3$ (since $n\geqslant 8$), in which case $n+1 = 3*(k-3)+5*(k'+2)$,
where $k-3\geqslant 0$. Hence p(n+1) holds.

3.1.2 Strong Induction

PROPOSITION 6. (Strong Induction Principle). Let p be a predicate on **natural**; if

i) p(0) is **true**, and
ii) $(\forall m, 0\leqslant m<n \Rightarrow p(m)) \Rightarrow p(n)$ is a P-tautology on **natural**, then p(n) is a P-tautology on **natural**.

EXAMPLE 6. Prove that all positive natural numbers can be written as the product of prime numbers. We define p(n) by "$n+1$ can be written as the product of prime numbers".
Basis of induction: $1 = 1$, hence p(0) holds. We consider 1 as a prime number.
Induction step: let n be a positive natural number; if $n+1$ is prime then p(n) holds else $n+1$ can be written as the product of two natural numbers, say m and m'; because $m<n+1$ and $m'<n+1$, we have p(m−1) and p(m'−1): hence p(n).

REMARK 1. Despite their difference in name and form, the three propositions given above are equally powerful, i.e. any predicate provable by one can be proved by the others (by eventually redefining the predicate to be proved). See exercise 3.

So far, we have seen methods of proof by induction which are applicable to properties of the set **natural** (or any set isomorphic to it). We intend to show that these methods can be used to prove properties of sets which are not necessarily isomorphic to **natural**. Let S be a set and p be a predicate on S; let q be a predicate on **natural** and k be a function from S to **natural** such that for any s in S, q(k(s)) = p(s). The proof of q by induction on **natural** can be understood as a proof of p by induction on S. For example, if S is the set of regular binary trees and p is the predicate defined by

p(s): the number of leaves of s exceeds the number of its internal nodes by 1,

one can define function k from S to **natural** by

k(s) = height of tree s,

and predicate q on **natural** by

q(h) = the number of leaves of any regular binary tree of height h exceeds the number of its internal nodes by 1,

and prove q by strong induction on the set **natural**.

The following section introduces a theorem of proof by induction which does not involve the set **natural** or any structure isomorphic to it.

3.2 Noetherian Induction

THEOREM 2. (Noetherian Induction Theorem, c.f. [2])
Let $<$ be a well-founded relation on set S, and let p be a predicate on S; if

$$(\forall t,\ t<s \Rightarrow p(t)) \Rightarrow p(s)$$

is a P-tautology on S, then p is a P-tautology on S.

Proof. We shall prove (reductio ad absurdum) that if $(\forall t,\ t<s \Rightarrow p(t)) \Rightarrow p(s))$ is a P-tautology on S then $S|\tilde{}p$ is empty. If $S|\tilde{}p$ is not empty, then it contains a $<$-minimal element, say s. For any element t in S such that $t<s$, p(t) holds; by hypothesis, this implies that p(s) holds, which contradicts the assumption that s belongs to $S|\tilde{}p$.

The importance of the Noetherian Induction Theorem is two-fold:

— It provides a method of proof which is more general than the three methods seen earlier.
— It shows that the rigid structure of the set **natural** (well-founded, simply ordered) is not necessary for proof by induction. In order for a proof by induction to be possible on set S, it suffices that set S be well-founded.

REMARK 2. The special case of Theorem 2 when the set S is well-ordered (vs. merely well-founded) is known as the *transfinite induction principle*.

All the principles of simple induction have two clauses to be proved: the basis of induction and the induction step. We wish to highlight the same feature in the premise of the Noetherian InductionTheorem, which is:

$$q(s) = (\forall t, \, t < s \Rightarrow p(t)) \Rightarrow p(s)).$$

Basis of induction: $q(s)$ must be a P-tautology on S; hence it must be **true** for the $<$-minimal elements of S; such elements exist because $<$ is a well-founded relation. Let u be a $<$-minimal element. The predicate $(\forall t, \, t < u \Rightarrow p(t))$ has the value **true**. Hence $q(u) = p(u)$: The proof of $p(u)$ corresponds precisely to the basis of induction.
Induction step: This is the proof of $q(s)$ when s is not $<$-minimal in S.

EXAMPLE 7. (Proof by Noetherian Induction). Let S be the set of regular binary trees, and let $<$ be the relation on S defined as $\{(t,s) \mid t$ is a subtree of $s\}$; we wish to prove by the Noetherian Induction Theorem that for any tree s in S, the number of leaves of s exceeds the number of its internal nodes by 1. It is easy to verify that $<$ is a well-founded relation.
Basis of induction: Let s be a $<$-minimal element of S; then, by definition of $<$, s is the tree made up of a single node; it has one leaf and no internal nodes.
Induction step: If s is not a leaf, then it has a left subtree and a right subtree (because s is regular): we call them ls and rs, respectively; we take the following notational conventions:

l, ll, lr: number of leaves of s, ls and rs, respectively;
i, il, ir: number of internal nodes of s, ls and rs, respectively.

We have:

$$ls < s, \text{ hence } ll = il + 1,$$
$$rs < s, \text{ hence } lr = ir + 1.$$

Furthermore,

$$l = ll + lr$$
$$i = il + ir + 1.$$

Hence, $l = i + 1$.

Note that the result proven by Noetherian induction in the example above could well have been proven by strong induction on the height of the tree. It is instructive to notice the distinction between the proof by Noetherian induction which deals with the very structure of the object it is dealing with (namely the tree) and the proof by strong induction which deals with a very *distant* abstraction of the tree: its height; see exercises 4 and 5.

3.3 Exercises

1. [A] Show by stepwise induction:
   a) $1**2 + 2**2 + \ldots + n**2 = n*(n+1)*(2n+1)/6$.
   b) $1**2 + 3**2 + \ldots + (2*n-1)**2 = n*(2*n-1)*(2*n+1)/3$.
   c) $1*2*3 + 2*3*4 + \ldots + n*(n+1)*(n+2) = n*(n+1)*(n+2)*(n+3)/4$.
   d) $1**3 + 2**3 + \ldots + n**3 = n* (n+1)**2 / 4$.

2. [A] Determine what is wrong with the following proof by stepwise induction: Its purpose is to show (?) that any finite set is a singleton (all its elements are equal). We will do induction on the cardinality of the set.
   Basis of induction: The property holds for a singleton.
   Induction step: let S_n be a set of cardinality n, $n > 1$; let $s_1, s_2, \ldots s_n$ be the elements of S_n; let S'_n and S''_n be the sets obtained from S_n by deleting (respectively) s_1 and s_n; since the induction property holds for S'_n and S'_n, we can write

$$s_1 = s_2 = \ldots = s_{n-1}$$
$$s_2 = s_3 = \ldots = s_n.$$

   Hence $s_1 = s_2 = \ldots = s_{n-1} = s_n$.

3. [B] Show that:
   a) Any property provable by stepwise induction can be proved by strong induction.
   b) Any property provable by strong induction can be proved by Noetherian induction.
   c) Any property provable by strong induction can be proved by stepwise induction (define $q(n) = p(1) \wedge p(2) \wedge \ldots p(n)$).

4. [B] (due to C L Liu, [8]) Prove by:
   a) Noetherian induction, then
   b) some method of simple induction, that any $2**n$ by $2**n$ defective chessboard

can be fully covered with triominoes without overlap; a defective chessboard is one such that one square is missing and a triomino is an L-shaped set of three squares.

5. [B] A tree is a graph which is both connected and cycle-free. Verify that in a tree the number of vertices exceeds the number of edges by 1, using:
   a) Noetherian induction, and
   b) some form of simple induction.
   c) Show on this example how Noetherian induction remains closer to the objects it is doing induction on.

4 Mathematical Deduction

4.1 Basic Definitions

DEFINITION 22. A *theory* t is defined when we are given the following:

— A set W, called the set of *well-formed formulas* of theory t.
— A subset T of W, called the set of *tautologies* of theory t.

Reflecting this definition, we shall represent a theory by the pair (W,T). If W is infinite, one may use a BNF description to represent all its elements; if T is infinite, it is customary to use a *deductive system* in order to represent all its elements in closed form. The interest of using deductive systems extends beyond the mere purpose of representing the tautologies of the theory at hand: More importantly, it gives insight into the process of proving that an element of W is or is not in T.

DEFINITION 23. A *deductive system* d is defined when we are given the following:

— A set W, called the set of *well-formed formulas* of system d.
— A subset A of W, called the set of *axioms* of system d.
— A set R of *inference rules*. Each inference rule is composed of a finite set of elements of W, say {p1, p2, ... pn}, and another element of W, say c; p1, p2, ... pn are called the *premises* of the rule; c is called its *conclusion*.

To reflect this definition, we shall represent a deductive system by the triplet (W,A,R). We may, sometimes, want to define abbreviations of well-formed formulas (e.g. (w⟹w′)⟹w′ abbreviated by w ∨ w′); each abbreviation is called a *definition,* and the set of definitions is then added to the description of the deductive system: (W,A,R,D). A definition is represented as follows: [⟨abbreviation⟩,⟨expression to be abbreviated⟩], for example: [w⟹w′, ˜w ∨ w′].

A rule whose premises are p1, p2, . . . pn and whose conclusion is c can be represented as [{p1, p2, . . . pn}, c]; however, for the sake of clarity, we usually represent it as follows:

$$
\begin{array}{c}
p1 \\
p2 \\
\cdots \\
pn \\
\hline
c.
\end{array}
$$

Once we are given a deductive system (W,A,R) (or (W,A,R,D)), it is interesting to characterize those elements of W that are theorems.

DEFINITION 24. A *deduction* in a deductive system d is a list w_1, w_2, . . . w_k of well-formed formulas of d such that for any i between 1 and k, w_i is either an axiom or the conclusion of some inference rule whose premises belong to the set $\{w_1, w_2, . . . w_{i-1}\}$.

DEFINITION 25. A *theorem* of the deductive system d is a well-formed formula w which appears on some deduction of d.

This definition yields that each axiom of d is a theorem of d.

DEFINITION 26. A well-formed formula w of d is said to be a *consequence* of a set V of well-formed formulas if and only if there exists a list w_1, w_2, . . . w_k in W such that w_k = w and for any i between 1 and k, w_i is either an axiom or an element of V or the conclusion of some inference rule of d whose premises belong to $\{w_1, w_2, . . . w_{i-1}\}$.

EXAMPLE 8. (Deductive System for the Propositional Logic, c.f. [5]). Let W be the set of well-formed formulas of propositional logic and T be the set of tautologies of propositional logic. In this example, we shall present a deductive system h = (W,A,R,D) for the theory t = (W,T); because truth tables enable one to answer most of the significant questions about propositions, the sole purpose of system h is illustrative.

Set W =
⟨well-formed formula⟩ ::= ⟨letter⟩ |
        ⟨well formed formula⟩ ⟹ ⟨well formed formula⟩ |
        ˜ ⟨well-formed formula⟩
⟨literal⟩ ::= a|b|c| . . . |x|y|z.

Set A =
  { u⟹(v⟹u),
    (u⟹(v⟹w)) ⟹ ((u⟹v)⟹(u⟹w)),
    (˜u⟹˜v) ⟹ (v⟹u) }.

Set R =
  { [{u, u⟹v}/v],   The Modus Ponens Rule
    [{f(u), u⟹v, v⟹u}/f(v)]   The Substitution Rule
  }.

Set D. =
  { [u ∧ v, ˜(u⟹˜v)],   And Abbreviation
    [u ∨ v, (u⟹v)⟹v],   Or Abbreviation
    [u = v, (u⟹v) ∧ (v⟹u)] Equal Abbreviation
  }.

$$h = (W,A,R,D).$$

Is (u⟹u) a theorem of h?

$$w1 = (u⟹((u⟹u)⟹u)) ⟹ ((u⟹(u⟹u))⟹(u⟹u));$$

this is the second axiom in which u and w are substituted by u and v is substituted by u⟹u.

$$w2 = (u⟹((u⟹u)⟹u));$$

this is an instance of the first axiom in which v is replaced by u⟹u.

$$w3 = (u⟹(u⟹u)) ⟹ (u⟹u);$$

w3 is the conclusion of the modus ponens rule for the premises w2 and w1.

$$w4 = u⟹(u⟹u);$$

this is an instance of the first axiom, with u and v being replaced by u.

$$w5 = (u⟹u);$$

w5 is the conclusion of the modus ponens rule for the premises w4 and w3.

Clearly, the list (w1, w2, w3, w4, w5) is a deduction in the deductive system h; hence w5 is a theorem of h.

Let us consider the list (v1, v2, v3) in W, where

$$v1 = (u{\Rightarrow}(v{\Rightarrow}u)),$$
$$v2 = u,$$
$$v3 = (v{\Rightarrow}u).$$

Let U be the set $\{u\}$; we see that v1 is an axiom of h, v2 is an element of U and v3 is the conclusion of the modus ponens rule for the premises v2 and v1; hence $(v{\Rightarrow}u)$ is a consequence of set U in the deductive system h.

4.2 Consistency and Completeness

Let $t = (W,T)$ be a theory and $d = (W,A,R)$ be a deductive system whose purpose is to support theory t (i.e. describe it in closed form). We define $G(A,R)$ (G stands for *generate)* to be the set of theorems that are generated from the axioms of A by the rules of R. Ideally, if system d is designed correctly, $G(A,R)$ is equal to T.

DEFINITION 27. System $d = (W,A,R)$ is said to be *complete* with respect to theory $t = (W,T)$ if and only if $G(A,R)$ is a superset (not necessarily a proper superset) of T.

DEFINITION 28. System $d = (W,A,R)$ is said to be *consistent* with respect to theory $t = (W,T)$ if and only if $G(A,R)$ is a subset (not necessarily a proper subset) of T.

The consistency of a deductive system is often defined independently of a theory: System d is said to be consistent if and only if no wff and its negation are both theorems of d. This definition was not adopted here because it assumes that the notion of negation is significant in the context of system d. Yet, the definition of deductive systems given in this chapter makes no mention of negation (see exercise 1).

Clearly, if system d is complete and consistent with respect to theory d then the relation $G(A,R) = T$ is satisfied.

4.3 Exercises

1. [A] List all the theorems of the deductive system $d = (W,A,R)$, where
   W $= \{a,b,c,d,e,f\}$,
   A $= \{a\}$,
   R $= \{[\{a\}/b], [\{a,b\}/c], [\{c\},d], [\{b,d\}/e], [\{b\}/f]\}$.
   Is this system consistent wrt theory $t = (W,W)$? Is this system complete with respect to $(W, \{a,b,c\})$?

2. [C] Verify that the following are theorems of the deductive system h given in Example 8 (section 4.1); briefly verify that they are tautologies of propositional logic.
   a) $u \Rightarrow \tilde{}\tilde{}u$.
   b) $\tilde{}u \Rightarrow (u \Rightarrow v)$.
   c) $(u \wedge v) \Rightarrow u$.
   d) $u \Rightarrow (u \vee v)$.
   e) $(\tilde{}u \Rightarrow u) \Rightarrow u$.

3. [C] Verify that, in the deductive system h (given in Example 8),
   a) $u \Rightarrow v$ is a consequence of $\{(u \Rightarrow w), (w \Rightarrow v)\}$.
   b) $v \Rightarrow (u \wedge v)$ is a consequence of $\{u\}$.

4 [C] Let m (due to E Mendelsson, [10]) be the deductive system defined as follows: m = (W,A,R,D), where W and D are identical to those of deductive system h (Example 8) and A and R are defined as follows:

$$Set\ A =$$
$$\{u \Rightarrow (v \Rightarrow u),\ (u \Rightarrow (v \Rightarrow w)) \Rightarrow ((u \Rightarrow v) \Rightarrow (u \Rightarrow w)),$$
$$((\tilde{}v \Rightarrow \tilde{}u) \Rightarrow ((\tilde{}v \Rightarrow u) \Rightarrow v))\}.$$
$$Set\ R =$$
$$\{[\{(u \Rightarrow v),u\}/v]\}.$$

Verify that the following are theorems of deductive system m.
   a) $\tilde{}\tilde{}u \Rightarrow u$.
   b) $\tilde{}u \Rightarrow (u \Rightarrow v)$.
   c) $u \wedge v \Rightarrow u$.
   d) $(\tilde{}v \Rightarrow \tilde{}u) \Rightarrow (u \Rightarrow v)$.
   e) $u \Rightarrow u$.

5 Problems

1. [A] Let S be the set defined as

$$S = \textbf{set}$$
$$a,\ b,\ c:\ \textbf{boolean}$$
$$\textbf{end};$$

Let w be the well-formed formula of predicate logic defined on S by $w(s) = a(s) \vee (b(s) \Rightarrow a(s) \wedge c(s))$.
   a) What is the space of w? How many free states does w have? Define, in the simplest possible terms, an interpretation of wff w.
   b) Consider the well-formed formula of propositional logic $w' = a \vee (b \Rightarrow a \wedge c)$. What is the space of w'? Define an interpretation of proposition w'.
   c) Summarize your conclusions.

2. [A] Discuss the significance of the following wff's on set S and show that they are tautologies; u and v are predicates on S.

$$(\forall s,u) \vee (\forall s,v) \Rightarrow (\forall s,u \vee v),$$
$$(\exists s,u \wedge v) \Rightarrow (\exists s,u) \wedge (\exists s,v).$$

Show, by a proper choice of S, u and v, that the reverse implications do not hold.

3. [A] Let S be

> S = **set**
> **crt**
>   a, b: **boolean;**
> **sub**
>   ~(a $\wedge$ ~b)
> **end,**

and let w be the wff defined on S by w(s) = (a(s)$\Rightarrow$b(s)).
a) Show that w is a P-tautology on S;
b) Let w' be the wff defined on S by w'(s) = (a(s) $\vee$ ~a(s)); show that w' is also a P-tautology on S. There is a fundamental attribute which distinguishes between these two P-tautologies: Discuss it.

4. [B] The Noetherian induction theorem provides that in order for proofs by induction to be feasible on set S, it suffices that S be well-founded. Show that this is a necessary condition. Give examples of sets on which no form of induction is possible.

5. [A] Describe a sufficient condition for a deductive system d to be consistent with respect to propositional logic.

6. [A] Let R be an I-relation equal to {(s,s')|r(s,s')}. Give a set-theoretic representation of **dom**(R), i.e. write **dom**(R) as {s|p(s)}.

6 Bibliography

For more on propositional logic, consult [3], [7], [10], [11] and [12]. See [7] for an in-depth study, and see [5] for more examples of deductive systems of the propositional logic.
  Predicate logic is concisely covered in [11], formally discussed in [10], [7] and [9]. [3] discusses the automatic verification of theorems in predicate logic.
  Simple induction is covered in [1], [8], [13] and [14]. Noetherian induction is covered in [2] and [9].
  Deductive systems are informally discussed in [6]. Formal presentations of deductive systems are given in [4], [5] and [13]. For more examples of deductive systems see [9], [10], [11] and [12].

 1: Anderson, R B. Proving Programs Correct. John Wiley, 1979.
 2: Burstall, R M. Proving Properties of Programs by Structural Induction. Computer Journal 12(1) (February 1969), pp 41-48.
 3: Chang, C L and R C Lee. Symbolic Logic and Mechanical Theorem Proving. Academic Press, 1973.
 4: Gries, D. The Science of Programming. Springer-Verlag, 1981.
 5: Hackstaff, L H. Systems of Formal Logic. Reidel, 1966.
 6: Kilgore, W J. An Introductory Logic. Holt, Rinehart and Winston, 1979.
 7: Kleene, S C. Mathematical Logic. John Wiley, 1967.
 8: Liu, C L. Elements of Discrete Mathematics. McGraw-Hill, 1977.
 9: Manna, Z. Mathematical Theory of Computation. McGraw-Hill, 1974.
10: Mendelson, E. Introduction to Mathematical Logic. D Van Nostrand, 1979.
11: Rogers, R. Mathematical Logic and Formalized Theories. North-Holland, 1971.
12: Stoll, R R. Set Theory and Logic. W H Freeman, 1966.
13: Thomason, R H. Symbolic Logic. Macmillan, 1970.
14: Wand, M. Induction, Recursion and Programming. Elsevier North-Holland, 1980.

Part II:
Specification, Abstraction and Verification

There is something uncanny about the power of a happily chosen ideographic language; for it often allows one to express relations which have never been noticed by anyone. Symbolism, then, becomes an organ of discovery rather than mere notation.

Suzanne K. Langer,
An Introduction to Symbolic Logic, *1967.*

Chapter 4 analyzes the nature and properties of specifications and derives from the analysis a simple representation for program specifications. Chapter 5 introduces the programming language SM-Pascal, which is a slightly modified version of a subset of Pascal (SM stands for *simple*); then it defines the notions of program execution and functional abstraction of programs. Chapter 6 defines program correctness and presents the symbolic execution method.

Chapter 4

Specification

The *specification* of a program is the expression of the requirements that a user imposes on a program he wishes to use. Requirements are usually of two kinds: performance requirements, such as response time, memory limitations, reliability or availability; and functional requirements, that is the functional relationships which must hold between the inputs submitted to the program and the outputs that it returns. Performance requirements are beyond the scope of this book; hence we shall consider only functional requirements. We shall further restrict our study of *terminating* programs, i.e. programs that for every input, return after a finite amount of time an output which is fully determined from the input. See problem 1 for a discussion of programs which do not fall into this category.

1 Basic Definitions

A user who wants to express his requirements on a program does so by defining the set of input/output pairs that he considers correct; hence a specification is a relation. A specification can be an E-relation or an I-relation depending on whether the set of inputs and the set of outputs are best considered identical or distinct.

DEFINITION 1. An *E-specification* is defined when we are given:
— A set IS called the *input space* of the specification.
— A set OS called the *output space* of the specification.
— an E-relation R from a subset of IS to a subset of OS called the *relation* of the specification.

Because of this definition, we shall describe an E-specification as (IS,OS,R). When IS and OS are implied, we will simply represent the specification by R. Notice that **dom**(R) (respectively **rng**(R)) is not necessarily equal to IS (respectively OS); rather, it is generally a subset of it. The appropriateness of this choice shall become clear later as we discuss the generation of specifications in section 3.

DEFINITION 2. An *I-specification* is defined when we are given:

— A set S called the *space* of the specification.
— An I-relation R on S, called the *relation* of the specification.

An I-specification will be represented as (S,R). We may sometimes describe an I-specification by its relation only (R), when set S is implicit from the context of the discussions.

Also, when the context does not lead to confusion or when it is not necessary to be specific, we shall use the generic term *specification* to refer to either an E-specification or an I-specification.

Exercises

1. [A] For each one of the specifications below, tell whether it would be best to use an I-specification or an E-specification. Briefly justify your choice.
   a) A program to sort an array.
   b) A program to search for an item in an array.
   c) A program to find the root (supposed to be unique) of a polynomial of degree n in some interval [a,b].
   d) A program to compute the number of leaves in a binary tree.
   e) A program to check whether a graph is connected.

2. [A] Same question as 1.
   a) A program to compute the square root.
   b) A program to read a list of n numbers and generate one of them that is greater than or equal to the median.
   c) A program to transfer a file from one medium to another.
   d) A program to check the syntax of a file (by some predefined rule).
   e) A program to swap the values of two variables (say of type **real**).

2 Representing Specifications

2.1 Representing E-specifications

E-specifications are expressed using sets and relations. The representation of sets was discussed in section 3.5 of Chapter 2. Once sets IS and OS are defined, the cartesian product IS×OS is implicitly defined. In order to describe a relation from IS to OS, one may want to write a predicate on set IS × OS. This requires that a variable from IS, say is, and a variable from OS, say os, be declared. An E-specification is represented as follows:

specification ⟨specification header⟩;
spa
      IS = ⟨set declaration⟩; (*input space*)
      OS = ⟨set declaration⟩; (*output space*)
sta
      is: IS; (*input state*)
      os: OS; (*output state*)
rel
      ⟨predicate⟩ (*predicate involving is and os*)
end.

The ⟨specification header⟩ represents a name, eventually followed by a parameter list if the specification is to be parameterized. Below is an example of E-specification.

EXAMPLE 1: Quadratic Equation.

specification quadratic (EpsilonX, EpsilonY: **real**);
(*actually EpsilonX and EpsilonY must be positive reals*)
spa
  Two-rooted-trinomials = **set**
  crt
    a, b, c: **real**;
  sub
    $a \neq 0 \ \wedge \ b*b - 4*a*c >$ EpsilonY
  end;
  Two-roots = **set**
  crt
    x′, x″: **real**;
  sub
    $x′ \leq x″$
  end;
sta
  t: Two-rooted-trinomials;
  r: Two-roots;
rel
  abs $(a(t)*x′(r)**2 \ + \ b(t)*x′(r) \ + \ c(t)) <$ EpsilonY $\wedge$
  abs $(a(t)*x″(r)**2 \ + \ b(t)*x″(r) \ + \ c(t)) <$ EpsilonY $\wedge$
  $x″(r) - x′(r) >$ EpsilonX
end.

The first and second conjuncts of the predicate written under the heading **rel** express that x′ and x″ are roots within a tolerance of EpsilonY. The third conjunct expresses that they are different by at least EpsilonX; it excludes programs which would return twice the same root.

2.2 Representing I-specifications

An I-specification is represented as follows:

> **specification** ⟨specification header⟩;
> **spa**
>   S = ⟨set declaration⟩; (*space*)
> **sta**
>   s, s′: S; (*input and output states*)
> **rel**
>   ⟨predicate⟩ (*predicate involving s and s′*)
> **end**.

Below is an example of I-specification.

EXAMPLE 2.

> **specification** integer-division;
> **spa**
>   triplets = **set**
>   **crt**
>   divisor, dividend, quotient: **natural**;
>   **sub**
>   divisor ≠ 0
>   **end**;
> **sta**
>   s, s′: triplets;
> **rel**
>   dividend(s) = divisor(s) * quotient(s′) + dividend(s′) ∧
>   dividend(s′) < divisor(s)
> **end**.

Note that the relation expressed in this specification is not a function because divisor(s′) is not fully determined from s. For example, ((3,16,0), (3,1,5)) and ((3,16,0), (9,1,5)) are both elements of the relation expressed in this specification.

2.3 Exercises

1. [B] Represent each one of the specifications given in exercise 1 of section 1; take into account the comments/hints given below for each.
   a) Use the list functions (Chapter 2, section 4) and assume the array is **real**.
   b) Assume the array is **real**.
   c) With some precision provided as parameter; assume degree 4.
   d) No comment.
   e) Assume a size of 10 nodes.

2. [B] Represent each one of the specifications given in exercise 2 of section 1; take into account the comments/hints given below for each.
   a) Assume a given tolerance.
   b) Assume you are given 50 real numbers.
   c) Assume the file is made up of 100 real numbers.
   d) The file contains 20 integers; it is syntactically correct if the signs of the integers alternate.
   e) No comment.

3 Developing Specifications

3.1 A Procedure

Specifications are potentially complex structures. Hence some provisions must be made to tackle their complexity in a stepwise fashion. We shall present a stepwise procedure for generating E-specifications. We leave it to the reader to derive a similar simple procedure for generating I-specifications.

— Generate sets IS and OS.
— Generate E-relations from subsets of IS to subsets of OS, which reflect properties that an input/output pair must meet in order to be correct.
— Intersect all these relations. Let R be the intersection; deliver the specification (IS, OS, R).

Sets IS and OS being arbitrarily vague (i.e. arbitrarily large in the sense of inclusion), their generation is easy. The generation of the E-relations from subsets of IS to subsets of OS is also intellectually manageable because they too can be arbitrarily vague. Each individual relation expresses a *weak* property; at no time is the user required to perceive the total specification in all its complexity. The third step of the procedure is straightforward; it is actually automatable.

3.2 Exercises

1. [B] Let *Arrays* be the set defined as follows:

Arrays = **set**
crt
    size: **integer**;
    vals: **array** [1.. size] of **real**;
sub
    size > 0
end,

and let s and s' be elements of *Arrays*.

a) We wish to generate a specification for a sorting program; the first requirement which comes to mind is that the output of the program be an ordered array: Derive the I-relation Ord on set *Arrays* which expresses this requirement.

b) Note that Ord is too vague a relation because if size(s') = 1 then (s,s'):Ord regardless of s. Derive the I-relation Unc on set *Arrays* which expresses that the size must be unchanged by application of the program.

c) Note that if s' is such that for any integer between 1 and size(s'), vals(s')[k] = k then (s,s'):(Ord ∩ Unc) for any s having the same size as s'. Derive the I-relation Perm on set *Arrays* which expresses the necessary additional requirement.

d) Noting that Perm is a subset of Unc, derive the intersection of Ord, Unc and Perm.

e) Write the final version of the specification.

4 Predicate-based Specifications

Many program verification methods place a heavy emphasis on the use of predicates to characterize correct states; as a result, a tradition for specifying programs using predicates has come about naturally. The purpose of this section is to show how predicate-based specifications relate to the relation-based mode of specification introduced in this chapter. For the sake of simplicity, we shall restrict our attention to I-specifications.

DEFINITION 3. A *predicate-based specification* is defined when we are given:

— A set S, called the *space* of the specification.
— A predicate Phi on S, called the *input predicate* of the specification.
— A predicate Psi on S, called the *output predicate* of the specification.

A predicate-based specification will be represented by the triplet (S,Phi,Psi).

DEFINITION 4. *Semantics of a predicate-based specification:* The predicate-based specification (S,Phi,Psi) defines the I-specification (S, {(s,s')| Phi(s) ∧ Psi(s')}).

It stems from this definition that for any predicate-based specification one can derive a relation-based specification which is equivalent; the relation-based specification so derived is called the *semantic value* of the predicate-based specification. The reverse transformation is also possible:

PROPOSITION 1. Let Sp = (S,R) be an I-specification. The semantic value of the predicate-based specification

$$Sp' = (S, \text{s:}\mathbf{dom}(R) \land s = s0, (s0,s):R)$$

is Sp.
Proof. By Definition 4, the semantic value of Sp' is

$$(S, \{(s,s')| \text{ s:}\mathbf{dom}(R) \land s = s0 \land (s0,s'):R\}).$$

This can be written as:

$$(S, \{(s,s')| \text{ s:}\mathbf{dom}(R) \land (s,s'):R\}),$$

which is equal to

$$(S, \{(s,s')| (s,s'):R\}),$$

i.e. (S,R). QED

Exercises

1. [A] Find the semantic value of the following predicate-based specifications.
   a) (**real**, s = s0, s = s0).
   b) (**real**, s = s0, s0 = log(s)).
   c) (**real**, s = s0 ∧ s<1, s = log(s0)).
   d) (**real**, s = s0 ∧ s>0 ∧ s≠3, s = log(s0)).
   e) (**real**, s = s0 ∧ (s = −2 ∨ s = 2), s = log(**abs**(s0+1))).

2. [B] Find the predicate-based specification which is equivalent to the following relation-based specification.
   a) (**real**, {(s,s')| s>0 ∧ s' = log(s)}).
   b) (**real**, {(0.,0.), (1.,1.), (1.,2.)}).

c) $(\textbf{real}, \{(s,s')|\ s>0\ \wedge\ s<4\ \wedge\ s'=\log(s)\})$.
d) $(\{1,2,3,4,5\}, \{(s,s')|\ s'<s\})$.
e) $(\{1,2,3,4,5\}, \{(s,s')|\ 1<s'<s\})$.

5 Problems

1. [C] Discuss the definition, representation and development of continuous program specifications. A continuous program is an implementation of a stimulus-response mechanism having three spaces (input, internal and output) and two functions (internal function and output function).

2. [B] The technique given in section 3 for developing specifications proceeds by generating many supersets of the target relation R then intersecting them. A dual approach would consist of generating many subsets of the target relation then computing their union. Discuss the latter technique and compare it to the former.

3. [B] *Enhancing the Representation of Sets:* Consider the specification Quadratic given in section 2.
   a) Discuss the pertinence of having built-in functions in the declaration of set Two-rooted-trinomials, such as the function discriminant *(dis)*, the function value *(val)*, etc . . .
   b) In opposition to the elementary functions (in this case a, b and c), the functions dis and val will be called the *secondary functions*. Discuss the syntax of the call of these functions; distinguish between the parameterless functions such as *dis* and the parameterized functions such as *val*. An appropriate representation for the structure of set would then be:

   > **set**
   > **crt** ⟨elementary function declarations⟩
   > **sec** ⟨secondary function declarations⟩
   > **sub** ⟨predicate involving elementary and/or secondary functions⟩
   > **end**.

See also section 1 of Chapter 8 for more on this notion.

4. [B] A *specification scheme* is the pair made up of:
   — A specification language, i.e. a notation for representing specifications,
   — A specification methodology, i.e. a procedure for deriving specifications.
   Provide a list of requirements that a specification scheme must meet.

6 Bibliography

Predicate-based specifications came about naturally along with the early program verification methods: [2] and [4].

For more information on recent developments in the specification of terminating as well as continuous programs, consult [5] and [8].

For advanced topics on specification languages, consult [1], [3], [6] and [7].

1: Burstall, R M and J A Goguen. The Semantics of Clear, a Specification Language. Lecture Notes in Computer Science, Vol 86. Springer-Verlag, 1980.

2: Floyd, R W. Assigning Meanings to Programs. Proceedings, The American Mathematical Society Symposium on Applied Mathematics. (1967), pp 19-31.

3: Goguen, J A and R M Burstall. An Ordinary Design. Internal Report, SRI International, Menlo Park, CA. November 1980.

4: Hoare, C A R. An Axiomatic Basis for Computer Programming. CACM 12(10) (October 1969), pp. 576-580, 583.

5: Ohno, Y (Editor). Requirements Engineering Environments. North-Holland, 1982.

6: Parnas, D L. A Technique for Software Module Specification with Examples. CACM 15(5) (May 1972), pp 330-336.

7: Roubine, O and L Robinson. SPECIAL Reference Manual. TR-CSG-45, SRI International, Menlo Park (CA) 1977.

8: Yeh, R T. Current Trends in Programming Methodology, Vol I. Prentice-Hall, 1977.

Chapter 5

Execution and Functional Abstraction

In this chapter a programming language is defined, under the name SM-Pascal; it is primarily a subset of Pascal with some syntactic and semantic adjustments whose purpose is to tune the language to our specific environment and interests. Issues relative to the functional abstraction of programs are then discussed.

1 SM-Pascal

A summary of the major features of SM-Pascal is given here; the full BNF description is given in Appendix A.

1.1 SM-Pascal's Data Structures

SM-Pascal has three kinds of *simple types* (see ⟨simple type⟩ in Appendix A):

— *scalar types*, such as traffic-lights = (green, orange, red).
— *subrange types*, such as nine-to-five = 9 .. 17.
— *basic types*, which are:

- **natural**, not available in Pascal, and
- **integer**,
- **real**,
- **boolean**, and
- **char**,

which are all available in Pascal.

SM-Pascal has four kinds of *structured types* (see ⟨structured type⟩ in Appendix A):

— *array type*, whose syntax and semantics are those of Pascal's array type.
— *set type*, which is fundamentally distinct from Pascal's set type. The syntax and semantics of SM-Pascal's set type are those given in section 3.5 of Chapter 2; an example is given below to refresh the reader's memory:

first-degree-polynomial = **set**
crt
  a, b: **real**;
sub
  $a \neq 0$
end.

— *collection type,* which is to be the same as Pascal's set type: It has a similar syntax (**collection of** instead of **set of**) and has the same semantics; an example of a collection type declaration is:

  fruits = **collection of** (apple, orange, banana, grape).

— *file type,* which is identical to Pascal's file type.

In contrast with Pascal, SM-Pascal has only unpacked structured types. Pascal's structure of **record** is not available in SM-Pascal, being replaced by SM-Pascal's **set** structure.

SM-Pascal also has Pascal's pointer type.

1.2 SM-Pascal's Control structures

Before we present SM-Pascal's control structures, let's agree to a notational convention.

REMARK 1. Let s be an element of the set *first-degree-polynomial* defined in the previous section. The syntax of SM-Pascal's set type provides that in order to access component "a" of element s, one has to write a(s). Using this notation in SM-Pascal leads to ambiguities: When a(s) appears in the statement part of a SM-Pascal program, it may be confused with a function call (function *a* called with parameter *s*). In order to remove this ambiguity, we shall use the notation *s.a.* This notation causes no confusion with Pascal's field designators because the type **record** is excluded from SM-Pascal. Along with the dot ("."") notation, we shall use the *with statement* with a meaning similar to that of Pascal's. Whenever no ambiguity is possible, we may directly reference the elementary functions of a set without a with statement. This is the case whenever the program has a single declaration in its variable declaration part (a very common case in this book). See, e.g. the program given in exercise 2.

SM-Pascal has three kinds of *simple statements* (see ⟨simple statement⟩ in Appendix A):

— *assignment statement.*
— *procedure call.*
— *empty statement.*

Pascal's *Goto* statement is excluded from SM-Pascal; furthermore, procedures and functions may not have procedures or functions as parameters. Also, in contrast with Pascal, the result type of a function declaration can be a structured type.

SM-Pascal has six kinds of *structured statements* (see ⟨structured statement⟩ in Appendix A):

— *begin-end statement,* such as: **begin** st **end.**
— *sequence statement,* such as: st1; st2.
— *conditional statement,* such as: **if** t **then** tc.
— *alternative statement,* such as: **if** t **then** tc **else** ec.
— *while statement,* such as: **while** t **do** lb.
— *with statement,* such as: **with** s **do** wb.

SM-Pascal does not offer Pascal's **case** statement, **repeat** statement or **for** statement; also, SM-Pascal programs have only two external files: **input** and **output.** Conceptually, these restrictions do not cause a loss of generality; they will, however, facilitate future discussions.

1.3 The Natural Ordering of SM-Pascal Statements

We introduce an ordering relation among the statements of a SM-Pascal program; this ordering ranks statements by increasing complexity, hence its name: relation *Cpx*. This relation shall be used for future proofs and discussions. Relation Cpx is the transitive closure of the following relation:

$$\{ (, st),$$
$$(st, \textbf{begin } st \textbf{ end}),$$
$$(st, st; st'),$$
$$(st, st'; st),$$
$$(tc, \textbf{if } t \textbf{ then } tc),$$
$$(tc, \textbf{if } t \textbf{ then } tc \textbf{ else } ec),$$
$$(ec, \textbf{if } t \textbf{ then } tc \textbf{ else } ec),$$

(lb, **while** t **do** lb),
(wb, **with** s **do** wb),
(pd, **procedure** ... **begin** pd **end**),
(pg, **program** ... **begin** pg **end.**)   }.

Relation Cpx is clearly a well-founded relation on the set of statements; hence we may use it for induction proofs. In the set of SM-Pascal statements, a Cpx-minimal statement is the empty statement. The empty statement is also the Cpx-first element of the set of SM-Pascal statements.

1.4 Exercises

1. [A] Parse the following expressions, on the basis of the BNF description of SM-Pascal (Appendix A).
   a) x + y + z + w.
   b) x * y + z < 1.
   c) x **mod** y + 1 **div** 4 = z.
   d) x < y **or** y > 0.
   e) − x * y − z + x ≠ 1.

2. [B] Formally verify that the following is a correct SM-Pascal program:

```
program P(input, output);
type
    S = set
    crt
        a, b: integer;
    sub
        b⩾0
    end;
var
    s: S;
begin
with s do (*can be deleted because it is implicit*)
    begin
    read(a); read(b);
    while b≠0 do
        begin
        a: = a+1; b: = b−1
        end;
    write(a)
    end
end.
```

2 Spaces, Execution and Functional Abstraction

It is assumed that the reader has some working knowledge of Pascal; hence we shall talk about executions of SM-Pascal programs without having clearly defined the semantics of SM-Pascal. Formal definitions of SM-Pascal's semantics will be given later in this and other chapters.

2.1 Preliminary Definitions

Let P be a SM-Pascal program; as such, P reads data from a single file, **input**; depending on the unit of information that program P reads in its input file, the latter may be viewed as a list of bits, a list of characters, a list of words, a list of numbers, a list or records, a list of lines, etc . . . . In general, the input file is best viewed as a list of items of information. We define the *input space* of program P as being the set of lists of input items (those items that P views as units of information to be read). Similarly, we define the *output space* of program P as being the set of lists of output items (those items that P views as units of information to be written). An element of the input space is called an *input state;* an element of the output space is called an *output state.*

When program P executes with some input state (is), one of many *exceptional conditions* may occur, namely:

— The program fails to terminate.
— The program attempts to read beyond the end of the input file.
— The program attempts to use a variable before assigning it a value.
— The program causes an overflow of the arithmetic unit.
— The program attempts an undefined operation such as: division by zero, logarithm of a negative number, square root of a negative number, etc..

When such an event occurs, one may not assign any meaning to the output state that the program has generated.

DEFINITION 1. The *domain* of program P is the set of input states which cause no exceptional condition.

We shall abuse the notation by using the same name to refer to the domain of a program and a function: **dom**(P). The justification of this convention will become clear as we introduce functional abstraction.

DEFINITION 2. An output state (os) belongs to the *range* of program P if and only if there exists an input state (is) in **dom**(P) such that execution of P on (is) generates (os).

Again, we abuse the notation by representing the range of program P by **rng**(P).

DEFINITION 3. The *functional abstraction* of program P is the E-function from **dom**(P) to **rng**(P) denoted [P] and equal to
{(is,os)| when P executes on (is), it causes no exceptional condition and generates (os)}.

Note that **dom**([P]) = **dom**(P) and that **rng**([P]) = **rng**(P). The functional abstraction of a program is an abstraction of its functional properties: All the non-functional information such as structure, performance and implementation is lost in the abstraction process.

2.2 Intermediate States and the Functional Abstraction of Statements

As long as we are interested in the functional abstraction of a program, we need only consider its domain, range and function. However, if we are to study the intermediate steps of its execution, we need to follow the sequence of values taken by the program variables throughout its execution.

Let P be a SM-Pascal program written as follows:

program P (**input, output**);
type S = **set** . . . **end**;
var s: S;
begin . . . . L: . . . . **end**.

The *proper space* (abbreviated P-space) of program P is set S; a *proper state* (abbreviated P-state) of program P at label L is a value that s has when the execution control of program P is at label L. Knowledge of a P-state of program P at label L is not sufficient to assess the progress of the computation and does not enable one to predict its future, unless one knows the current input and output states.

DEFINITION 4. Let P be a SM-Pascal program and let IS, S and OS be its input space, proper space and output space respectively. The *extended space* (abbreviated E-space) of program P is

$$IS \times S \times OS.$$

An *extended state* of program P at label L is a triplet (is,s,os) in the set IS × S × OS such that at label L, s is the current P-state of P, (is) and (os) are its current input state and current output state (each **read** execution performs a **cdr** operation on the input state, and each **write** execution performs an **app** operation on the output file; the formal semantics of procedures **read** and **write** are given later in this chapter).

EXAMPLE 1. Consider the following program.

> **program** P(**input, output**);
> **label**   1;
> **type**   C = **char**;
> **var**   c: C;
> **begin**   read(c); write(c); read(c); 1: **write**(c) **end**.

The input space (IS) and output space (OS) are both equal to L*(**char**). The P-space of P is C; a P-state of P at label 1 is, for example 'b' (for the initial input state 'cbe') and an E-state at the same label is, for example, ('e', 'b', 'c') (for the same initial input state). The domain of P is DM = {is:L*(**char**)| lng(is)≥2}; its range is RN = {os:L*(**char**)| lng(os) = 2}; its functional abstraction is

[P] =
{(is,os)| lng(is)≥2 ∧ lng(os) = 2 ∧ car(is) = car(os) ∧ car.cdr(is) = car.cdr(os)}.

Let P be a SM-Pascal program whose E-space is ES and let st be a statement in its statement part (see BNF description of ⟨statement part⟩ in Appendix A).

> DEFINITION 5. The *functional abstraction of statement* st (denoted by [st]) is the I-function on ES equal to

{(es,es')| if statement st starts execution at E-state es, then it causes no exceptional condition and terminates in E-state es'}.

Furthermore, we pose by definition, **dom**(st) = **dom**([st]) and **rng**(st) = **rng**([st]).

2.3 Procedures and Parameters

2.3.1 Parameterless Procedures

Let R be the SM-Pascal procedure declared as follows:

> **procedure** R;
> **label** L;
> **type** T = **set** .. **end**;

> **var** t: T;
> **begin** . . . . L: . . . . . . **end**.

T is called the *proper space* (or P-space) of procedure R; a *proper state* (or P-state) of procedure R at label L is a value that t may take when the control of the procedure is at label L.

Let P be the program (or procedure) calling R and let ES be its E-space. The *extended space* (or E-space) of procedure R is ES′ = ES×T; an *extended state* (or E-state) of procedure R at label L is the pair (es,t), where es is an E-state of P at label L and t is a P-state of R at label L. Procedure R computes an I-function on ES, and any statement in its statement part computes an I-function on ES′.

A parameterless function whose result type (see ⟨result type⟩ in Appendix A) is, say, U is an E-function from the E-space of its calling program to U (considered as a set).

2.3.2 Parameterized Procedures

In Pascal, the purpose of parameters is to show what particular variables of the calling program might affect the execution of the called procedure and what variables might be affected by it. Let P be the calling program and R be the called procedure. We denote by ES the E-space of P. Any time a particular variable of P affects the execution of R, one may think of the whole E-space of P as affecting it; symmetrically, any time a particular variable of P is affected by the execution of R, one may want to think of the whole E-space of P as being affected. Hence in SM-Pascal the view is taken that when program P calls procedure R, P implicitly passes its E-space ES to R, both as a value parameter and as a **var** parameter. This view is all the more fitting as SM-Pascal puts more emphasis on the space of a program as a whole rather than on individual variables. Hence, as far as semantics go, a parameterized procedure is equivalent to a parameterless procedure; they both compute an I-function on the E-space of the calling program.

Yet, SM-Pascal admits the use of parameters in procedure declarations and procedure calls. Parameters are viewed as contributing information to the description of the I-function to be computed: The use of parameters in the calls **read**(a) and **read**(b) is viewed as a simple notational convention for using the same procedure definition (**read**) to represent two conceptually distinct procedures, namely **reada** and **readb**. For all its weakness, the view taken here will make future discussions of procedures a great deal simpler. The reader who is interested in more information regarding procedure calls and parameter passing is referred to the bibliographic sources given in section 5.

Similarly, a parameterized function is considered as an E-function from the E-space of its calling program/procedure to its result type considered as a set.

2.4 Exercises

1. [A] Determine the input space and the domain of the following programs.
   a) **program** Pa(**input, output**); **var** c: **char**; **begin read**(c); c: = 'z' **end**.
   b) **program** Pb(**input, output**); **var** x: **real**; **begin write**(x) **end**.
   c) **program** Pc(**input, output**); **var** x: **integer**; **begin read**(x); x: = 1/x **end**.
   d) **program** Pd(**input, output**); **var** x: **real**; **begin read**(x); **write(sqrt**(x)) **end**.
   e) **program** Pe(**input, output**); **var** c: **char**; **begin read**(c); **read**(c); **read**(c) **end**.

2. [B] Determine the input space, output space, domain, range and functional abstraction of the following programs.
   a) **program** Pa(**input, output**); **var** c: **char**;
               begin read(c); **read**(c); **write**(c); **write**(c) **end**.
   b) **program** Pb(**input, output**); **var** c: **char**;
               begin write(c); **read**(c) **end**.
   c) **program** Pc(**input, output**); **var** c: **char**;
               begin read(c); **read**(c); **read**(c); c: = 'a' **end**.
   d) **program** Pd(**input, output**); **var** x: **real**;
               begin read(x); **write(sqrt**(x)); **end**.
   e) **program** Pe(**input, output**); **var** x: **real**;
               begin read(x); **if** x>0 **then write(sqrt**(x)) **else write**('−1') **end**.

3. [B] Let P be a program whose input space is IS, output space is OS and proper space is S (proper state: s), defined as follows:

$$S = \textbf{set}$$
$$\text{a, b: } \textbf{integer};$$
$$\text{p: } \textbf{boolean}$$
$$\textbf{end} \ .$$

Compute the functional abstraction of the following statement (**with** s **do** is implied).
   a) a: = a+1.
   b) p: = **true**.
   c) **while** b>0 **do begin** b: = b−1; a: = a+1 **end**.
   d) a: = a+b; b: = 0.
   e) **while** p **do begin** p: = a>b **end**.

4. [A] Let P be a program whose input space is IS, proper space is S and output space is OS and let st be a statement in its statement part which calls no **read** or **write** procedure. Redefine the notion of functional abstraction for this special case of statement by deleting the input and output states. Deduce the new form of functional abstraction for all the statements given in exercise 3.

5. [B] Let P be the following program with input space IS and output space OS:

```
program P(input, output);
type
  S= set
    a, b: real
  end;
var
  s: S;
procedure Swap;
  label 1;
  type T= real;
  var t: T;
  begin t:=a; a:=b; 1: b:=t end;
begin
read(a); read(b);
Swap;
write(a); write(b)
end.
```

a) Give a reasonable definition of IS and OS in the light of the program, then determine **dom**(P) and **rng**(P).
b) Give the E-space of P.
c) Give the P-space and the E-space of Swap.
d) Give an example of a P-state of Swap at label 1.
e) Give an example of an E-state of Swap at label 1.

6. [B] Consider the program of Example 5. Give the functional abstraction of:
— Procedure Swap's statement part.
— Procedure Swap.
— Program P.

3 Generation of Functional Abstractions

This section discusses the generation of functional abstractions of programs and statements. The basic idea of the method presented here is to deduce the functional abstraction of complex statements from the functional abstractions of their components. The axioms and rules generated for this method will be assembled in a deductive system named FA (for Functional Abstraction). We shall discuss the generation of functional abstractions of simple and structured statements, then programs and procedures. All the rules and axioms given below are to be understood within the following notational context: We are given a program P, with input space IS, proper space S and output space OS. The E-space of P, which is IS×S×OS, is named ES; in order to represent expressions on set ES we shall use the variable es = (is,s,os).

3.1 Simple Statements

a0: The Assignment Statement Axiom

$$[s := E(s)] = [:\textbf{def}(E), (is,E(s),os)],$$

where E is an internal expression on S and **def**(E) is its domain of definition. Note the distinction between the use of brackets on the left of the equal sign, to designate the functional abstraction of a statement and on the right, to designate a pE-formula.

a1: The Empty Statement Axiom

$$[\ \ ] = [\textbf{true}, es];$$

this provides that [ ] is the identity on ES.

r0: The Procedure Call Rule

$$\frac{[\textbf{procedure } R \ldots \textbf{begin} \ldots \textbf{end}] = f}{[R] = f.}$$

The sentence "**procedure** R . . . **begin** . . . **end**" (above the line) represents the declaration of procedure R, whereas the sentence "R" (below the line) represents a call of procedure R in the statement part of the calling program. In section 3.3 we discuss how to establish the theoremhood of a well-formed formula such as [**procedure** R . . . **begin** . . . **end**] = f.

3.2 Structured Statements

a2: The Begin-End Axiom

$$[\textbf{begin } st \textbf{ end}] = [st].$$

a3: The Sequence Statement Axiom

$$[st1; st2] = [st1]*[st2].$$

a4: The Conditional Statement Axiom

$$[\textbf{if } t \textbf{ then } tc] = [t,es]*[tc] \cup [{}^\sim t,es].$$

Function [t,es]*[tc] is the restriction of function [tc] to predicate t, hence its domain is a subset of ES|t; on the other hand, the domain of [~t,es] is ES|~t; therefore ([t,es]*[tc] ∪ [~t,es]) is indeed a function.

a5: The Alternative Statement Axiom

$$[\textbf{if } t \textbf{ then } tc \textbf{ else } ec] = [t,es]^*[tc] \cup [\tilde{\ }t,es]^*[ec]$$

A similar argument to the one given above establishes that ([t,es]*[tc] ∪ [~t,es]*[ec]) is indeed a function.

r1: The While Statement Rule
    There exists an I-function f on ES such that

p0: [~t,es]*f = [~t,es]
p1: f = [if t then lb]*f
p2: ([t,es]*[lb])⁺ is a well-founded relation on dom(f) and for any (es) ir
    ES − dom(f), the while statement w = (while t do lb) does not terminate

[while t do lb] = f.

This rule is explained in detail in section 3.5.

a6: The With Statement Axiom

$$[\textbf{with } s \textbf{ do } wb] = [s.wb],$$

where s.wb is the statement obtained from wb by replacing each occurrence of elementary function designator a by s.a (see ⟨elementary function designator⟩ in Appendix A).

3.3 Programs and Procedures

r2: The Procedure Declaration Rule
    R is a procedure with proper space T declared within program P whose E-space is ES; the E-space of procedure R is then ES×T. Let pd be the statement part of procedure R and let (es,t) be a variable E-state of P. The functional abstraction of pd is an I-function on ES×T whereas the functional abstraction of procedure R is an I-function on ES:

[pd] = [p, (E,E′)]

[procedure R; ... begin pd end] = [p,E].

Predicate p on ES×T is a function of es only, because the initial value of t is undefined; hence it can be viewed as a predicate on ES. Similarly, E is an internal expression on ES whereas E′ is an external expression from ES to T. Therefore [p,E] is an I-function on ES. The rule of function declaration can be derived in a similar fashion. See problem 2.

r3: The Program Rule

Program P has input space IS, proper space S and output space OS, and statement part pg; let (is,s,os) be a variable E-state of p. The functional abstraction of pg is an I-function on IS×S×OS whereas the functional abstraction of the whole program is an E-function from a subset of IS to a subset of OS.

$$\frac{[\text{pg}] = [\text{p,(IE,E,OE)}],}{[\textbf{program } P; \dots \textbf{ begin } \text{pg } \textbf{end}] = \{(\text{is,os})|\ \text{p(is)} \wedge \text{os} = \text{OE(is,())}\}}$$

where p, IE and E are expressions with one free variable (is) and OE is an expression with two free variables (is and os).

A similar argument to that given in rule r2 is needed to establish that p, IE and E are all functions of (is) only; as for expression OE, it is a function of (is) and (os).

3.4 Input and Output Procedures

a7: The Read Axiom

$$[\textbf{read}(\text{s.a})] = [\textbf{lng}(\text{is}) \geqslant 1, (\textbf{cdr}(\text{is}), \text{Rd(s,is,a)}, \text{os})],$$

where Rd(s,is,a) is the proper state s′ defined by a(s′)= **car**(is) and b(s′)= b(s) for any variable (elementary function) identifier b distinct from a.

a8: The Write Axiom

$$[\textbf{write}(\text{s.a})] = [\textbf{true}, (\text{is, s, } \textbf{app}(\text{os, a(s)}))].$$

3.5 The While Statement Theorem

This section presents a theorem regarding the functional abstraction of while statements and explains the While Statement Rule (r1). For a deeper study of while statements consult Chapters 8 and 9 and Appendices B and C.

First, a comment is in order regarding the domain of a while statement. Let w be the statement (**while** t **do** lb) on E-space ES; in order for some (es) in ES to be in the domain of statement w, the execution of w on (es) must terminate, cause no overflow, no division by zero, no use of undefined value, no attempt to read past the end of the input file, etc . . . Among all these exceptional conditions, the only one that lends itself to elegant formalization and is machine independent is the condition of termination. Therefore, we shall always, in our theoretical studies of while statements, equate the domain of a while statement with its termination domain. This decision is reflected in premise p2 of rule r1 which checks whether the termination domain of w (as a statement) and the domain of f (as a function) are identical. Once f is established as the functional abstraction of w by means of rule r1, one may *multiply* (relative product) f on the left by [p,es] if one believes that predicate p ensures freedom from other forms of exceptional conditions, and assume that [p,es]*f, rather than f, is the actual functional abstraction of w.

The theorem below (whose original version is due to Mills et al, [7]) provides necessary and sufficient conditions for an I-function f on ES to be the functional abstraction of a while statement w on ES. This theorem is the basis of rule r1.

THEOREM 1. Let w = (**while** t **do** lb) be a statement on E-space ES and let f be an I-function on ES. Then f = [w] if and only if:

a) [~t,es]*f = [~t,es],
b) f = [**if** t **then** lb] * f
c) ([t,es]*[lb])$^+$ is a well-founded relation on **dom**(f) and for any (es) in ES − **dom**(f), w does not terminate whenever started with (es).

Proof. The proof of necessity is straightforward and is not needed to support rule r1; hence it shall be skipped.

We shall, however, prove sufficiency, which depends on the semantics of while statements. Let (a), (b) and (c) hold and let (es) be an element of **dom**(f). The first question we wish to address is whether statement w terminates if it is started with (es). From condition (b) it stems that [**if** t **then** lb] is closed on **dom**(f) (i.e. if (es) is in **dom**(f), then so is [**if** t **then** lb](es)); we conclude that [t,es]*[lb], which is a subset of [**if** t **then** lb] is also closed on **dom**(f). We assume that execution of w on (es) does not terminate and find that it would generate a sequence in **dom**(f) which is infinite and decreasing by relation ([t,es]*[lb])$^+$. This is in contradiction with hypothesis (c). Therefore **dom**(f) ⊆ **dom**(w).

When started with an element (es) in ES, statement w terminates in state

[w](es). We have to show that [w](es) = f(es). Because the range of [w] is
ES|~t, we can write

$$[w] = [w]*[~t,es].$$

In particular, we have:

$$[w](es) = ([w]*[~t,es])(es).$$

By virtue of hypothesis (a), we transform the right hand side into:

$$([w]*([~t,es]*f))(es).$$

By associativity of the relative product, we write this as:

$$(([w]*[~t,es])*f)(es).$$

Because the range of [w] is ES|~t, this becomes

$$([w]*f)(es).$$

Now, because w terminates when started with (es), [w] is equal to a finite
relative product of functions equal to [**if** t **then** lb]. The expression above
becomes:

$$((([\textbf{if } t \textbf{ then } lb] * \ldots * [\textbf{if } t \textbf{ then } lb]) * f) \,(es).$$

Because of the associativity of the relative product and hypothesis (b), this
becomes:

$$f(es).$$

Whenever (es) is chosen in **dom**(f), it belongs to **dom**(w) and [w](es)=f(es).
On the other hand, whenever (es) is chosen outside **dom**(f), it does not belong
to **dom**(w), due to condition (c). Hence [w]=f.   QED

REMARK 2. If f and g are two I-functions on ES and t is a predicate on ES,
then, obviously,

$$f=g \Rightarrow [t,es]*f = [t,es]*g \wedge [~t,es]*f = [~t,es]*g.$$

Conversely,

$$[t,es]*f = [t,es]*g \wedge [~t,es]*f = [~t,es]*g \Rightarrow f=g$$

because

$$f = [t,es]^*f \cup [\tilde{}t,es]^*f, \text{ and}$$
$$g = [t,es]^*g \cup [\tilde{}t,es]^*g.$$

Hence premise p1 of rule r1 is equivalent to the conjunction of:

p1a: $[t,es] * f = [t,es] * [\textbf{if } t \textbf{ then } lb] * f$, and
p1b: $[\tilde{}t,es] * f = [\tilde{}t,es] * [\textbf{if } t \textbf{ then } lb] * f$.

Now,

$$[\tilde{}t,es] * [\textbf{if } t \textbf{ then } lb] = [\tilde{}t,es],$$

hence p1b is an identity and p1 can be replaced by p1a alone in rule r1. Also, because $[t,es] * [\textbf{if } t \textbf{ then } lb] = [t,es] * [lb]$, p1a can be written as:

p′1: $[t,es] * f = [t,es] * [lb] * f$.

The rule we obtain from the While Statement Rule by replacing p1 by p′1 is called the *Modified While Statement Rule* (denoted: rule r′1).

r1:   The Modified While Statement Rule
      There exists an I-function f on ES such that:

p0: $[\tilde{}t,es]^*f = [\tilde{}t,es]$
p′1: $[t,es]^*f = [t,es]^*[lb]^*f$
p2: $([t,es]^*[lb])^+$ is a well-founded relation on **dom**(f) and for any es
      in ES − **dom**(f), statement w does not terminate.

[**while** t **do** lb] = f.

3.6 The Theorem of Functional Abstraction

Let FA = (W,A,R) be the deductive system defined as follows:

Well-Formed Formulas, W:

Below is a partial BNF description of W. Many non-terminals have not been defined either because they appear in SM-Pascal's BNF description (Appendix A) or because they are self-explanatory.

⟨well-formed formula⟩ ::= ⟨predicate⟩ |
  ⟨function expression⟩ = ⟨function expression⟩

⟨function expression⟩ ::= ⟨function term⟩ |
  ⟨function expression⟩ ∪ ⟨program term⟩

⟨functional term⟩ ::= ⟨function factor⟩ |
  ⟨function term⟩ * ⟨function factor⟩

⟨function factor⟩ ::= ⟨function name⟩ |
  ⟨function representation⟩ |
  ⟨functional abstraction⟩ |
  (⟨function expression⟩)

⟨functional abstraction⟩ ::= [⟨SM-Pascal program⟩] |
  [⟨SM-Pascal procedure declaration⟩] |
  [⟨SM-Pascal statement⟩]

Axioms, A:

A = {a0, a1, a2, a3, a4, a5, a6, a7, a8}, the axioms introduced in sections 3.1, 3.2 and 3.4.

Rules, R:
R = {r0, r1, r2, r3}, the rules introduced in sections 3.1, 3.2 and 3.3.

On the basis of the deductive system FA = (W,A,R), we obtain the *meta-theorem of functional abstraction.*

THEOREM 2. Function p is the functional abstraction of program (or procedure or statement) P if [P] = p is a theorem of system FA.

No formal proof is given for this theorem. All the discussions surrounding the axioms and rules given above constitute a proof. This theorem is an act of faith in the consistency of the deductive system FA. Note the use of "if" rather than "iff": No statement is made about the completeness of system FA. In order to enhance the reader's confidence in this system, we devote the next section to the study of examples of application.

3.7 Examples of Theorems of System FA

EXAMPLE 2. (Axiom a0)
Input space: IS, state: is; proper space: **real**, state: s; output space: OS, state: os; es is an abbreviation of (is,s,os). Determine [s: = log(s)].By axiom a0,

$$[s:= \log(s)] = [s>0, (is,\log(s),os)].$$

EXAMPLE 3. (Axiom a3)
Same context as Example 2, determine $[s:= 1/(1-s); s:= \textbf{log}(s)]$.
By axiom a3,

$$[s:=1/(1-s); s:= \textbf{log}(s)]= [s:= 1/(1-s)] * [s:= \textbf{log}(s)].$$

By axiom a0,

$$= [s\neq 1, (is, 1/(1-s), os)] * [s>0, (is, \log(s), os)].$$

By the rule of product of pE-formulas,

$$= [s\neq 1 \wedge 1/(1-s)>0, (is, \log(1/(1-s)), os)].$$

This can be simplified to:

$$[s<1, (is, -\log(1-s), os)].$$

EXAMPLE 4. (Axiom a4)
Same context as Example 2, determine

$$[\textbf{if } s<0 \textbf{ then } s:= -s].$$

By axiom a4, this is equal to:

$$[s<0,es] * [s:= -s] \cup [s\geqslant 0,es].$$

By axiom a0, we transform this function to:

$$[s<0,es] * [\textbf{true}, (is, -s, os)] \cup [s\geqslant 0,es].$$

Performing the relative product, we get:

$$[s<0, (is, -s, os)] \cup [s\geqslant 0, es].$$

By the formula of function union, we get:

$$[\textbf{true}, \textbf{ite}(s<0, (is,-s,os), (is,s,os))],$$

which can also be written as

$$[\textbf{true}, (is, \textbf{abs}(s), os)].$$

EXAMPLE 5. (Axiom a5)
Proper space,

$$S = \textbf{set}$$
$$a, b: \textbf{integer}$$
$$\textbf{end};$$

proper state, s; the rest of the context identical to Example 2. Determine

$$[\textbf{if } a>b \textbf{ then } a:= \log(b-a) \textbf{ else } b:= \textbf{sqrt}(a)].$$

By axiom a0,

$$[a:= \log(b-a)] = [b(s)-a(s)>0, \text{ (is, } (\log(b(s)-a(s)), \text{ } b(s)), \text{ os})].$$

Multiplying this by $[a(s)>b(s), \text{ es}]$ on the left, we get:

$$[a(s)>b(s) \wedge b(s)-a(s)>0, \text{ (is, } (\log(b(s)-a(s)),b(s)), \text{ os})],$$

which is the empty function.
   By axiom a0,

$$[b:= \textbf{sqrt}(a)] = [a(s)\geqslant 0, \text{ (is, } (a(s),\textbf{sqrt}(a(s))), \text{ os})].$$

Multiplying this by $[a(s)\leqslant b(s), \text{ es}]$ on the left, we get

$$[a(s)\leqslant b(s) \wedge a(s)\geqslant 0, \text{ (is, } (a(s), \textbf{sqrt}(a(s))), \text{ os})].$$

By axiom a5, we have:

$$[\textbf{if } a>b \textbf{ then } a:= \log(b-a) \textbf{ else } b:= \textbf{sqrt}(a)]$$
$$= \{ \} \cup [0\leqslant a(s)\leqslant b(s), \text{ (is, } (a(s),\textbf{sqrt}(a(s))), \text{ os})]$$
$$= [0\leqslant a(s)\leqslant b(s), \text{ (is, } (a(s),\textbf{sqrt}(a(s))), \text{ os})].$$

EXAMPLE 6. (Axiom a6 and Rule r'1)
Same context as Example 5. Determine

$$[\textbf{with } s \textbf{ do while } b\neq 0 \textbf{ do begin } a:= a+1; b:= b-1 \textbf{ end}].$$

By axiom a6, this function is equal to:

$$[\textbf{while } s.b\neq 0 \textbf{ do begin } s.a:= s.a+1; s.b:= s.b-1 \textbf{ end}].$$

This statement does not include any **read** or **write** statement, hence (is) and (os) are not modified by it: For the sake of simplicity, we shall concentrate our discussions on the proper space S. We apply rule r'1 with the following function:

$$f = [b(s) \geqslant 0, (a(s)+b(s), 0)].$$

First, we check premise p0:

$$[b(s)=0,s] * [b(s) \geqslant 0, (a(s)+b(s),0)]$$
$$= [b(s)=0 \wedge b(s) \geqslant 0, (a(s)+b(s),0)]$$
$$= [b(s)=0, (a(s),b(s))]$$
$$= [\tilde{\ }(b(s) \neq 0), s];$$

hence p0 is proved.

Now, by axioms a0, a2 and a3, we can write

[**begin** s.a:= s.a+1; s.b:= s.b−1 **end**] = [**true**, (a(s)+1, b(s)−1)].

Multiplying on the left by [b(s) ≠ 0,s], we get:

[b(s) ≠ 0,s] * [**true**, (a(s)+1, b(s)−1)] = [b(s) ≠ 0, (a(s)+1, b(s)−1)].

We now verify premise p'1 of rule r'1:

$$[b(s) \neq 0, (a(s)+1, b(s)-1)] * [b(s) \geqslant 0, (a(s)+b(s),0)]$$
$$= [b(s) \neq 0 \wedge b(s)-1 \geqslant 0, (a(s)+1+b(s)-1,0)]$$
$$= [b(s) \geqslant 1, (a(s)+b(s),0)] .$$

On the other hand,

[b(s) ≠ 0,s] * [b(s) ≥ 0, (a(s)+b(s),0)] = [b(s) > 0, (a(s)+b(s),0)].

Because [b(s) ≥ 1, (a(s)+b(s),0)] = [b(s) > 0, (a(s)+b(s),0)], we deduce premise p'1 of rule r'1.

Now, we discuss premise p2:

$$[b(s) \neq 0,s] * [\textbf{begin } s.a:= s.a+1; s.b:= s.b-1 \textbf{ end}]$$
$$= \{(s,s') | \ b(s) \neq 0 \wedge a(s')=a(s)+1 \wedge b(s')=b(s)-1\}.$$

The transitive closure of this relation is:

$$R = \{(s,s') \mid b(s) \neq 0 \; \wedge \; a(s') > a(s) \; \wedge \; b(s') < b(s) \; \wedge$$
$$a(s') + b(s') = a(s) + b(s) \; \}.$$

The domain of f is

$$D = \{s \mid b(s) \geqslant 0\}.$$

Clearly, R is a well-founded relation on D. Furthermore, for any s such that $b(s) < 0$, the while statement fails to terminate. The Modified While Statement Rule (r'1) provides:

$$[\textbf{while } s.b \neq 0 \textbf{ do begin } s.a := s.a + 1; \; s.b := s.b - 1 \textbf{ end}]$$
$$= [b(s) \geqslant 0, \; (a(s) + b(s), \; 0)].$$

EXAMPLE 7. (Rule r3)
We propose to compute the functional abstraction of the following program:

```
program Add (input, output);
type
  S = set
    a, b: integer
  end;
var
  s: S;
begin
  (* with s do is implicit here *)
  read(a); read(b);
  while b ≠ 0 do begin a: = a + 1; b: = b − 1 end;
  write(a)
end.
```

Input space, $IS = L^*(\textbf{integer})$; output space, $OS = L^*(\textbf{integer})$; proper space, S. Extended state is (is,s,os), abbreviated by (es).
    For the sake of clarity we shall take the following notational conventions:

$$\textbf{car}(is) = is1$$
$$\textbf{car} \bullet \textbf{cdr}(is) = is2$$
$$\textbf{cdr} \bullet \textbf{cdr}(is) = \textbf{cdr}2(is).$$

By virtue of axiom a7,

> v0: [**read**(a)] = [**lng**(is)≥1, (**cdr**(is), (**car**(is),b(s)), os)].

By virtue of axiom a7,

> v1: [**read**(b)] = [**lng**(is)≥1, (**cdr**(is), (a(s), **car**(is)), os)].

By virtue of axiom a3,

> v2: [**read**(a); **read**(b)]
> = [**lng**(is)≥1, (**cdr**(is), (**car**(is), b(s)), os)]
>   * [**lng**(is)≥1, (**cdr**(is), (a(s), **car**(is)), os)]
> = [**lng**(is)≥1 ∧ **lng**(**cdr**(is))≥1, (**cdr2**(is), (is1, is2), os)]
> = [**lng**(is)≥2, (**cdr2**(is), (is1, is2), os)].

By virtue of the previous example, we have

> v3: [**while** b≠0 **do begin** a:= a+1; b:= b−1 **end**]
> = [b(s)≥0, (is, (a(s)+b(s), 0), os)].

By virtue of axiom a3,

> v4: [**read**(a); **read**(b); **while** b≠0 **do begin** a:= a+1; b:= b−1 **end**]
> = [**lng**(is)≥2, (**cdr2**(is), (is1,is2), os)]
>   * [b(s)≥0, (is, (a(s)+b(s),0), os)]
> = [**lng**(is)≥2 ∧ is2≥0, (**cdr2**(is), (is1+is2,0), os)].

By virtue of axiom a8,

> v5: [**write**(a)] = [**true**, (is, s, **app**(os,a(s)))].

By virtue of axiom a3,

> v6: [**read**(a); **read**(b); **while** b≠0 **do begin** a:= a+1; b:= b−1 **end**; **write**(a)]
> = [**lng**(is)≥2 ∧ is2≥0, (**cdr2**(is), (is1+is2,0), os)]
>   * [**true**, (is, s, **app**(os, a(s)))]
> = [**lng**(is)≥2 ∧ is2≥0, (**cdr2**(is), (is1+is2,0), **app**(os,is1+is2))].

By virtue of the program rule,

> v7: [Add] = {(is,os) : IS×OS| **lng**(is)≥2 ∧ is2≥0
>   ∧ os= **app**((), is1+is2) }.

Note that **app**((),is1+is2) is the list of length 1 containing is1+is2. By inspecting the sequence (v0, v1, v2, v3, v4, v5, v6, v7), one can convince oneself that v7 is a logical consequence of {v3 }; since v3 is a theorem of system FA (previous example), then so is v7. See exercise 3 for a similar example.

3.8 Exercises

1. [B] Let P be a program on input space IS, output space OS and proper space S defined as follows:

$$
\begin{aligned}
&S = \textbf{set}\\
&\quad a, b: \textbf{integer};\\
&\quad q: \textbf{boolean}\\
&\textbf{end}.
\end{aligned}
$$

Using system FA, compute the functional abstraction of the following statements.
   a) q:= (a=b).
   b) q:= (a=b); a:= 1/b.
   c) **if** a<0 **then** a:= −a.
   d) **if** a>0 **then** b:= a **else** b:= −a.
   e) **while** a≠b **do** q:= ~q.

2. [B] Same context and same question as exercise 1.
   a) a:= a−b.
   b) a:= **trunc(sqrt**(a)); b:= **trunc(log**(a)).
   c) **if** a>b **then** b:= a.
   d) **if** a>b **then** b:= a **else** a:= b.
   e) **while** b>0 **do begin** a:= a+b; b:= b−1 **end**.

3. [C] Using the deductive system FA, compute the functional abstraction of the following programs. The statement **with** s **do** is omitted. (Hint: See Examples 6 and 7).

```
program Add (input, output);
type
   S = set
     a, b: integer
   end;
var
   s: S;
begin
   read(a); read(b);
   while b>0 do begin a:= a+1; b:= b−1 end;
   write(a)
end.
```

Compare its functional abstraction with that of Example 7, section 3.7. (Hint: Write the function of the while statement as 2 union).

4. [B] Find the E-space and functional abstraction of the following program.

```
program Prod1(input, output);
type
  S = set
    a, b, p: integer
  end;
var
  s: S;
begin
  read(a); read(b); p:= 0;
  while b≠0 do begin b:= b−1; p:= p+a end;
  write(p)
end.
```

5. [C] Find the E-space and functional abstraction of the following program. Let k be a integer constant.

```
program Prod2(input, output);
const
  p0 = k;
type
  S = set
    a, b, p: integer
  end;
var
  s: S;
begin
  read(a); read(b); p:= p0;
  while b>0 do begin b:= b−1; p:= p+a end;
  write(p)
end.
```

Compare your results with exercise 4.

6. [B] Find the E-space and functional abstraction of the following program.

```
program Copy1(input, output);
type
  S = set
    c, d: char
  end;
```

```
var
  s: S;
begin
  read(c); read(d);
  write(c); write(d)
end.
```

7. [B] Find the E-space and functional abstraction of the following program.

```
program Sort(input, output);
type
  S = set
    a, b: char
  end;
var
  s: S;
begin
  read(a); read(b);
  if a<b then begin write(a); write(b) end
  else begin write(b); write(a) end
end.
```

8. [B] Find the E-space and functional abstraction of the following program.

```
program Re(input, output);
type
  S = set
    i: integer;
    c: char
  end;
var
  s: S;
begin
  i:= 1; while i≤100 do begin read(c); i:=i+1 end
end.
```

9. [B] Find the E-space and functional abstraction of the following program.

```
program V(input, output);
type S = char;
var s: S;
begin while true do read(s) end.
```

10. [B] Find the E-space and functional abstraction of the following program.

```
program ident(input, output);
type
```

```
    S = set
       a, b: char
    end;
var
    s: S;
    procedure swap;
    type T = char;
    var t: T;
    begin t: = a; a: = b; b: = t end;
begin
    read(a); read(b); swap; write(b); write(a)
end.
```

11. [B] Find the E-space and functional abstraction of the following program.

```
    program Max(input, output);
    type
       S = set
          a, b: integer
       end;
    var
       s: S;
    begin
       read(a); read(b);
       while b<a do b: = b+1;
       write(b)
    end.
```

12. [B] Find the E-space and functional abstraction of the following program.

```
    program Sub(input, output);
    type
       S = set
          a, b: integer
       end;
    var
       s: S;
    begin
       read(a); read(b);
       while b≠0 do begin a: = a−1; b: = b−1
       end;
       write(a)
    end.
```

4 Problems

1. [A]
   a) Define the spaces and domains of a program which handles many input files and many output files; redefine the functional abstraction of such a program.
   b) Same question as (a), if some files are used for input and output.

2. [B] Let P be a program with E-space ES and let F be a function whose result type (see ⟨result type⟩ in Appendix A) is U, and whose statement part (see ⟨statement part⟩) is st.
   a) Let S′ be the space declared in the type definition part of function F; would it be faithful to the spirit of section 2 to call S′ the proper space of F? Give a more appropriate definition of the proper space of F.
   b) Is it better to define the functional abstraction of a SM-Pascal function as an I-function or an E-function? Give a formal definition.
   c) Derive a Function Declaration Rule along the lines of rules r2 and r3.

3. [A]
   a) Generalize the Read Statement Axiom to include two variables, then three, using the function Rd introduced in the Read Statement Axiom and the Sequence Axiom.
   b) Generalize the Write Statement Axiom to include two variables, then three.

5 Bibliography

For a BNF description of Pascal, consult [4].

The approach underlying system FA has some similarities with symbolic execution: Consult [2] and [5] for the use of symbolic execution in program verification and program testing.

Alternative approaches to the evaluation of functional abstraction of statements are given in [6] and [7]. The While Statement Theorem (section 3.5) is due to [7].

For more information on the axiomatization of procedure calls, consult [1] and [3].

1: Gries, D. The Science of Programming. Springer-Verlag, 1981.
2: Hantler, S L and J C King. An Introduction to Proving the Correctness of Programs. Computing Surveys 8(3) (September 1976), pp 331-353.
3: Hoare, C A R. Procedures and Parameters: An Axiomatic Approach. Symposium on Semantics of Programming Languages. Springer-Verlag, 1971, pp 102-116.
4: Jensen, K and N Wirth. Pascal User Manual and Report. Springer-Verlag, 1974.
5: King, J C. Symbolic Execution and Program Testing. *CACM* 19(7) (July 1976), pp 385-394.
6: Linger, R C, H D Mills and B I Witt. Structured Programming: Theory and Practice. Addison-Wesley, 1979.
7: Mills, H D , R H Austing, V R Basili, J D Gannon, R G Hamlet, J E Kohl and B Schneiderman. The Calculus of Computer Programming. To be published by Allyn and Bacon.

Chapter 6

Program Correctness and the Symbolic Execution Method

1 Formulas of Program Correctness

Let IS = {a,b,c,d,e,f}, OS = {0,1,2,3,4,5} and let

$$R = \{(a,0), (a,1), (b,0), (c,1), (c,2), (d,0), (d,2)\}.$$

We call Sp the specification (IS,OS,R). Let P be the program having IS for input space, OS for output space and whose functional abstraction is

$$[P] = \{(a,1), (b,0), (c,1), (d,2)\}.$$

By providing the specification Sp, the user indicates that the only elements of IS he considers possibly submitting to program P are those in **dom**(R), namely: a, b, c or d. Clearly, program P is defined for each one of these values and the output that it returns for each is satisfactory by the standards of specification Sp. Hence, we can judge that P is correct wrt Sp. Following the same argument, one can convince oneself that program Q whose functional abstraction is

$$[Q] = \{(a,1), (b,0), (c,1), (d,2) (e,5), (f,0)\}$$

is also correct wrt Sp. The fact that program Q is defined outside the domain of R does not prevent it from being correct.

Let P' be the program having IS for input space, OS for output space and whose functional abstraction is

$$[P'] = \{(a,0), (c,2), (d,0)\}.$$

Even though all the pairs of [P'] are in the relation of specification Sp, P' cannot be considered correct since it is not defined for the input state b. Yet, by including b in the domain of the specification the user indicates that he may submit it to the program. We then say that P′ is partially correct wrt specification Sp. Also, if we consider program Q′ whose functional abstraction is

$$[Q′] = \{(a,0), (c,2), (d,0), (f,3)\},$$

we notice that for all s in the domain of Q′ and the domain of R, $(s,[Q′](s))$ is in relation R. Q′ is also considered partially correct.

Let P″ be the program having IS and OS for input space and output space (respectively) and whose functional abstraction is

$$[P″] = \{(a,1), (b,2), (c,3), (d,0)\}.$$

We see that program P″ is defined for every value of the domain of Sp. If the user of program P″ submits any one of elements a, b, c or d, the program may (as in the case of a or d) or may not (b or c) return a correct state, but at least it does terminate. We then say that P″ terminates wrt Sp. Following the same argument, one can convince oneself that program Q″ whose functional abstraction is

$$[Q″] = \{(a,1), (b,2), (c,3), (d,0), (e,0), (f,1)\}$$

also terminates wrt Sp.

Below are formal definitions of the three notions informally introduced above.

DEFINITION 1. Let Sp = (IS,OS,R) be a specification and let P be a program whose input space is IS and output space is OS. Program P is said to be *correct* wrt Sp iff

$$is:\textbf{dom}(R) \implies is:\textbf{dom}([P]) \wedge (is,[P](is)):R$$

is a P-tautology on IS.

If P is correct wrt Sp, we also say that P is a *solution* of Sp. To contrast it with partial correctness, the property of correctness is sometimes referred to as *total correctness*.

DEFINITION 2. Let Sp = (IS,OS,R) be a specification and let P be a program whose input space is IS and output space is OS. Program P is said to be *partially correct* wrt Sp iff

$$\text{is:}\mathbf{dom}(R) \ \wedge \ \text{is:}\mathbf{dom}([P]) \ \Rightarrow \ (\text{is},[P](\text{is})){:}R$$

is a P-tautology on IS.

Partial correctness is a very weak property: A program whose functional abstraction is empty (i.e. causes an exceptional condition for every input state) is partially correct wrt any specification!

DEFINITION 3. Let $Sp = (IS,OS,R)$ be a specification and let P be a program whose input space is IS and output space is OS. Program P is said to *terminate* (or *be defined*) wrt Sp iff:

$$\text{is:}\mathbf{dom}(R) \ \Rightarrow \ \text{is:}\mathbf{dom}([P])$$

is a P-tautology on IS.

The following properties stem immediately from these definitions:

— If P is correct wrt Sp then it terminates wrt Sp.
— If P is correct wrt Sp then it is partially correct wrt Sp.
— If P is partially correct and terminates wrt Sp then it is correct wrt Sp.
— If P terminates wrt (IS,OS,R) then it is correct wrt (IS,OS,$\mathbf{dom}(R)\times$ OS).

Below is a characterization of correctness. It is equivalent to Definition 1, if perhaps slightly less intuitive at first sight. Its interpretation is given below, in Remark 1.

PROPOSITION 1. (Characterization of Correctness, due to Mills *et al* [5]). Let $Sp = (IS,OS,R)$ be a specification and P be a program having IS and OS for input space and output space. Program P is correct wrt Sp iff

$$\mathbf{dom}(R\cap[P]) \ = \ \mathbf{dom}(R).$$

Proof. First of all, it must be noted that the assertion

$$\text{``}\mathbf{dom}(R\cap[P])=\mathbf{dom}(R)\text{''}$$

is equivalent to the assertion

$$\text{``}\mathbf{dom}(R) \ \subseteq \ \mathbf{dom}(R\cap[P])\text{''}$$

because the assertion

$$\text{"dom}(R \cap [P]) \subseteq \text{dom}(R)\text{"}$$

is valid regardless of R and P. Hence we shall prove the equivalence between the following propositions:

    a) **dom**(R) $\subseteq$ **dom**(R $\cap$ [P]).
    b) is:**dom**(R) $\Rightarrow$ is:**dom**([P]) $\wedge$ (is,[P](is)):R.

Proof of a$\Rightarrow$b:
Let (is) be an element of **dom**(R). By hypothesis (a), (is) is an element of **dom**(R $\cap$ [P]). Hence there exists os such that (is,os) belongs to (R $\cap$ [P]). From (is,os):[P] we deduce is:**dom**([P]) and os = [P](is). Replacing os by [P](is) in the proposition (is,os):R, we obtain the result sought.

Proof of b$\Rightarrow$a:
Let (is) be an element of **dom**(R). According to (b), (is,[P](is)):R; on the other hand, (is,[P](is)):[P] by definition. Hence is:**dom**(R $\cap$ [P]).

                                                   QED

REMARK 1. Note that **dom**(R $\cap$ [P]) is the set of input states for which program P works according to the requirements of specification Sp = (IS,OS,R). On the other hand, **dom**(R) is the set of input states for which program P must work according to the requirements of specification Sp. The characterization of Mills merely expresses that a program is correct if it works for all the input states for which it must work!

One can develop set-theoretic formulas for partial correctness and termination. They are given below.

PROPOSITION 2. Program P (input space IS, output space OS) is partially correct wrt Sp = (IS,OS,R) iff

$$\text{dom}(R \cap [P]) = \text{dom}(R) \cap \text{dom}([P]).$$

For an outline of the proof, see problem 4.

PROPOSITION 3. Program P (input space IS, output space OS) terminates wrt Sp = (IS,OS,R) iff

$$\text{dom}(R) \subseteq \text{dom}([P]).$$

Proof. This formula is a simple paraphrase of the definition of termination.

The correctness, partial correctness and termination of statements can be defined using I-specifications, in a way similar to that of programs. Also, similar set-theoretic formulas of correctness can be derived for statements.

REMARK 2. It is important to note that E-specifications are usually used for the specification of programs (whose functional abstraction is an E-function, as we recall), whereas I-specifications are usually used for the specification of statements (whose functional abstraction is an I-function).

Exercises

1. [A] Let IS be {a,b,c,d,e} and OS be {0,1,2,3}; let R be the relation {(a,0),(a,1),(b,1),(b,2),(d,3)}. For each of the following programs on input space IS and output space OS tell whether it is correct, partially correct or defined wrt Sp=(IS,OS,R).
   a) Program Pa, such that [Pa] = {(a,0),(b,2),(d,3),(e,2)}.
   b) Program Pb, such that [Pb] = {(a,0),(d,3)}.
   c) Program Pc, such that [Pc] = {(a,3),(b,0),(d,3),(e,0)}.
   d) Program Pd, such that [Pd] = {(a,0),(b,0),(c,1),(d,3)}.
   e) Program Pe, such that [Pe] = {}.

2. [A] Let S=**integer** be the P-space of program P and let R be the I-relation on S defined by R = {(s,s')| $s \geq 2 \wedge s' > s$}. For each of the following statements, indicate whether it is correct, partially correct or defined wrt (S,R).
   a) Statement Sa, such that [Sa] = [$s \geq 0$, s+2].
   b) Statement Sb, such that [Sb] = [$s \geq 4$, s+4].
   c) Statement Sc, such that [Sc] = [$s > 0$, s].
   d) Statement Sd, such that [Sd] = [$s > 10$, s].
   e) Statement Se, such that [Se] = [**true**, s−1].

3. [B] Let S be the set:

$$S = \textbf{set}$$
$$\text{a, b: } \textbf{integer}$$
$$\textbf{end.}$$

Let R be the I-relation on S defined by

$$R = \{(s,s')| \ a(s) > b(s) \wedge a(s') + b(s') \geq a(s) + b(s)\}.$$

For each of the following statements on P-space S, indicate whether it is correct, partially correct or defined wrt (S,R).
   a) Statement Sa, such that [Sa] = [$a(s) \geq b(s)$, (a(s)+1,b(s)−1)].

b) Statement Sb, such that [Sb] = $[a(s) = b(s)+1, (a(s)+1,b(s)+1)]$.
c) Statement Sc, such that [Sc] = $[a(s) = b(s)+3, (a(s)-1,b(s))]$.
d) Statement Sd, such that [Sd] = $[\mathbf{true}, (a(s)+2,b(s)-1)]$.
e) Statement Se, such that [Se] = $[\mathbf{false}, s]$.

2 The Symbolic Execution Method

Let Sp = (IS,OS,R) be a specification and let P be a program whose input space is IS and output space is OS. Proving the correctness of program P wrt E-specification Sp by symbolic execution consists of

— computing the functional abstraction of P, then
— verifying the correctness of P wrt Sp.

The proof of individual statements wrt I-specifications is done in a similar fashion.

Below are examples of proofs of programs by symbolic execution.

EXAMPLE 1.
Specification: Sp = (IS,OS,R), where

IS = L*(**integer**).
OS = L*(**integer**).
R = $\{(is,os)\mid$ **lng**(is) = 4 $\wedge$ **car•cdr**(is) $\geq$ 5 $\wedge$ **car**(os) = **car**(is) + **car•cdr**(is)$\}$.

Program:

```
program Add(input,output);
type
   S = set
      a, b: integer
   end;
var
   s:S;
begin
   read(a); read(b);
   while b≠0 do begin a:=a+1; b:=b-1 end;
   write(a)
end.
```

This program is identical to that of Example 7, Chapter 5. Its functional abstraction is:

[Add] =
$\{(is,os)|$ **lng**$(is)\geq 2 \wedge$ **car•cdr**$(is)\geq 0 \wedge os =$ **app**$((),$ **car**$(is)+$**car•cdr**$(is))\}.$

Taking the notational conventions of Example 7, Chapter 5, we have:

R ∩ [Add] = $\{(is,os)|$ **lng**$(is)=4 \wedge$ **lng**$(is)\geq 2 \wedge is2\geq 0 \wedge$
$is2\geq 5 \wedge os1 = is1+is2 \wedge os =$ **app**$((),is1+is2)\}.$

This can be simplified to become:

$= \{(is,os)|$ **lng**$(is)=4 \wedge is2\geq 5 \wedge os = (is1+is2)\}.$

Clearly, the domain of this relation is identical to that of R, namely:

$\{is|$ **lng**$(is)=4 \wedge is2\geq 5\}.$

Hence program Add is correct wrt Sp; consequently, it is also partially correct and defined wrt Sp.

EXAMPLE 2.
Specification: Sp' = (IS,OS,R'), where

IS and OS are defined as in Example 1 and relation R' is:
R' = $\{(is,os)|$ **lng**$(is)\geq 2 \wedge os1 = is1+is2\}.$

The program considered is program Add, given in Example 1. We have,

R' ∩ [Add] = $\{(is,os)|$ **lng**$(is)\geq 2 \wedge is2\geq 0 \wedge os =$ **app**$((),is1+is2))\},$

whose domain,

$\{is|$ **lng**$(is)\geq 2 \wedge is2\geq 0\},$

is not the same as the domain of R', which is

$\{is|$ **lng**$(is)\geq 2\}.$

Hence program Add is not correct wrt Sp'. It may, however, be partially correct:

$$\mathbf{dom}([\text{Add}]) = \{\text{is}|\ \mathbf{lng}(\text{is})\geqslant 2\ \wedge\ \text{is}2\geqslant 0\},$$

hence

$$\mathbf{dom}(R')\ \cap\ \mathbf{dom}([\text{Add}]) = \{\text{is}\ |\ \mathbf{lng}(\text{is})\geqslant 2\ \wedge\ \text{is}2\geqslant 0\},$$

which is the same as

$$\mathbf{dom}(R'\cap[\text{Add}]).$$

Hence Add is partially correct wrt Sp. Finally, because $\mathbf{dom}(R')$ is not a subset of $\mathbf{dom}([\text{Add}])$, program Add is not defined wrt Sp'.

EXAMPLE 3. It is left to the reader to verify that program Add is not even partially correct but that it terminates wrt Sp" = (IS,OS,R"), where

$$R'' = \{(\text{is,os})|\ \mathbf{lng}(\text{is})=4\ \wedge\ \text{is}2\geqslant 5\ \wedge\ \text{os}=\text{is}\}.$$

Exercises

1. [B] Let IS and OS be equal to the set L*(**integer**) and R be the relation

$$\{(\text{is,os})|\ \mathbf{lng}(\text{is})\geqslant 2\ \wedge\ \mathbf{car}(\text{os})=\mathbf{car}(\text{is})*\mathbf{car.cdr}(\text{is})\}.$$

Let M be the program having IS and OS for input space and output space, respectively, and defined by:

```
program M(input, output);
type
  S = set
    a, b, p: integer
  end;
var
  s:S;
begin
  read(a); read(b); p: = 0;
  while a ≠ 0 do begin p: = p+b; a: = a−1 end;
  write(p)
end.
```

a) Explain why R is not a function.
b) Determine the functional abstraction of program M.
c) Does M terminate wrt Sp = (IS,OS,R)?
d) Is M partially correct wrt Sp?
e) Modify the domain of R so as to make M correct wrt Sp.

2. [B] Let IS and OS be equal to the set L*(**integer**) and R be the relation

$$\{(is,os) \mid \textbf{lng}(is) = 1 \ \wedge \ \textbf{car}(is) \geqslant 0 \ \wedge \ \textbf{car}(os) = (\textbf{car}(is))!\}.$$

Let F be the program having IS and OS as input space and output space and defined by:

```
program F(input, output);
type
  S = set
     in, fc, n: integer
  end;
var
  s:S;
begin
  read(n); in: = 3; fc: = 2;
  while in≤n do begin fc: = fc*in; in: = in+1 end;
  write(fc)
end.
```

a) Explain why R is not a function.
b) Determine the functional abstraction of program F.
c) Does program F terminate wrt Sp = (IS,OS,R)?
d) Is F partially correct wrt Sp?
e) Modify program F so as to make it correct wrt Sp.

3. [B] Let S be the set:

```
S = set
   n, fc: integer
end,
```

and let st be the SM-Pascal statement on S:

```
while n ≠ 0 do
   begin
   fc: = fc*n;
   n: = n−1
   end.
```

For each I-relation R on S given below, say whether st is correct, partially correct or defined wrt Sp = (S,R).

a) $\{(s,s')\mid n(s) \geqslant 0 \;\wedge\; fc(s') = n(s)!\}$.
b) $\{(s,s')\mid fc(s') = fc(s)*n(s)!\}$.
c) $\{(s,s')\mid n(s) \geqslant 0 \;\wedge\; fc(s) = 1 \;\wedge\; fc(s') = n(s)!\}$.
d) $\{(s,s')\mid n(s) \geqslant 0 \;\wedge\; fc(s') = fc(s)*n(s)!\}$.
e) $\{(s,s')\mid (n(s) = 0 \vee n(s) = 1) \;\wedge\; fc(s') = 1\}$.

4. [B] Let S be the set

$$S = \textbf{set}$$
$$a, b: \textbf{integer}$$
$$\textbf{end,}$$

and let st be the SM-Pascal statement on S

while $a < b$ **do** $a := a + 1$.

For each binary relation R on S given below, indicate whether st is correct, partially correct or defined wrt Sp = (S,R). Notational convention: max(s) (respectively min(s)) denotes the largest (respectively the smallest) of a(s) and b(s).

a) $\{(s,s')\mid max(s) = max(s')\}$.
b) $\{(s,s')\mid a(s') = max(s)\}$.
c) $\{(s,s')\mid a(s) > b(s) \;\wedge\; min(s) = min(s')\}$.
d) $\{(s,s')\mid min(s) = min(s')\}$.
e) $\{(s,s')\mid a(s) \leqslant b(s) \;\wedge\; a(s) = b(s')\}$.

3 Problems

1. [B]
   a) Prove that program P terminates wrt (IS,OS,R) if it is totally correct wrt (IS,OS, **dom**(R)×OS).
   b) Let P be a program partially correct wrt (IS,OS,R). Express the partial correctness of P wrt (IS,OS,R) as the total correctness of P wrt some other specification.

2. [C] Let P be a program which is correct wrt (IS,OS,R) and let R' be a subset of R and R'' a superset of R. Justify your answers to the following questions:
   a) Is P partially correct wrt (IS,OS,R')?
   b) Is P partially correct wrt (IS,OS,R'')?
   c) Is P correct wrt (IS,OS,R')? If not, what additional condition is necessary to make it so?
   d) Is P correct wrt (IS,OS,R'')? If not, what additional condition is necessary to make it so?

e) Deduce from your answers some comments regarding program maintenance: When and how is a program to be modified to meet new specifications whose relation is a subset (or a superset) of the relation of the current specification?

3. [C] Let P be a program which is partially correct wrt (IS,OS,R) and let R' be a subset of R and R" be a superset of R. Justify your answers to the following questions:
   a) Is P partially correct wrt (IS,OS,R')?
   b) Is P partially correct wrt (IS,OS,R")?
   c) Under what condition is P correct wrt (IS,OS,R')?
   d) Under what condition is P correct wrt (IS,OS,R")?
   e) Deduce from your answers some comments regarding program maintenance.

4. [B] Let R and p be two I-relations on some set S.
   a) Show that: $\mathbf{dom}(R \cap p) \subseteq \mathbf{dom}(R) \cap \mathbf{dom}(p)$.
   b) Find examples of R and p such that: $\mathbf{dom}(R \cap p) \subset \mathbf{dom}(R) \cap \mathbf{dom}(p)$.
   c) On the basis of question (a), weaken the characterization of partial correctness given in Proposition 1.
   d) Let st be a statement on space S. We define two formulas:

$$\text{(i)} \quad \mathbf{dom}(R) \cap \mathbf{dom}([st]) \subseteq \mathbf{dom}(R \cap [st]).$$
$$\text{(ii)} \quad s: \mathbf{dom}(R) \wedge s: \mathbf{dom}([st]) \Rightarrow (s, [st](s)): R.$$

   Prove (i)$\Rightarrow$(ii).
   e) Prove (ii)$\Rightarrow$(i).

5. [C] Let

```
S = set
crt
    l, h, m: integer; (*low, high, middle*)
    v: real; (*value*)
    a: array [1..100] of real;
    w: integer; (*where?*)
sub
    0≤w≤100 ∧ 1≤l≤101 ∧ 0≤h≤100
end,
```

and let Sr (search) be the following SM-Pascal statement on S:

```
begin
l: = 1; h: = 100; w: = 0;
while l≤h do
    begin
    m: = (l+h)/2;
```

$$\textbf{if } a[m] = v \textbf{ then } w := m$$
$$\textbf{else}$$
$$\quad \textbf{if } a[m] < v \textbf{ then } l := m+1$$
$$\quad \textbf{else } h := m-1$$
$$\textbf{end}$$
$$\textbf{end}.$$

Let R be the I-relation on S defined by

$$R =$$
$$\{(s,s') \mid w(s') = 0 \ \wedge \ (\forall i, \ 1 \leqslant i \leqslant 100 \Rightarrow a(s)[i] \neq v(s))\}$$
$$\cup$$
$$\{(s,s') \mid 1 \leqslant w(s') \leqslant 100 \ \wedge \ a(s)[w(s')] = v(s)\}.$$

a) Interpret the significance of R. Is R a function?
b) Comment on the difficulty to generate the functional abstraction of Sr.
c) Is the value of $l([Sr](s))$, $m([Sr](s))$ or $h([Sr](s))$ important from the view-point of relation R?
d) Can one prove the correctness of Sr by symbolic execution without computing $l([Sr](s))$, $m([Sr](s))$ and $h([Sr](s))$?
e) Comment on the weakness of symbolic execution.

6. [B] Prove, using Definition 2, that a program P is partially correct wrt a specification (IS,OS,R) iff:

$$R**0 * [P] \subseteq R.$$

Prove the equivalence of this formula with that of Proposition 2.

4 Bibliography

The characterization given in Proposition 1 is due to [5]. For more background on function theoretic methods of program verification, consult [4] or [5]. For early references on symbolic execution, consult [1], [2] or [3].

1: Boyer R S, B Elspas and K N Levitt. SELECT-A System for Testing and Debugging Programs by Symbolic Execution. Proceedings, International Conference on Reliable Software. Los Angeles, April 1975, pp 234-245.
2: Hantler S L and J C King. An Introduction to Proving the Correctness of Programs. Computing Surveys 8(3) (September 1976), pp 331-353.
3: King J C. Symbolic Execution and Program Testing. CACM 19(7) (July 1976), pp 385-394.
4: Linger R C, H D Mills and B I Witts. Structured Programming: Theory and Practice. Addison-Wesley, 1979.
5: Mills H D, R H Austing, V R Basili, J D Gannon, R G Hamlet, J E Kohl and B Schneiderman. The Calculus of Computer Programming. To be published by Allyn and Bacon.

Part III: Verifying Programs by Induction

Ce que l'on conçoit bien s'énonce clairement, et les mots pour le dire viennent aisément

Boileau

What is well conceived can be expressed clearly, and the words to say it come easily.

A program is potentially a complex structure. By its attempt to derive the functional abstraction of programs, the symbolic execution confronts program complexity head-on because it concerns itself with all the functional details of the program. In addition to being irrelevant to the specification given, some details can be very complex: Try, for example, to evaluate $l([Sr](s))$, $m([Sr](s))$ or $h([Sr](s))$ in problem 5, Chapter 6. In Part III we shall use induction in order to tackle the complexity of programs. As a static object, a program presents two *axes* of complexity: its *control structure,* that is its statement part (see ⟨statement part⟩, Appendix A) and its *data structure,* that is its E-space. As a dynamic object, a program presents yet two more axes of complexity: its *trace of execution,* as materialized by the sequence of labels crossed during execution, and its *length of execution* as measured in terms of number of iterations or depth of recursion. All the methods introduced and discussed in Part III prove the correctness of programs by induction along some axis of complexity.

Chapter 7

Induction on the Control Structure: The Invariant Assertion Method

The *invariant assertion method* deduces the correctness of complex statements from the correctness of simpler statements. In this chapter, we shall discuss the proof of partial correctness then the proof of total correctness of programs using the principle of induction on the complexity of their statement parts.

1 Proof of Partial Correctness

The purpose of this section is to design the deductive system s.IA (IA stands for *invariant assertion;* this name will be justified later). Before we develop the deductive system itself, we shall discuss the *theory* underlying it. (See the definition of *theory* in section 4.1, Chapter 3).

1.1 The Theory t.IA

A theory is defined when we are given a set W of well-formed formulas and a set T in W of tautologies. Below is a definition of t.IA.

Well-formed formulas. Let st = **begin** s: = s+1 **end** be a statement on space S = **real**; if s is known to be greater than 2 before execution of st then it is greater than 3 after; this sentence can be abbreviated by

$$s > 2 \ \{st\} \ s > 3.$$

This type of expression (due to Hoare, [10]) is called an IA-formula; more generally, an IA-formula on the extended space ES has the form:

$$p \ \{st\} \ q$$

where p and q are predicates on ES and st is a statement on ES.

Tautologies. The semantics of an IA-formula such as

$$p \{st\} q$$

is as follows:

$$(\forall es, p(es) \land es{:}\mathbf{dom}([st])) \Rightarrow q([st](es))).$$

Implicit in this definition is the clause es:ES on both sides of the $\Rightarrow$ sign, without which the formula makes no sense. From this semantic definition, it stems that

— IA-formulas are simply a notational extension of predicate logic.
— The IA-formula

$$p \{st\} q$$

(considered as a well-formed formula of predicate logic) is valid if and only if statement st is partially correct with respect to the I-specification (ES, {(es,es')| p(es) $\land$ q(es')}).

1.2 The Deductive System s.IA

We have seen above that IA-formulas can be understood as well-formed formulas of predicate logic; technically, this means that the proof of their validity could proceed according to the guidelines laid out in Chapter 3. There is, however, a hitch: [st], the functional abstraction of st, may be arbitrarily difficult to determine and handle. This is precisely where induction intervenes. Instead of proving the validity of

$$p \{st\} q$$

by interpreting it as a well-formed formula of predicate logic, we attempt to establish its validity by writing it as the consequence (in some deductive system) of simpler formulas. These simpler formulas constitute assertions about the correctness of building components of statement st, which are simpler than st (by relation Cpx, defined in Chapter 5).

The deductive system, called s.IA, that we generate in this section has the same set of well-formed formulas as t.IA; its axioms and rules are designed in such a way as to generate all the tautologies of t.IA without inconsistencies.

The general context of the axioms and rules to be given below is the following: input space IS, input state (is); proper space S, proper state (s); output space OS, output state (os); extended space ES = IS×S×OS, extended state es = (is,s,os).

1.2.1 Axioms

a0: Any P-tautology of predicate logic on ES.

a1: The Empty Statement Axiom

$$p \{\} p.$$

a2: The Assignment Statement Axiom

$$p \bullet E \{s:=E(s)\} p$$

The significance of this axiom is the following: if p is true of E(s) before execution of the assignment statement, then p is true of s after.

a3: The Read Statement Axiom
A **read** statement is a generalized case of assignment statement: One which affects not only the proper state (s), but also the input state (is). It assigns **car**(is) to the variable (elementary function) read leaving all other variables intact, and applies function **cdr** to (is). Using the expression Rd(s,a,is) introduced in section 3.4 of Chapter 5, we define an internal expression Er[a] on set ES by

$$Er[a](is,s,os) = (\textbf{cdr}(is), \ Rd(s,a,is), \ os);$$

then we write the axiom

$$p \bullet Er[a] \{\textbf{read}(a)\} p.$$

a4: The Write Statement Axiom
A **write** statement is also an assignment statement on ES. It modifies the output state (os) only. We define expression Wt on ES by

$$Wt[a](is,s,os) = (is, \ s, \ \textbf{app}(os,a(s)))$$

and we write the axiom

$$p \bullet Wt[a] \{\textbf{write}(a)\} p.$$

1.2.2 Rules

The inference rules of system s.IA are designed on the basis of induction on the set of statements of the program: The correctness of complex (by relation Cpx) statements is deduced from the correctness of their components, which are simpler (in the sense of Cpx).

r0: The Procedure Call Rule

$$\frac{p \; \{\textbf{procedure } R; \; \ldots \; \textbf{end}\} \; q}{p \; \{R\} \; q.}$$

r1: The Begin-End Statement Rule

$$\frac{p \; \{st\} \; q}{p \; \{\textbf{begin } st \; \textbf{end}\} \; q.}$$

r2: The Sequence Statement Rule

$$\frac{\begin{array}{l} p \; \{st\} \; int \\ int \; \{st'\} \; q \end{array}}{p \; \{st; \; st'\} \; q;}$$

int is called the *intermediate predicate.*

r3: The Conditional Statement Rule

$$\frac{\begin{array}{l} p \wedge t \; \{tc\} \; q \\ p \wedge {\sim}t \Rightarrow q \end{array}}{p \; \{\textbf{if } t \; \textbf{then } tc\} \; q.}$$

r4: The Alternative Statement Rule

$$\frac{\begin{array}{l} p \wedge t \; \{tc\} \; q \\ p \wedge {\sim}t \; \{ec\} \; q \end{array}}{p \; \{\textbf{if } t \; \textbf{then } tc \; \textbf{else } ec\} \; q.}$$

r5: The While Statement Rule
There exists a predicate inv such that

$$\frac{\text{inv} \wedge \text{t \{lb\} inv}}{\text{inv \{\textbf{while} t \textbf{do} lb\} inv} \wedge \text{\textasciitilde t.}}$$

Predicate inv(stands for *invariant*) is a very central figure in the verification of while statements. It has traditionally been called a *loop invariant* of the while statement. We shall adopt this name even though the adjective *increasing* is more appropriate to describing this predicate than the adjective *invariant:* See Appendix B.

r6: The With Statement Rule

$$\frac{\text{p \{s.wb\} q}}{\text{p \{\textbf{with} s \textbf{do} wb\} q,}}$$

where s.wb is obtained from wb by replacing all occurrences of elementary function names, say a, by s.a.

r7: The Procedure Declaration Rule
E-space of calling program: ES; current states: es; p-space of called procedure: T; current state: t;

$$\frac{\text{p(es) \{pd\} q (es,t)}}{\text{p(es) \{\textbf{procedure} \ldots \textbf{begin} pd \textbf{end}\} ($\exists$t,q(es,t))}}$$

r8: The Program Rule

$$\frac{\text{p(is)} \wedge \text{os} = () \text{ \{pg\} q(s,os)}}{\text{p(is) \{\textbf{program} \ldots \textbf{begin} pg \textbf{end}\} ($\exists$ s, q(s,os)).}}$$

r9: The Consequence Rule

$$\frac{\begin{array}{c}\text{p' \{st\} q'} \\ \text{p} \Rightarrow \text{p'} \\ \text{q'} \Rightarrow \text{q}\end{array}}{\text{p \{st\} q.}}$$

The Consequence Rule owes its validity to the semantics of IA-formulas; it allows us to rewrite some rules and axioms presented above:

r'2: The Modified Sequence Statement Rule

$$\frac{\begin{array}{l} p \{st\} q \\ p' \{st'\} q' \\ q \Rightarrow p' \end{array}}{p \{st;st'\} q'.}$$

r'5: The Modified While Statement Rule

$$\frac{\begin{array}{l} p \Rightarrow inv \\ inv \wedge t \{lb\} inv \\ inv \wedge \tilde{\ }t \Rightarrow q \end{array}}{p \{\textbf{while } t \textbf{ do } lb\} q.}$$

Notice that the two first premises of the rule constitute respectively the basis of induction and the induction step of a proof by induction to the effect that predicate inv holds after any number (including 0) of iterations.

r'7: The Modified Procedure Declaration Rule

$$\frac{\begin{array}{l} p(es) \{pd\} q'(es,t) \\ (\exists t, q'(es,t)) \Rightarrow q(es) \end{array}}{p(es) \{\textbf{procedure} \ldots \textbf{begin } pd \textbf{ end}\} q(es),}$$

where t is the proper state of the procedure.

r'8: The Modified Program Rule

$$\frac{\begin{array}{l} p(is) \wedge os = () \{pg\} q'(s,os) \\ (\exists s, q'(s,os)) \Rightarrow q(os) \end{array}}{p(is) \{\textbf{program} \ldots \textbf{begin } pg \textbf{ end}\} q(os).}$$

a'1: The Empty Statement Rule

$$\frac{p \Rightarrow q}{p \{\} q.}$$

a'2: The Assignment Statement Rule

$$\frac{p \Rightarrow q \bullet E}{p \{s: = E(s)\}\ q.}$$

a'3: The Read Statement Rule

$$\frac{p \Rightarrow q \bullet Er[a]}{p \{read(a)\}\ q.}$$

a'4: The Write Statement Rule

$$\frac{p \Rightarrow q \bullet Wt[a]}{p \{write(a)\}\ q.}$$

1.3 The First Theorem of Invariant Assertion: Partial Correctness

THEOREM 1. Let P be a program on E-space $ES = IS \times S \times OS$ and st be a statement of P. If

$$p \{P\}\ q$$

is a theorem of s.IA then program P is partially correct with respect to the E-specification $(IS,OS,\{(is,os)\,|\,p(is) \wedge q(os)\})$.
If

$$p \{st\}\ q$$

is a theorem of s.IA then statement st is partially correct with respect to the I-specification $(ES,\{(es,es')\,|\ p(es) \wedge q(es')\})$.

No formal proof of the theorem is given; the axioms and rules of system s.IA are designed to reflect the semantics usually associated with the constructs involved. Note that this theorem provides sufficient but not necessary conditions for the partial correctness of programs or statements; we do not exclude that a program (or statement) be correct, yet not provably correct, by system s.IA. In other words, Theorem 1 is an act of faith in the consistency of system s.IA but not in its completeness. Indeed it is much easier to convince oneself of the consistency of system s.IA than it is to convince oneself of its completeness.

REMARK 1. When an IA-formula such as

$$p \{st\} q$$

is not a theorem of system s.IA, one may want to prove that it is actually not valid. The simplest way to do so is to translate it back to predicate logic, as

$$(\forall s, p(s) \land s:\mathbf{dom}([st]) \Rightarrow q([st](s)))$$

and find a state s such that $p(s) \land s:\mathbf{dom}[st]$ holds whereas $q([st](s))$ does not hold.

1.4 Examples of Application

In order to enhance the reader's understanding and confidence in system s.IA, some examples are given below; these examples exercise most of the axioms and rules of the system.

EXAMPLE 1. (Rule a'2)
We consider the proper space S = **real** and the variable s in S. Is

$$v: \quad s \neq 0 \{s := s*s\} s > 0$$

a theorem of s.IA?
    We consider

$$v0: \quad s \neq 0 \Rightarrow s*s > 0$$

and we note that the sequence (v0,v) is a deduction in s.IA because:

— v0 is an axiom of s.IA (an instance of a0),
— v is the consequence of v0 by rule a'2.

Hence v is a theorem.

EXAMPLE 2. (Rule a'3)
We consider the set

$$S = \mathbf{set}$$
$$\quad a, b: \mathbf{integer}$$
$$\mathbf{end}.$$

Let IS and OS be L*(**integer**) and let s, is, os be variables in S, IS and OS respectively. Is the formula

$$\text{v:}\quad \text{is} = (3,4,1) \wedge a(s) = 2 \;\{\textbf{read}(b)\}\; a(s) < b(s)$$

a theorem of s.IA?

The expression Er[b] that the **read** statement defines on set ES can be described as follows:

$$Er[b] = (\;\; \textbf{cdr}(is),\; (a(s),\; \textbf{car}(is)),\; os\;\;).$$

We consider the formula

$$\text{v0:}\quad \text{is} = (3,4,1) \wedge a(s) = 2 \;\Rightarrow\; a(s) < \textbf{car}(is).$$

Clearly, (v0,v) is a deduction in s.IA because

— v0 is an axiom of s.IA (an instance of a0),
— v is the consequence of v0 by rule a'3.

Hence v is a theorem of s.IA.

EXAMPLE 3. (Rule a'4)
In the same context as above, we wish to establish the theoremhood of

$$\text{v:}\quad \textbf{lng}(os) \geqslant 3 \;\{\textbf{write}(b)\}\; \textbf{lng}(os) \geqslant 4.$$

The expression Wt[b] that the **write** statement defines on set ES can be described as follows:

$$Wt[b] = (\;\; is,\; s,\; \textbf{app}(os,b(s))\;\;).$$

Clearly,

$$\text{v0:}\quad \textbf{lng}(os) \geqslant 3 \;\Rightarrow\; \textbf{lng}(\textbf{app}(os,b(s))) \geqslant 4$$

is an axiom of system s.IA since it is a P-tautology on ES, due to the semantics of functions **lng** and **app**.

Rule a'4 provides that (v0,v) is a deduction in s.IA, hence v is a theorem in s.IA.

EXAMPLE 4. (Rule r2)
Proper space, S = **real**; proper state, s. Prove that

$$v: s = s0 \; \{s: = 1/(1-s); \; s: = \log(s)\} \; s = -\log(1-s0)$$

is a theorem of s.IA.
Let v0 and v1 be formulas defined as follows:

$$v0: s = s0 \; \{s: = 1/(1-s)\} \; s = 1/(1-s0),$$
$$v1: s = 1/(1-s0) \; \{s: = \log (s)\} \; s = -\log (1-s0).$$

Rule r2 provides that if v0 and v1 are theorems then so is v. We define:

$$v00: s = s0 \Rightarrow 1/(1-s) = 1/(1-s0)$$

and

$$v10: s = 1/(1-s0) \Rightarrow \log(s) = -\log(1-s0).$$

Clearly, (v00,v10,v0,v1,v) is a deduction in system s.IA, hence v is a theorem.

EXAMPLE 5. (Rule r3)
Proper space,

$$S = \textbf{set}$$
$$a, b: \textbf{integer}$$
$$\textbf{end};$$

proper state, s. Prove the following formula:

$$v: \quad s = s0 \; \{\textbf{if} \; a > b \; \textbf{then} \; b: = a\} \; b(s) = \max(a(s0),b(s0)).$$

We define

$$v0: \quad s = s0 \wedge a(s) > b(s) \; \{b: = a\} \; b(s) = \max(a(s0),b(s0))$$

and

$$v1: \quad s = s0 \wedge \sim(a(s) > b(s)) \Rightarrow b(s) = \max(a(s0),b(s0)).$$

Rule r3 provides that if v0 and v1 are theorems then so is v. The internal expression on S that the statement (b: = a) defines is

$$E(s) = (a(s),a(s)).$$

We define the formula

$$v00: \quad s = s0 \ \wedge \ a(s) > b(s) \ \Rightarrow \ a(s) = \max(a(s0), b(s0)).$$

Clearly, (v00,v0,v1,v) is a deduction in s.IA because v00 and v1 are axioms (instances of a0), v0 is the conclusion of v00 by rule a′2 and v is the conclusion of v0 and v1 by rule r3. Formula v is a theorem of system s.IA.

EXAMPLE 6. (Rule r4)
Proper space:

$$S = \textbf{set}$$
$$a, b, c: \textbf{integer}$$
$$\textbf{end};$$

proper state: s. Prove the following formula:

v: **true** {**if** $a > b$ **then** $c := a$ **else** $c := b$} $c(s) = \max(a(s), b(s))$.

We define the following formulas, inspired by rule r4:

v0:   **true** $\wedge$ $a(s) > b(s)$ {$c := a$} $c(s) = \max(a(s), b(s))$,
v1:   **true** $\wedge$ $\tilde{\ }(a(s) > b(s))$ {$c := b$} $c(s) = \max(a(s), b(s))$.

The expression defined by the assignment statement $(c := a)$ (respectively $(c := b)$) is $(a(s), b(s), a(s))$ (respectively $(a(s), b(s), b(s))$); we define the following formulas, inspired by the application of rule a′2 to formulas v0 and v1:

v00: $a(s) > b(s) \ \Rightarrow \ a(s) = \max(a(s), b(s))$,
v11: $\tilde{\ }(a(s) > b(s)) \ \Rightarrow \ b(s) = \max(a(s), b(s))$.

Clearly, (v00,v11,v0,v1,v) is a deduction and v is a theorem in s.IA.

EXAMPLE 7. (Rule r′5)
Proper space:

$$S = \textbf{set}$$
$$\textbf{crt}$$
$$a, b, q: \textbf{integer};$$
$$\textbf{sub}$$
$$a \geqslant 0 \ \wedge \ b \geqslant 0$$
$$\textbf{end}.$$

Proper state: s. Prove the following formula:

v: s = s0 $\wedge$ q(s) = 0
$\qquad$ {**while** b$\geqslant$a **do begin** q: = q+1; b: = b−a **end**}
$\qquad\qquad$ b(s0) = q(s)*a(s0)+b(s) $\wedge$ b(s)<a(s0)

In order to apply the Modified While Statement Rule (r′5) to formula v, we have to derive a predicate which is a loop invariant for the iteration; the generation of the loop invariant stems from a thorough comprehension of the statement. We choose

$$\text{inv(s): } b(s0) = q(s)*a(s0)+b(s) \ \wedge \ a(s) = a(s0),$$

then we write the three premises of rule r′5.

v0: $\quad$ s = s0 $\wedge$ q(s)=0 $\Rightarrow$ b(s0)=q(s)*a(s0)+b(s) $\wedge$ a(s)=a(s0),
v1: $\quad$ b(s0)=q(s)*a(s0)+b(s) $\wedge$ a (s)=a(s0) $\wedge$ b(s)$\geqslant$a(s)
$\qquad\qquad$ {q: = q+1; b: = b−a}
$\qquad\qquad\qquad$ b(s0)=q(s)*a(s0)+b(s) $\wedge$ a(s)=a(s0),
v2: $\quad$ b(s0) = q(s)*a(s0)+b(s) $\wedge$ a(s)=a(s0) $\wedge$ ~(b(s)$\geqslant$a(s))
$\qquad\qquad\qquad$ $\Rightarrow$ b(s0)=q(s)*a(s0)+b(s) $\wedge$ b(s) <a(s0).

In order to apply the Sequence Statement Rule to formula v1, we need to derive an intermediate predicate; we choose:

$$\text{int(s): } b(s0) = (q(s)-1)*a(s0)+b(s) \ \wedge \ a(s) = a(s0) \ \wedge \ b(s) \geqslant a(s).$$

We define the formulas:

v10: $\quad$ b(s0)=q(s)*a(s0)+b(s) $\wedge$ a(s)=a(s0) $\wedge$ b(s)$\geqslant$a(s)
$\qquad\qquad$ {q:=q+1}
$\qquad\quad$ b(s0) = (q(s)−1)*a(s0)+b(s) $\wedge$ a(s)=a(s0) $\wedge$ b(s)$\geqslant$a(s),

and

v11: $\quad$ b(s0)=(q(s)−1)*a(s0)+b(s) $\wedge$ a(s)=a(s0) $\wedge$ b(s)$\geqslant$a(s)
$\qquad\qquad$ {b: = b−a}
$\qquad\qquad$ b(s0)=q(s)*a(s0)+b(s) $\wedge$ a(s)=a(s0).

In order to apply rule a′2 to v01 and v11, we generate the formulas

v100: $\quad$ b(s0)=q(s)*a(s0)+b(s) $\wedge$ a(s)=a(s0) $\wedge$ b(s)$\geqslant$a(s)
$\qquad\quad$ $\Rightarrow$ b(s0)=((q(s)+1)−1)*a(s0)+b(s) $\wedge$ a(s)=a(s0) $\wedge$ b(s)$\geqslant$a(s),

v110: $b(s0) = (q(s)-1)*a(s0)+b(s) \wedge a(s)=a(s0) \wedge b(s)\geqslant a(s)$
$\Rightarrow b(s0) = q(s)*a(s0)+b(s)-a(s) \wedge a(s)=a(s0)$.

Clearly, (v100,v110,v10,v11,v1,v2,v0,v) is a deduction, hence v is a theorem of s.IA.

REMARK 2. The reader may think that the clause $b(s)\geqslant a(s)$ appearing on the left side of formula v11 (Example 7) is superfluous. In fact it is necessary to ensure that the state reached after execution of (b: = b−a) still belongs to S. See the semantic definition of IA-formulas, in section 1.1.

EXAMPLE 8. (Rules r0 and r7)
We are given a program P with P-space S defined as follows:

$$S = \textbf{set}$$
$$a, b: \textbf{real}$$
$$\textbf{end}.$$

Furthermore, we are given a procedure R defined by

```
procedure R;
type T = real;
var t:T;
begin
pd (*where pd is some SM-Pascal statement*)
end.
```

Let v′ be the following formula:

v′:   **true** {pd} $a(s)=t \wedge b(s)=t**2$.

Prove that the formula v defined by:

v: **true** {R} $b(s)=a(s)**2$

is a logical consequence of {v′} in system s.IA. This proof is quite simple and is left as an exercise.

EXAMPLE 9. (Rule r8)
The proof developed in this example is rather complex. It is done in some level of detail to show at least one example of a proof of a complete program using the invariant assertion method.

Let D (stands for division) be the program below:

```
program D(input, output);
type
  S = set
  crt
    a, b, q: integer;
  sub
    a⩾0 ∧ b⩾0
  end;
var
  s: S;
begin read(a); read(b); q: = 0;
while b⩾a do begin q: = q+1; b: = b−a end;
write(b); write(q)
end.
```

We define:

Input space, $IS = L^*(\textbf{natural})$; input state, (is).
Output space, $OS = L^*(\textbf{natural})$; output state, (os).

Let SD (stands for: specification for a division) be the E-specification

(IS,
  OS,
  {(is,os)| **car•cdr**(is) = **car•cdr**(os)***car**(is)+**car**(os)
      ∧ **car**(os)<**car**(is)}).

This specification expresses that (is) contains the divisor and dividend (in this order) and (os) must contain the remainder and quotient (in this order) of an integer division of two non-negative numbers.

Theorem 1 provides that if

v: is = is0

$$\{D\}$$

car•cdr(is0) = **car•cdr**(os)***car**(is0)+**car**(os) ∧ **car**(os)<**car**(is0)

is a theorem of s.IA then D is partially correct with respect to SD. On the basis of the modified program rule, we generate the following formulas:

v0:   is = is0 ∧ os = ( )

                    {**read**(a); **read**(b); q: = 0;
                    while b⩾a **do**
                      begin
                      q: = q+1;
                      b: = b−a
                    end;
                  write(b); **write**(q)}

car•cdr(is0) = q(s)***car**(is0) + b(s) ∧ b(s) < **car**(is0) ∧ os = **app**(**app**(( ),b(s)),q(s)).

v1:   (∃ s, **car•cdr**(is0) = q(s)***car**(is0) + b(s) ∧ b(s) < **car**(is0)
      ∧ os = **app**(**app**(( ),b(s)),q(s)))
  ⇒   **car•cdr**(is0) = **car•cdr**(os)***car**(is0) + **car**(os)
      ∧ **car**(os) < **car**(is0).

On the basis of the Sequence Statement Rule (applied twice to v0) we generate the following formulas:

v00:   is = is0 ∧ os = ( )

                    {**read**(a);**read**(b); q: = 0}
                         os = ( ) ∧ s = (**car**(is0), **car.cdr**(is0), 0).

v01:   os = ( ) ∧ s = (**car**(is0),**car•cdr**(is0),0)
             {**while** b⩾a **do begin** q: = q+1;b: = b−a **end**}
             car•cdr(is0) = q(s)***car**(is0) + b(s) ∧ b(s) < **car**(is0) ∧ os = ( ).

v02:   **car•cdr**(is0) = q(s)***car**(is0) + b(s) ∧ b(s) < **car**(is0) ∧ os = ( )
                    {**write**(b);**write**(q)}
                car•cdr(is0) = q(s)***car**(is0) + b(s) ∧ b(s) < **car**(is0)
                        ∧ os = **app**(**app**(( ),b(s)),q(s)).

On the basis of the Consequence Rule (applied to v01) we generate the following formulas:

v010:   os = ( ) ∧ s = (**car**(is0),**car•cdr**(is0),0)
       ⇒s = (**car**(is0),**car•cdr**(is0),0) ∧ q(s) = 0 ∧ os = ( )

v011:   s = (**car**(is0),**car•cdr**(is0),0) ∧ q(s) = 0 ∧ os = ( )
          {**while** b⩾a **do begin** q: = q+1; b: = b−a **end**}
          car•cdr(is0) = q(s)***car**(is0) + b(s) ∧ b(s) < **car**(is0) ∧ os = ( ).

Let's consider the sequence (v011,v010,v01,v02,v00,v1,v0,v); v1 and v010 are axioms of s.IA, v is the conclusion of v0 and v1 by rule r'8; v0 is the conclusion of v00, v01 and v02 by rule r2; v01 is the conclusion of v010 and v011 by the Consequence Rule. Hence v is a logical consequence of {v011,v02,v00} in system s.IA. Now, v011 is an instance of the theorem proved in Example 7, and v00 and v02 are easily provable using the Read Statement and Write Statement Axioms (their proof is left as an exercise). Hence v is a theorem.

This proof is relatively complex (relative to the complexity of the program at hand); it has attempted to grasp all the semantics of the program at hand, including the handling of the input and output files.

1.5 Exercises

1. [A] Prove formulas v00 and v02 of Example 9, section 1.4.

2. [A] Prove or disprove the following formulas defined on space S:

$$\text{set}$$
$$\text{a, b: \textbf{integer}}$$
$$\textbf{end};$$

s is a state.
a) $a(s) = 1 \lor a(s) = -1 \{a:=a*a\} a(s) = 1$.
b) $s = s0 \{a:=b;b:=a\} b(s) = a(s0)$.
c) $s = s0 \{a:=b;b:=a\} a(s) = b(s0)$.
d) $s = s0 \{a:=a-1;b:=b+1\} a(s)+b(s) = a(s0)+b(s0)$.
e) $a(s) \geqslant b(s) \{a:=a-b\} a(s) \geqslant 0$.

3. [A] On the same space as exercise 2, prove or disprove:
a) $a(s) < b(s) \{\textbf{if } a \leqslant b \textbf{ then } a:=b \textbf{ else } b:=a+2\} a(s) = b(s)$.
b) $a(s) \leqslant b(s) \{\textbf{if } a > b \textbf{ then } b:=b+1 \textbf{ else } a:=a-1\} a(s) \leqslant b(s)$.
c) $a(s) \leqslant b(s) \{\textbf{if } a < b \textbf{ then } a:=b \textbf{ else } b:=2*b-a\} a(s) = b(s)$.
d) $s = s0 \{\textbf{if } a < 1 \textbf{ then } a:=a+1\} a(s) > a(s0)$.
e) $b(s) = 1 \{\textbf{if } b \leqslant 1 \textbf{ then } a:=b-1\} b(s)-1 \geqslant 0$.

4. [A] On the same space as exercise 2, prove or disprove:
a) $s = s0 \land b(s) > 0 \{a:=a-b\} a(s) < a(s0) \land b(s) \geqslant 0$.
b) $\textbf{true} \{a:=0;b:=-1\} a(s) \geqslant -1$.
c) $\textbf{false} \{a:=3\} a(s) < 3$.
d) $s = s0 \land b(s) > 0 \{a:=a-1;b:=b-1\} a(s)+b(s) = a(s0)+b(s0)$.
e) $s = s0 \{a:=a+1;b:=b+1\} a(s)-b(s) = a(s0)-b(s0) \land b(s) > b(s0)$.

5. [B] On the same space as exercise 2, prove or disprove the following:
   a) $a(s) = 1 \vee a(s) = -1$
   $$\{if\ a \geqslant 1\ then\ a := a+1\ else\ a := a-1\}$$
   $$a(s) = 2 \vee a(s) = -2 \vee a(s) = 0.$$
   b) $a(s) \geqslant 0$ {while a>0 do a:=a−1} $a(s) = 0.$
   c) **true** {while a>0 do a:=a−1} $a(s) = 0.$
   d) $a(s) = b(s)$ {while a = b do begin a:=a+1; b:=b+1 end} $a(s) \neq b(s).$
   e) $a(s) < b(s)$ {while a ≠ b do begin a:=a+1; b:=b−2 end} $a(s) = b(s).$
      (hint: choose inv(s) = $(a(s) < b(s))$).

6. [B] On the same space as exercise 2, prove the following:
   a) **true** {while true do} $a(s) = b(s0).$
   b) $s = s0$ {while b≠0 do begin a:=a+1;b:=b−1 end} $a(s) = a(s0) + b(s0).$
   c) $s = s0 \wedge b(s) \geqslant 0$
      $$\{while\ b>0\ do\ begin\ a:=a+1;b:=b-1\ end\}$$
      $$a(s) = a(s0) + b(s0).$$
   d) $s = s0$ {while b≠0 do begin a:=a−1; b:=b−1 end} $a(s) = a(s0) − b(s0).$
   e) $s = s0 \wedge b(s) \geqslant 0$
      $$\{while\ b>0\ do\ begin\ a:=a-1;\ b:=b-1\ end\}$$
      $$a(s) = a(s0) - b(s0).$$

7. [B] On the same space as exercise 2, prove the following formulas:
   a) $b(s) < 0$ {while b≠0 do b:=b−1} $b(s) = 0.$ (hint: inv(s) = (b(s)<0)).
   b) $s = s0$ {while a<b do a:=a+1} $a(s) \geqslant a(s0).$
   c) $s = s0 \wedge a(s0) < b(s0)$ {while a<b do a:=a+1} $a(s) = b(s).$
   d) $s = s0 \wedge a(s0) > b(s0)$ {while a<b do a:=a+1} $a(s) > b(s).$
   e) $s = s0 \wedge a(s0) \leqslant b(s0)$ {while a≠b do a:=a+1} $a(s) = b(s).$

8. [B] Let S be

> set
> crt
>   n: **integer**;
>   i: 1 .. n+1;
>   a: **array** [1..n] **of integer**;
>   all: **boolean**;
> sub
>   n ⩾ 2
> end.

Prove or disprove the following formulas in system s.IA. Note: Eq(s) is an abbreviation for

$$a(s)[1] = a(s)[2] = \ldots a(s)[n(s)].$$

a) $s = s0 \land all(s0) \land i(s0) = 2$
$\quad$ {**while** $i \leqslant n$ **do begin** all: = all **and** $a[i] = a[1]$; i: = i+1 **end**}
$\qquad\qquad\qquad\qquad\qquad\qquad\qquad\qquad\qquad$ $all(s) = Eq(s0)$.

b) $s = s0 \land i(s0) = 2$
$\quad$ {**while** $i \leqslant n$ **do begin** all: = all **and** $a[i] = a[1]$; i: = i+1 **end**}
$\qquad\qquad\qquad\qquad\qquad\qquad\qquad\qquad$ $all(s) = (all(s0) \land Eq(s0))$.

c) $s = s0 \land all(s0) \land i(s0) = 2$ {**while** $i \leqslant n$ **and** all **do** i: = i+1} $all(s) = Eq(s0)$.

d) $s = s0 \land i(s) = n(s)$
$\quad$ {**while** $i > 1$ **do begin** all: = all **and** $a[i] = a[1]$; i: = i−1 **end**}
$\qquad\qquad\qquad\qquad\qquad\qquad\qquad\qquad$ $all(s) = all(s0) \land Eq(s0)$.

e) $s = s0 \land i(s) = n(s) - 1 \land all(s)$
$\quad$ {**while** $i \geqslant 1$ **do begin** all: = all **and** $a[i] = a[n]$; i: = i−1 **end**}
$\qquad\qquad\qquad\qquad\qquad\qquad\qquad\qquad\qquad$ $all(s) = Eq(s0)$.

9. [B] Let S be

$\qquad\qquad\qquad\qquad$ **set**
$\qquad\qquad\qquad\qquad$ **crt**
$\qquad\qquad\qquad\qquad\quad$ n, i, f: **integer**;
$\qquad\qquad\qquad\qquad$ **sub**
$\qquad\qquad\qquad\qquad\quad$ $n \geqslant 0$
$\qquad\qquad\qquad\qquad$ **end**.

Prove or disprove the following formulas:

a) $s = s0 \land i(s0) = 1 \land f(s0) = 1$
$\quad$ {**while** $i \leqslant n$ **do begin** f: = f*i; i: = i+1 **end**}
$\qquad\qquad\qquad\qquad\qquad\qquad\qquad\qquad$ $f(s) = n(s0)!$.

b) $s = s0 \land i(s) = 1$ {**while** $i \leqslant n$ **do begin** f: = f*i; i: = i+1 **end**} $f(s) = f(s0)*n(s0)!$.

c) $s = s0 \land i(s) \leqslant n(s) \land f(s) = 1$
$\quad$ {**while** $i \leqslant n$ **do begin** f: = f*i; i: = i+1 **end**}
$\qquad\qquad\qquad\qquad\qquad\qquad\qquad$ $f(s) = n(s0)!/(i(s0) - 1)!$.

d) $s = s0 \land i(s) = 1 \land f(s) = 1$
$\quad$ {**while** $i < n$ **do begin** i: = i+1; f: = f*i **end**}
$\qquad\qquad\qquad\qquad\qquad\qquad\qquad\qquad$ $f(s) = n(s0)!$.

e) $s = s0 \land i(s) = n(s)$ {**while** $i \geqslant 1$ **do begin** f: = f*i; i: = i−1 **end**} $f(s) = n(s0)!$.

10. [B] Let S be

$\qquad\qquad\qquad\qquad$ **set**
$\qquad\qquad\qquad\qquad$ **crt**
$\qquad\qquad\qquad\qquad\quad$ n, f: **integer**;
$\qquad\qquad\qquad\qquad$ **sub**
$\qquad\qquad\qquad\qquad\quad$ $n \geqslant 0$
$\qquad\qquad\qquad\qquad$ **end**.

Prove or disprove the following formulas:
a) s = s0 ∧ f(s) = 1 {**while** n>0 **do begin** f: = n*f; n: = n−1 **end**} f(s) = n(s0)!.
b) s = s0

$$\{\textbf{while } n>0 \textbf{ do begin } f:=n*f; n:=n-1 \textbf{ end}\}$$
$$f(s) = f(s0)*n(s0)! \ \wedge \ n(s) = 0.$$

c) s = s0 {**while** n>0 **do begin** f: = f*n; n: = n−1 **end**} n(s) = 0 ∧ f(s) = n(s0)!.
d) s = s0 ∧ f(s) = n(s) {**while** n>1 **do begin** n: = n−1; f: = n*f **end**} f(s) = n(s0)!.
e) s = s0 ∧ f(s) = 1

$$\{\textbf{while } n>1 \textbf{ do begin } n:=n-1; f:=f*n \textbf{ end}\}$$
$$f(s) = (n(s0)-1)!.$$

11. [B]
    a) Let S be

$$
\begin{aligned}
&\textbf{set}\\
&\textbf{crt}\\
&\quad \text{a, b, p: } \textbf{integer;}\\
&\textbf{sub}\\
&\quad b \geqslant 0\\
&\textbf{end.}
\end{aligned}
$$

Prove the formula
s = s0

$$\{\textbf{while } b \neq 0 \textbf{ do begin } b:=b-1; p:=p+a \textbf{ end}\}$$
$$p(s) = p(s0)+a(s0)*b(s0) \ \wedge \ b(s) = 0.$$

    b) Let S be

$$
\begin{aligned}
&\textbf{set}\\
&\textbf{crt}\\
&\quad \text{a, b, q: } \textbf{integer;}\\
&\textbf{sub}\\
&\quad a \geqslant 0 \ \wedge \ b \geqslant 0\\
&\textbf{end.}
\end{aligned}
$$

Prove the formula

s = s0 ∧ q(s) = 0
$$\{\textbf{while } a \geqslant b \textbf{ do begin } q:=q+1; a:=a-b \textbf{ end}\}$$
$$a(s0) = q(s)*b(s0)+a(s) \ \wedge \ a(s) < b(s0).$$

    c) Let S be

$$
\begin{aligned}
&\textbf{set}\\
&\textbf{crt}\\
&\quad \text{n: } \textbf{integer;}\\
&\quad \text{i: } 1..n+1;\\
&\quad \text{a: } \textbf{array } [1..n] \textbf{ of real;}\\
&\quad \text{sum: } \textbf{real;}
\end{aligned}
$$

sub
    n ≥ 1
end.

Prove the formula

s = s0 ∧ sum(s) = 0 ∧ i(s) = 1
        {**while** i ≤ n **do begin** sum: = sum + a[i]; i: = i + 1 **end**}
                sum(s) = a(s0)[1] + a(s0)[2] + ... + a(s0)[n(s0)].

d) Let S be

set
crt
    n: **integer**;
    i: 1..n + 1;
    a: **array** [1..n] **of real**;
    sort: **boolean**;
sub
    n ≥ 1
end.

Prove the formula

s = s0 ∧ sort(s) ∧ i(s) = 2
        {**while** i ≤ n **do begin** sort: = sort **and** a[i − 1] ≤ a[i]; i: = i + 1 **end**}
                sort(s) = (a(s0)[1] ≤ a(s0)[2] ≤ ... a(s0)[n(s0)]).

e) Let S be

set
crt
    n: **integer**;
    i: 1..n + 1;
    a: **array** [1..n] **of real**;
    m: **real**;
sub
    n ≥ 1
end.

Prove the formula

s = s0 ∧ m = a(s)[1] ∧ i(s) = 2
        {**while** i ≤ n **do begin if** a[i] > m **then** m: = a[i]; i: = i + 1 **end**}
                m = max(a(s0)[1], a(s0)[2], ... a(s0)[n(s0)]) ∧ i(s) = n(s0) + 1.

12. [A] Complete the proof of Example 8.

13. [B] Show that the following program is partially correct wrt the specification

(L*(integer),   L*(integer),   {(is,os) | car(os) = max(car(is), car.cdr(is))}   ).

```
program M(input, output);
type
    S = set
    a, b, m: integer
  end;
  var
   s: S;
  begin
  read(a); read(b);
  if a>b then m: = a else m: = b;
  write(m)
  end.
```

2 Proof of Total Correctness

2.1 The Theory t.IA*

Theory t.IA* is defined by (W,T), where W is the set of formulas which have
the form

$$\{p\} \; st \; \{q\},$$

where p and q are predicates on the extended space ES of statement st. Such
a formula is called an IA*-formula. The syntax of an IA*-formula involving a
program (rather than a statement) is formally similar. The definition of T (the
set of theorems of t. 1A*) depends on the semantics of 1A*-formulas: The
semantics of an IA*-formula such as

$$\{p\} \; st \; \{q\}$$

are as follows:

$$(\forall es, \; p(es) \Rightarrow es:\textbf{dom}([st]) \; \wedge \; q([st](es))).$$

Implicit in this definition is the clause es:ES on both sides of the sign $\Rightarrow$.

From this definition it stems that:

— IA*-formulas are nothing but a notational extension of predicate logic.
— the IA*-formula {p} st {q} (considered as a formula of predicate logic) is valid if and only if statement st is (totally) correct with respect to the I-specification (ES, {(es,es′)| p(es) ∧ q(es′)}). A similar interpretation can be given for the case when we are dealing with a program rather than a mere statement.

2.2 The Deductive System s.IA*

s.IA* = (W,A,R), where W is the same as that of theory t.IA*, and A and R are given below; they are designed with the goal of generating all the elements of T without inconsistencies. As in previous cases of deductive systems, we shall be more concerned about the consistency of s.IA* than about its completeness with respect to t.IA*.

The context of the axioms and rules to be given below is the following: input space IS, input state is; proper space S, proper state s; output space OS, output state os; extended space ES = IS×S×OS, extended state es = (is,s,os). Whenever no input/output operations are involved, we focus our attention on the proper space S and proper state s.

2.2.1 Axioms

a0: any P-tautology on ES.

a1: The Empty Statement Axiom

$$\{p\}\ \{p\}.$$

a2: The Assignment Statement Axiom

$$\{p{\bullet}E \ \wedge\ \mathbf{:def}(E)\}\ s{:}=E(s)\ \{p\}.$$

a3: The Read Statement Axiom
Using the notation introduced in axiom a3 of section 1.2.1 (for system s.IA), we write:

$$\{p{\bullet}Er[a] \ \wedge\ \mathbf{lng}(is){\geqslant}1\}\ \mathbf{read}(a)\ \{p\}.$$

a4: The Write Statement Axiom
Using the notation introduced in axiom a4 of section 1.2.1 (for system
s.IA), we write:

$$\{p \bullet Wt[a]\} \ \textbf{write}(a) \ \{p\}.$$

2.2.2 Rules

r0: The Procedure Call Rule

$$\frac{\{p\} \ \textbf{procedure} \ R; \ \dots \ \textbf{end} \ \{q\}}{\{p\} \ R \ \{q\}.}$$

r1: The Begin-End Statement Rule

$$\frac{\{p\} \ st \ \{q\}}{\{p\} \ \textbf{begin} \ st \ \textbf{end} \ \{q\}.}$$

r2: The Sequence Statement Rule

$$\frac{\{p\} \ st \ \{int\} \quad \{int\} \ st' \ \{q\}}{\{p\} \ st; \ st' \ \{q\}.}$$

r3: The Conditional Statement Rule

$$\frac{\{p \wedge t\} \ tc \ \{q\} \quad p \wedge \ {\sim}t \Rightarrow q}{\{p\} \ \textbf{if} \ t \ \textbf{then} \ tc \ \{q\}.}$$

r4: The Alternative Statement Rule

$$\frac{\{p \wedge t\} \ tc \ \{q\} \quad \{p \wedge \ {\sim}t\} \ ec \ \{q\}}{\{p\} \ \textbf{if} \ t \ \textbf{then} \ tc \ \textbf{else} \ ec \ \{q\}.}$$

r5: The While Statement Rule
There exists a predicate inv on ES and a relation lt (less than) on ES such that

$$v0: p \Rightarrow inv$$
$$v1: \{inv \land t \land s = s1\} \; lb \; \{inv \land (s,s1):lt\}$$
$$v2: lt \text{ is a well-founded relation on ES}$$
$$v3: inv \land \tilde{\ }t \Rightarrow q$$

$$\overline{\{p\} \textbf{ while } t \textbf{ do } lb \; \{q\}}$$

r6: The With Statement Rule

$$\{p\} \; s.wb \; \{q\}$$
$$\overline{\{p\} \textbf{ with } s \textbf{ do } wb \; \{q\}.}$$

r7: The Procedure Declaration Rule
With the same context as rule r7, section 1.2.2,

$$\{p(es)\} \; pd \; \{q(es,t)\}$$
$$\overline{\{p(es)\} \textbf{ procedure } \ldots \textbf{ begin } pd \textbf{ end } \{(\exists t, q(es,t))\}}$$

r8: The Program Rule
With the same context as rule r8, section 1.2.2,

$$\{p(is) \; \land \; os = (\;)\} \; pg \; \{q(s,os)\}$$
$$\overline{\{p(is)\} \textbf{ program } \ldots \textbf{ begin } pg \textbf{ end } \{(\exists s, q(s,os))\}}$$

r9: The Consequence Rule

$$\{p'\} \; st \; \{q'\}$$
$$p \Rightarrow p'$$
$$q' \Rightarrow q$$
$$\overline{\{p\} \; st \; \{q\}.}$$

The Consequence Rule allows us to rewrite many of the axioms and rules presented above:

r'2: The Modified Sequence Statement Rule

$$\frac{\begin{array}{l} \{p\}\ st\ \{q\} \\ \{p'\}\ st'\ \{q'\} \\ q \Rightarrow p' \end{array}}{\{p\}\ st;\ st'\ \{q'\}.}$$

r'7: The Modified Procedure Declaration Rule

$$\frac{\begin{array}{l} \{p(es)\}\ pd\ \{q'(es,t)\} \\ (\exists\,t,\ q'(es,\ t)) \Rightarrow q(es) \end{array}}{\{p(es)\}\ \textbf{procedure} \ldots \textbf{begin}\ pd\ \textbf{end}\ \{q(es)\}.}$$

r'8: The Modified Program Rule

$$\frac{\begin{array}{l} \{p(is)\ \wedge\ os\ =\ (\ )\}\ pg\ \{q'(s,os)\} \\ (\exists\,s,\ q'(s,os)) \Rightarrow q(os) \end{array}}{\{p(is)\}\ \textbf{program} \ldots \textbf{begin}\ pg\ \textbf{end}\ \{q(os)\}.}$$

a'1: The Empty Statement Rule

$$\frac{p \Rightarrow q}{\{p\}\ \{q\}}$$

a'2: The Assignment Statement Rule

$$\frac{p \Rightarrow q \bullet E\ \wedge\ :\textbf{def}(E)}{\{p\}\ s := E(s)\ \{q\}}$$

a'3: The Read Statement Rule

$$\frac{p \Rightarrow q \bullet Er[a]\ \wedge\ \textbf{lng}(is) \geqslant 1}{\{p\}\ \textbf{read}(a)\ \{q\}}$$

a'4: The Write Statement Rule

$$p \Rightarrow q \bullet Wt[a]$$
$$\overline{\{p\} \; \textbf{write}(a) \; \{q\}.}$$

2.3 The Second Theorem of Invariant Assertions: Total Correctness

THEOREM 2. Let P be a program on E-space $ES = IS \times S \times OS$ and let st be a statement of P. If $\{p\} \; P \; \{q\}$ is a theorem of s.IA* then P is (totally) correct wrt the E-specification

$$(IS, OS, \{(is, os) \mid p(is) \wedge q(os)\} \,).$$

If $\{p\} \; st \; \{q\}$ is a theorem of s.IA* then st is (totally) correct wrt the I-specification $(S, \{(es, es') \mid p(es) \wedge q(es')\} \,)$.

Theorem 2 provides a sufficient (but not necessary) condition of correctness; it is an act of faith in the consistency of the deductive system s.IA* with respect to theory t.IA*, but not in its completeness.

Below are some examples of applications of Theorem 2.

EXAMPLE 10. (Rule a'2)
Proper space $S = \textbf{real}$, proper state s; verify

$$v: \{s \neq 4 \wedge s > 1\} \; s := 1/\textbf{sqrt}(s) \; \{s \neq 1/2\}.$$

The premise needed for rule a'2 is

$$v0: s \neq 4 \wedge s > 1 \Rightarrow s > 0 \wedge 1/\textbf{sqrt}(s) \neq 1/2.$$

Clearly, (v0,v) is a deduction in system s.IA*; hence v is a theorem.

EXAMPLE 11. (Rules a'3 and r2)
Input space $IS = L*(\textbf{integer})$, input state (is); proper space $S = \textbf{integer}$, proper state s; output space $OS = L*(\textbf{integer})$, output state (os); verify

$$v: \{is = is0 \wedge \textbf{lng}(is0) \geqslant 2\} \; \textbf{read}(a); \; \textbf{read}(a) \; \{a(s) = \textbf{car} \bullet \textbf{cdr}(is0)\}.$$

On the basis of rule r2, we generate the following formulas:

v0: $\{is = is0 \wedge \textbf{lng}(is0) \geqslant 2\}$

$$\textbf{read}(a)$$

$$\{is = \textbf{cdr}(is0) \wedge \textbf{lng}(is0) \geqslant 2\},$$

v1: $\{is = \textbf{cdr}(is0) \wedge \textbf{lng}(is0) \geqslant 2\}$

$$\textbf{read}(a)$$

$$\{a(s) = \textbf{car} \cdot \textbf{cdr}(is0)\}.$$

The application of rule a'3 to v0 yields the generation of

v00: $is = is0 \wedge \textbf{lng}(is0) \geqslant 2$
$\Rightarrow \textbf{cdr}(is) = \textbf{cdr}(is0) \wedge \textbf{lng}(is0) \geqslant 2 \wedge \textbf{lng}(is) \geqslant 1.$

The application of rule a'3 to v1 yields the generation of

v10: $is = \textbf{cdr}(is0) \wedge \textbf{lng}(is0) \geqslant 2$
$\Rightarrow \textbf{car}(is) = \textbf{car} \bullet \textbf{cdr}(is0) \wedge \textbf{lng}(is) \geqslant 1.$

In the sequence (v10,v00,v1,v0,v), v10 and v00 are axioms, v1 is the conclusion of v10 by a'3, v0 is the conclusion of v00 by a'3 and v is the conclusion of v1 and v0 by r2; hence this sequence is a deduction and v is a theorem.

EXAMPLE 12. (Rule r4)
For the sake of illustration, we shall take an example containing two nested loops; for the sake of simplicity, we shall reduce the embedded loop structure to a minimal skeleton, whose only function is to . . . terminate. The statement does not involve any **read** or **write**, hence we shall focus our attention on the proper space, which is:

$$S = \textbf{set}$$
$$i, j: \textbf{natural}$$
$$\textbf{end}.$$

The statement is:

```
Dble-loop =
while i⩾1 do
    begin
    i: = i−1; j: = 100;
    while j⩾1 do j: = j−1
    end.
```

We wish to prove the formula

$$v: \{\textbf{true}\} \text{ Dble} - \text{loop } \{i(s) = 0\}.$$

In order to apply the While Statement Rule, we must generate a loop invariant inv and a well-founded relation lt on S; we choose

$$inv(s) = \textbf{true},$$
$$lt = \{(s,s') \mid i(s) < i(s')\}.$$

On the basis of these choices, we generate the following formulas

$$v0: \textbf{true} \Rightarrow \textbf{true},$$
$$v1: \{i(s) \geqslant 1 \ \wedge \ s = s1\} \text{ lb } \{i(s) < i(s1)\},$$
$$v2: \text{lt is a well-founded relation on S},$$
$$v3: \widetilde{\ }(i(s) \geqslant 1) \Rightarrow i(s) = 0.$$

Applying the Begin-End Rule and the Sequence Statement Rule to v1, we generate the following formulas:

$$v10: \{i(s) \geqslant 1 \ \wedge \ s = s1\} \ i: = \ i - 1 \ \{i(s) < i(s1)\},$$
$$v11: \{i(s) < i(s1)\} \ j: = 100; \ \textbf{while } j \geqslant 1 \ \textbf{do } j: = j - 1 \ \{i(s) < i(s1)\}.$$

The Assignment Statement Rule applied to v10 yields

$$v100: \quad i(s) \geqslant 1 \ \wedge \ s = s1 \Rightarrow i(s) - 1 < i(s1).$$

Note that the condition $i(s) \geqslant 1$ ensures that $i(s) - 1 \geqslant 0$, hence the computed value of s remains in S. Applying the Sequence Statement Rule to v11, we generate

$$v110: \quad \{i(s) < i(s1)\} \ j: = 100 \ \{i(s) < i(s1)\}$$
$$v111: \quad \{i(s) < i(s1)\} \ \underline{\textbf{while}} \ j \geqslant 1 \ \textbf{do } j: = j - 1 \ \{i(s) < i(s1)\}.$$

Before we apply the While Statement Rule to v111, we choose a loop invariant inv′ and an ordering relation lt′:

$$inv'(s) = i(s) < i(s1),$$
$$lt' = \{(s,s') \mid j(s) < j(s')\}.$$

Then the premises of the While Statement Rule become

v1110: $i(s) < i(s1) \Rightarrow i(s) < i(s1)$,
v1111: $\{i(s) < i(s1) \land j(s) \geqslant 1 \land s = s2\}$ $j := j - 1$ $\{i(s) < i(s1) \land j(s) < j(s2)\}$,
v1112: lt' is a well-founded relation on ES,
v1113: $i(s) < i(s1) \land \tilde{\ }(j(s) \geqslant 1) \Rightarrow i(s) < i(s1)$.

Applying the Assignment Statement Rule to v1111, we get

$$v11110: i(s) < i(s1) \land j(s) \geqslant 1 \land s = s2$$
$$\Rightarrow i(s) < i(s1) \land j(s) - 1 < j(s2).$$

Note that condition $j(s) \geqslant 1$ on the left hand side of the $\Rightarrow$ sign is useful to ensure that the computed value of j $(j(s) - 1)$ is not out of range (< 0), hence s remains in S.

It is left to the reader to verify that (v11110, v1113, v1112, v1111, v1110, v111, v110, v100, v11, v10, v3, v2, v1, v0, v) is indeed a deduction in system s.IA*; hence v is a theorem.

2.4 Incremental Proofs of Total Correctness

Let st be a statement (or a program) on space S and p and q be predicates on S; we assume that

$$u: \{p\}\ st\ \{q\}$$

is a theorem of s.IA*. We are interested in proving:

$$v: \{p\}\ st\ \{q \land r\}$$

where r is another predicate on S. The question that comes to mind regarding the proof of v is: Can one take advantage of the proof of formula u in proving formula v?

The theorem given below essentially answers this question.

THEOREM 3. (Incremental Proof Theorem, due to Manna and Pnuelli, 1974).
Suppose that the formula

$$u: \{p\}\ st\ \{q\}$$

has been deduced in system s.IA*. Let r be a reflexive and transitive relation on the E-space of st. If for every formula of the form

$$u': \{p'\}\ s := E(s)\ \{q'\}$$

used in the proof of u, it is possible to deduce

$$u'': \{p' \wedge s = s0\} \; s: = E(s) \; \{q' \wedge (s,s0):r\},$$

then

$$v: \{p \wedge s = s0\} \; st \; \{q \wedge (s,s0):r\}$$

is a theorem of system s.IA*.

Proof. On the set of SM-Pascal statements on ES (the E-space of st), we define the following predicate:

$$t(st) = \text{the theorem above holds for statement st.}$$

We shall prove the validity of predicate t by Noetherian induction on the set of statements ordered with relation Cpx. We shall consider in turn all the forms that st might have:

— st is an empty statement: t(st) holds because r is reflexive (this is the basis of induction since the empty statement is Cpx-minimal).
— st is a Begin-End statement or a with statement: t(st) stems from the Begin-End Rule and the With Statement Rule, respectively.
— st is a sequence statement: t(st) stems from the Sequence Statement Rule and the transitivity of r.
— st is a conditional statement: t(st) stems from the Conditional Statement Rule and the reflexivity of r.
— st is an alternative statement: t(st) stems from the Alternation Statement Rule.
— st is a while statement: t(st) stems from the While Statement Rule and the reflexivity and the transitivity of r.
— st is an assignment statement: t(st) holds by hypothesis.

QED

Below is an example of incremental proof; for another example, see exercise 4.

EXAMPLE 13. Let S be

```
set
crt
  a, b: integer;
sub
  a>0 ∧ b>0
end,
```

and let st be the statement

$$\text{while } a \neq b \text{ do if } a > b \text{ then } a := a - b \text{ else } b := b - a.$$

We wish to prove

$$\{s = s0\} \text{ st } \{a(s) = b(s) \; \wedge \; a(s) = gcd(s0)\},$$

where gcd(s0) is the greatest common divisor of a(s0) and b(s0). Because s = s0 is equivalent to

$$s = s0 \; \wedge \; \textbf{true}$$

and $a(s) = b(s) \; \wedge \; a(s) = gcd(s0)$ is equivalent to

$$a(s) = b(s) \; \wedge \; gcd(s) = gcd(s0),$$

the formula above can be rewritten as:

$$v: \{\textbf{true} \; \wedge \; s = s0\} \text{ st } \{a(s) = b(s) \; \wedge \; gcd(s) = gcd(s0)\}.$$

In order to prove v, we will prove

$$u: \{\textbf{true}\} \text{ st } \{a(s) = b(s)\},$$

then apply Theorem 3 with the relation:

$$r = \{(s,s') | \; gcd(s) = gcd(s')\},$$

which is clearly reflexive and transitive.

In order to apply the While Statement Rule to u, we generate a loop invariant and a well-founded relation relation lt; we choose:

$$\begin{aligned} &inv(s) = \textbf{true} \\ &lt = \{(s,s') | \; a(s) + b(s) < a(s') + b(s')\}. \end{aligned}$$

The premises of the rule are:

$$\begin{aligned} u0: \quad &\textbf{true} \Rightarrow \textbf{true} \\ u1: \quad &\{\textbf{true} \; \wedge \; s = s1 \; \wedge \; a(s) \neq b(s)\} \\ &\quad \text{if } a > b \text{ then } a := a - b \text{ else } b := b - a \\ &\quad \{\textbf{true} \; \wedge \; a(s) + b(s) < a(s1) + b(s1)\}. \end{aligned}$$

u2:   It is a well-founded relation on S
u3:   **true** $\wedge$ $\tilde{}(a(s) \neq b(s))$ $\Rightarrow$ $a(s) = b(s)$.

Applying the Alternative Statement Rule to u1, we generate

u10: $\{s = s1 \ \wedge \ a(s) > b(s)\}$ a:$=$ a$-$b $\{a(s) + b(s) < a(s1) + b(s1)\}$
u11: $\{s = s1 \ \wedge \ a(s) < b(s)\}$ b:$=$ b$-$a $\{a(s) + b(s) < a(s1) + b(s1)\}$

Applying the Assignment Statement Rule to u10 yields

u100: $s = s1 \ \wedge \ a(s) > b(s)$ $\Rightarrow$ $a(s) < a(s1) + b(s1)$.

Applying the Assignment Statement Rule to u11 yields

u110: $s = s1 \ \wedge \ a(s) < b(s)$ $\Rightarrow$ $b(s) < a(s1) + b(s1)$.

It is left to the reader to check that (u110, u100, u11, u10, u0, u1, u2 u3, u)
is indeed a deduction in s.IA*. Now, due to the properties of gcd, one can
deduce v10 from u10 and v11 from u11, where:

v10: $\{s = s1 \ \wedge \ a(s) > b(s)\}$

$$a: = a - b$$
$$\{a(s) + b(s) < a(s1) + b(s1) \ \wedge \ gcd(s) = gcd(s1)\}$$

v11: $\{s = s1 \ \wedge \ a(s) < b(s)\}$

$$b: = b - a$$
$$\{a(s) + b(s) < a(s1) + b(s1) \ \wedge \ gcd(s) = gcd(s1)\}.$$

Hence, by Theorem 3, v is a theorem of s.IA*.

2.5 Exercises

1. [A] Prove or disprove in system s.IA* the following formulas on space S.

$$S = \textbf{set}$$
$$a, b: \textbf{real}$$
$$\textbf{end}.$$

a) $\{a(s) \geqslant 0\}$ b:$=$ log(a) $\{\textbf{true}\}$.
b) $\{a(s) > 0\}$ b:$=$ log(a) $\{\textbf{true}\}$.
c) $\{a(s) > 0\}$ a:$= 1/a$; b:$=$ log$(1-a)$ $\{a(s) > 0\}$.
d) $\{a(s) > 1\}$ a:$= 1/a$; b:$=$ log$(1-a)$ $\{a(s) > 0\}$.
e) $\{\textbf{true}\}$ a:$=$ b $\{\textbf{true}\}$.

2. [A] Prove or disprove in system s.IA* the following formulas on space

$$
\begin{aligned}
&S = \textbf{set} \\
&\textbf{crt} \\
&\quad \text{a, b: } \textbf{integer;} \\
&\textbf{sub} \\
&\quad b \geqslant 0 \\
&\textbf{end.}
\end{aligned}
$$

a) $\{s = s0\}$ **while** $b \geqslant 3$ **do** $b := b - 1$ $\{a(s) = a(s0)\}$.
b) $\{s = s0\}$ **while** $b \geqslant 0$ **do begin** $a := a + 1$; $b := b - 1$ **end** $\{a(s) = a(s0) + b(s0)\}$.
c) $\{s = s0 \wedge b(s) \geqslant 0\}$
   while $b \neq 0$ **do begin** $a := a + 1$; $b := b - 1$ **end**
   $$\{a(s) = a(s0) + b(s0)\}.$$
d) $\{s = s0 \wedge b(s) \geqslant 0\}$
   while $b > 0$ **do begin** $a := a + 1$; $b := b - 1$ **end**
   $$\{a(s) = a(s0) + b(s0)\}.$$
e) $\{s = s0\}$ **while** $b > 0$ **do begin** $a := a + 1$; $b := b - 1$ **end** $\{b(s) = b(s0)\}$.
f) $\{s = s0\}$ **while** $a \leqslant b$ **do** $a := a + 1$ $\{a(s) = \max(a(s0), b(s0))\}$.

3. [B] We consider the input space L*(**integer**), the output space L*(**integer**) and the proper space:

$$
\begin{aligned}
&S = \textbf{set} \\
&\quad \text{a, b: } \textbf{integer} \\
&\textbf{end.}
\end{aligned}
$$

It is implicit that all input files are finite; the name **eof** can be understood as an abbreviation of **lng**(is) = 0. Prove or disprove the following formulas in system s.IA*.
a) $\{$**true**$\}$ **while not eof do read**(a) $\{$**true**$\}$.
b) $\{$is = is0$\}$ **while not eof do begin read**(a); **write**(a) **end** $\{$os = is0$\}$
c) $\{$es = es0$\}$ **while** $b \neq 0$ **do begin write**(a); $b := b - 1$ **end** $\{$**true**$\}$
d) $\{$**true**$\}$ **read**(a); **read**(b); **read**(a); **write**(b) $\{$car(os) = car.cdr(is)$\}$.

4. [C] Consider the space:

$$
\begin{aligned}
&S = \textbf{set} \\
&\textbf{crt} \\
&\quad \text{a, b: } \textbf{integer;} \\
&\textbf{sub} \\
&\quad a > 0 \wedge b > 0 \\
&\textbf{end.}
\end{aligned}
$$

Let G be the statement on S defined by

while a ≠ b **do**
   begin
   while a>b **do** a: = a − b;
   while b>a **do** b: = b − a
   end.

a) Prove the following formula in s.IA*:

$$u: \{\textbf{true}\}\ G\ \{a(s) = b(s)\}.$$

b) Use Theorem 3 to deduce that v defined below is valid.

$$v: \{s = s0\}\ G\ \{a(s) = \gcd(s0)\}.$$

c) Comment on the usefulness of the theorem of incremental proofs of total correctness.

3 Problems

1. [B] Let S be a set and let u: p {st} q be a theorem of system s.IA (where p, q and st are all defined on S). For each of the following formulas, discuss whether it can be deduced from u or explain under what condition the deduction is possible.
   a) $p \wedge r$ {st} $q \wedge r$.
   b) $p \vee r$ {st} $q \vee r$.

2. [B] In the same context as problem 1, assume that

$$u: p\ \{st\}\ q$$

and

$$u': p'\ \{st\}\ q'$$

are theorems of system s.IA; discuss the validity of
   a) $p \wedge p'$ {st} $q \wedge q'$.
   b) $p \vee p'$ {st} $q \vee q'$.
   c) $p \vee p'$ {st} $q \wedge q'$.

3. [B] Same problem as 1, for system s.IA*.

4. [B] Same problem as 2, for system s.IA*.

5. [B] Let st be a statement on space S and R be an I-relation on S. Express the partial correctness of st with respect to R using the IA notation; express the total

correctness of st with respect to R using the IA* notation; express the termination of st with respect to R, using the IA* notation; generalize your results to programs and E-specifications.

6. [B] Let

$$v: p \{st1;st2\} q$$

be a formula of system s.IA. We are interested in generating an intermediate predicate to prove it.

a) One possible approach to generate an intermediate predicate is based on an analysis of p and st1 exclusively; the predicate obtained is called the *strongest postcondition* of p and st1; we denote it by sp[p,st1]; derive its formula in predicate logic.

b) Another approach is based on an analysis of st2 and q; the predicate obtained is called the *weakest precondition* of st2 and q. We denote it by wp[st2,q]; derive its formula.

c) Show that if v is a theorem of s.IA then sp[p,st1] $\Rightarrow$ wp[st2,q].

7. [C] Discuss the significance and means of proof of the completeness of systems s.IA and s.IA* with respect to t.IA and t.IA* respectively. (Hint: See [5]).

8. [C] Let

```
S = set
crt
    n: integer;
    i, j: 0..n+1;
    a: array [1..n] of real;
    t: real;
sub
    n ≥ 1
end.
```

Let B be the following statement on S:

```
while i≤n do
    begin
    j:=n;
    while j≥i do
        begin
        if a[j−1]>a[j] then
        begin
        t:=a[j−1]; a[j−1]:=a[j]; a[j]:=t
        end;
```

$$j := j - 1$$
end;
$$i := i + 1$$
end.

a) Prove the following formula in system s.IA*:

$$u: \{i(s) = 2\} \ B \ \{ord(s)\},$$

where ord(s) is an abbreviation for

$$a(s)[1] \leqslant a(s)[2] \leqslant \ldots a(s)[n(s)].$$

b) We wish to prove the total correctness of B with respect to the I-specification (S, $\{(s,s')|\ i(s) = 2 \ \wedge \ ord(s') \ \wedge \ perm(s,s')\}$), where perm(s,s') means a(s') is some permutation of a(s). Is it possible to apply the theorem of incremental proofs of total correctness to the proof of formula u in order to obtain a proof of

$$v: \{i(s) = 2 \ \wedge \ s = s0\} \ B \ \{ord(s) \ \wedge \ perm(s0,s)\}?$$

c) Derive a slightly generalized version of the theorem and apply it to the proof at hand.

4 Bibliography

The invariant assertion method was first described in [10] and has attracted a great deal of attention ever since: See [1], [3], [7], [9] and [15], to mention only a few references. Extensions of the invariant assertion method are numerous: [21] derives a set of similar deductive rules for the verification of total correctness of non-structured programs; [11], [14] and [18] discuss similar deductive systems for proving the correctness of parallel programs; [12] discusses the implementation of an automatic program verification system based on the invariant assertion method; [16] uses the deductive rules of the invariant assertion method to derive rules for formal program synthesis; [20] uses a similar deductive system to prove the fault-tolerance of programs and [17] uses a similar deductive system to prove the self-checking property of programs. The theoretical aspects of the method have also been the focus of a great deal of attention: [19] investigates the attributes of the Floyd-Hoare logic with respect to the semantic definition of programming languages; [13] derives a larger framework of which proofs by the invariant assertion method are only a subset; [5] discusses the completeness of a deductive system for the proof of correctness of Algol-like programs; [8] extends the results of [5] to recursive programs; similar completeness results are shown in [6] and [7]; [4] shows the existence of programming language constructs for which it is not possible to obtain consistent and complete sets of Hoare-like axioms. Finally, [2] presents a very extensive survey of the invariant assertion method and its theoretical underpinnings.

1: Anderson, R B. Proving Programs Correct. John Wiley, 1979.
2: Apt, K R. Ten Years of Hoare's Logic: A Survey, Part I. ACM-TOPLAS 3(4) (October 1981), pp 431-483.

3: Berg, H K, W E Boebert, W R Franta and T G Moher. A Survey of Formal Methods of Program Verification and Specification. Prentice-Hall, 1982.

4: Clarke, E M. Programming Language Constructs for which it is Impossible to Obtain Good Hoare-like Axioms. Technical Report No 76-287, Computer Science Department, Cornell University, 1976.

5: Cook, S A. Soundness and Completeness of an Axiom System for Program Verification. SIAM Journal on Computing 7(1) (February 1978), pp 70-90.

6: DeBakker, J W and L G L Th Meertens. On the Completeness of the Inductive Assertion Method. Mathematical Center, Amsterdam, December 1973.

7: DeBakker, J W. Mathematical Theory of Program Correctness. Prentice-Hall, 1980.

8: Gorelick, G. A Complete Axiomatic System for Proving Assertions About Recursive and non-Recursive Programs. Technical report No 75, Computer Science Department, University of Toronto, January 1975.

9: Gries, D. The Science of Programming. Springer-Verlag, 1981.

10: Hoare, C A R. An Axiomatic Basis for Computer Programming. CACM 12(10) (October 1969), pp 576-580, 583.

11: Hoare, C A R. Parallel Programming: An Axiomatic Approach. Computer Languages 1(2) (June 1975), pp 151-160.

12: Igarashi, S, R L London and D C Luckham. Automatic Program Verification I: A Logical Basis and its Implementation. Acta Informatica 4(2) (May 1975), pp 145-182.

13: Kroger, F. Infinite Proof Rules for Loops. Acta Informatica 14(4) (1980), pp 371-390.

14: Lamport, L. The Hoare Logic of Concurrent Programs. Acta Informatica 14(1) (1980), pp 21-37.

15: Manna, Z. Mathematical Theory of Computation. McGraw-Hill, 1974.

16: Manna, Z and R Waldinger. Studies in Automatic Programming Logic. North-Holland, 1977.

17: Metze, G et al. Self-checking Programs: An Axiomatization of Program Validation by Executable Assertions. FTCS-11 Portland (ME), June 1981, pp 118-120.

18: Owicki, S and D Gries. An Axiomatic Proof Technique for Parallel Programs. Acta Informatica Vol 6 (1976), pp 319-340.

19: Pratt, V R. Semantical Considerations on Floyd-Hoare Logic. Proceedings, Seventeenth Symposium on the Foundations of Computer Science. Houston (TX), 1976, pp 109-121.

20: Schlichting, R D and F B Schneider. Verification of Fault-Tolerant Software. Technical Report No TR 80-446, Computer Science Department, Cornell University, November 1980.

21: Wang, A. An Axiomatic Basis for Proving Total Correctness of Go-to Programs. BIT Vol 16 (1976), pp 88-102.

Chapter 8

Induction on the Data Structure: The Intermittent Assertion Method

The *intermittent assertion method* proves properties of SM-Pascal while statements by Noetherian induction on their E-space: If statement st meets some condition when it executes on a simple element of the E-space then it meets the same condition when it executes on a complex element.

Before the Noetherian Induction Theorem is invoked, some analysis of the while statement is needed. This preliminary analysis depends to a great extent on the particular statement and its E-space; this makes a general formalization of the method difficult. Hence we shall use examples to introduce the intermittent assertion method. At the end of the chapter, we shall discuss some generalities about the method.

1 Example 1: Counting the Leaves of a Binary Tree

This example has traditionally been used to explain the intermittent assertion method. Its object is a statement that computes the number of leaves in a regular binary tree, i.e. a binary tree such that every internal node has two subtrees. Let

$$
\begin{aligned}
S = \ &\textbf{set} \\
&\text{current: treetype;} \\
&\text{stack: stacktype;} \\
&\text{count: } \textbf{integer} \\
&\textbf{end,}
\end{aligned}
$$

where treetype and stacktype are defined as follows.

$$
\begin{aligned}
&\text{treetype} = \ \uparrow \text{nodetype;} \\
&\text{nodetype} = \ \textbf{set} \\
&\textbf{crt} \\
&\quad \text{content: } \textbf{char;} \\
&\quad \text{left, right: treetype;}
\end{aligned}
$$

```
      sec
         function leaf: boolean;
            begin leaf: = (left = nil) and (right = nil) end;
      sub
         (left = nil)  =  (right = nil)  (*tree is regular*)
      end.
```

REMARK 1. Notice the introduction of a new section in the description of *sets:* the section *secondary functions* headed by the keyword **sec**. It introduces functions which are constructed from the elementary functions of the set. On the basis of the introduction of secondary functions, we must generalize the syntax of sets to:

```
         set
         crt ⟨elementary function declarations⟩
         sec ⟨secondary function declarations⟩
         sub ⟨predicate⟩
         end.
```

Of course, when a set has no secondary functions, the whole section of secondary functions may be deleted and one is left with the usual notation. Because of its limited use, the section of secondary functions is not considered in the BNF syntax given in Appendix A. It follows the rules of Pascal's function or procedure declarations. Another illustration of the use of secondary functions is given in problem 3, Chapter 4.

```
      stacktype = set
      crt
         k: integer;
         a: array [1..k] of treetype;
         i: integer;
      sec
         function empty: boolean;
            begin empty: = (i = 0) end;
         function top: treetype;
            begin top: = a[i] end;
         procedure pop(var x: treetype);
            begin x: = a[i]; i: = i − 1 end;
         procedure push(x: treetype);
            begin i: = i + 1; a[i]: = x end;
```

sub
  $i \geqslant 0 \land i \leqslant k \land k \geqslant 1$ (*and k is large enough*)
end.

REMARK 2. Secondary functions serve two distinct purposes, clearly high-lighted by the two sets described above:

— abstraction, i.e. the convenience of calling pre-defined functions (such as leaf, on *nodetype)* rather than invoking tedious formulas (such as left = **nil and** right = **nil**).
— encapsulation, i.e. the security of affecting the elementary functions of the set through a small collection of well-defined, well-controlled, well-checked procedures (such as procedures pop and push, on *stacktype)*.

We define an I-function pp on stacktype by:

  domain: the set of non-empty stacks,
  expression: the stack obtained by calling pop once.

We also define an E-function psh from (stacktype × treetype) to stacktype by:

  expression: the stack obtained by pushing the second argument of the function onto the first.

Let s be an element of S and let Lf be the following statement whose P-space is S.

```
Lf=
1: while not stack.empty do
   begin
   stack.pop(current);
   if current.leaf then count: = count + 1
   else
      begin
      stack.push(current↑. left);
      stack.push(current↑. right)
      end
   end.
```

The loop body of this statement will be denoted by lb. We want to prove the following property about the functional abstraction of Lf:

V: $(\forall s, count(s) = 0 \wedge stack(s) = \langle tree0 \rangle \Rightarrow count([Lf](s)) = lv(tree0))$,

where $lv(t)$ is the number of leaves in the tree t and $\langle t \rangle$ designates the stack containing the single element t.

REMARK 3. Note that V has the form

$$(\forall s, p(s) \Rightarrow q([Lf](s))).$$

One may want to ask: Can this formula be interpreted as the correctness of Lf with respect to some specification? First, one must observe that **dom**([Lf]) = S. Hence s:**dom**([Lf]) is the constant predicate **true**. Therefore

$$(\forall s, p(s) \Rightarrow q([Lf](s)))$$

can be rewritten as:

$$(\forall s, p(s) \Rightarrow s:\mathbf{dom}([Lf]) \wedge q([Lf](s))).$$

Clearly, this expresses the correctness of Lf wrt (S,R), where R is:

$$\{(s,s') \mid p(s) \wedge q(s')\}.$$

In general, whenever we study a while statement, say w, on space S, we shall assume that $S = \mathbf{dom}(w)$. In the next chapter we prove that this restriction does not affect the generality of our study.

Let l be the I-function on S defined by:

domain: the set of states that program Lf reaches at label 1 while the stack is not empty.
expression: the state reached after state s, at label 1 (after some number of iterations), when the top of the stack has been *pop*-ed and processed. In other words, E(s) is characterized by
— E(s) is a state reached at label 1 after state s.
— $stack(E(s)) = pp(stack(s))$.

In order to prove V, we introduce a lemma:

V': $(\forall s, \tilde{}empty(stack(s)) \Rightarrow count(l(s)) = count(s) + lv(top(stack(s))))$.

Before we prove V', let's show that V can be deduced from V': By definition of l, we can say that if stack(s) contains a single element, say tree0, then $[Lf](s) = l(s)$; hence we deduce from V' that

V'': $(\forall s, \text{stack}(s) = \langle \text{tree0} \rangle \Rightarrow \text{count}([Lf](s)) = \text{count}(s) + \text{lv}(\text{tree0}))$.

Clearly, V stems from V''.

Now, in order to prove the validity of V', we define

v(s): $\sim\text{empty}(\text{stack}(s)) \Rightarrow \text{count}(l(s)) = \text{count}(s) + \text{lv}(\text{top}(\text{stack}(s)))$

and we can invoke the Noetherian Induction Theorem to prove that v is a P-tautology on S. This requires, of course, that we define a well-founded relation on S; we choose:

$$< \; = \; \{(s',s) \mid \sim\text{empty}(\text{stack}(s)) \wedge \sim\text{empty}(\text{stack}(s')) \wedge$$
$$\text{top}(\text{stack}(s')) \text{ is a subtree of top}(\text{stack}(s))\}.$$

(Note: We represent pairs of relation $<$ by (s',s) whereas we are used to representing pairs by (s,s'). This switch will alleviate notations in this proof). The Noetherian Induction Theorem provides that in order to prove that v is a tautology, we have to prove:

$$(\forall s, (\forall s', s' < s \Rightarrow v(s')) \Rightarrow v(s)).$$

Basis of induction: s is minimal; hence either empty(stack(s)), in which case v(s) is vacuously true, or:

$$(\sim\text{empty}(\text{stack}(s)) \wedge \text{leaf}(\text{top}(\text{stack}(s))))),$$

in which case $l(s) = [lb](s)$ (i.e. the top of the stack is processed by a single iteration). Hence,

$$\begin{aligned}
\text{count}(l(s)) &= \text{count}([lb](s)) \\
&= \text{count}(s) + 1 \\
&= \text{count}(s) + \text{lv}(\text{top}(\text{stack}(s))).
\end{aligned}$$

Induction step: s is not minimal; hence $\sim\text{empty}(\text{stack}(s))$ and top(stack(s)) is an internal node. Because $\sim\text{empty}(\text{stack}(s))$, the loop body is executed at least once on s, yielding:

$$[lb](s) = (\ top(stack(s)),$$
$$psh(psh(pp(stack(s)),$$
$$left(top(stack(s)))),$$
$$right(top(stack(s)))),$$
$$count(s)).$$

Note that $top(stack([lb](s))) = right(top(stack(s)))$; hence $[lb](s) < s$. By induction hypothesis, $v([lb](s))$ holds:

$v([lb](s))$: ~$empty(stack([lb](s)))$
$\Rightarrow count(l([lb](s))) = count([\,lb](s)) + lv(right(top(stack(s))))$.

Since ~$empty(stack([lb](s)))$ holds, so does the right hand side of the $\Rightarrow$ sign:

u0: $count(l([lb](s))) = count([lb](s)) + lv(right(top(stack(s))))$.

Furthermore, one can see that, by definition of l,

$$top(stack(l([lb](s)))) = left(top(stack(s))).$$

Hence, $l([lb](s)) < s$. By induction hypothesis, v holds for $l([lb](s))$:

$v(l([lb](s)))$: ~$empty(stack(l([lb](s))))$
$\Rightarrow count(l(l([lb](s)))) = count(l([lb](s))) + lv(left(top(stack(s))))$.

Since ~$empty(stack([lb](s)))$ holds, so does the right hand side of the $\Rightarrow$ sign:

u1: $count(l(l([lb](s)))) = count(\ l([lb](s))) + lv(left(top(stack(s))))$.

We have to prove $v(s)$; since ~$empty(stack(s))$ holds, we have to prove

$$count(l(s)) = count(s) + lv(top(stack(s))).$$

Clearly, this stems from the following results:

u0
u1
$l(l([lb](s))) = l(s)$, by definition of l
$count(s) = count([lb](s))$
$lv(top(stack(s))) = lv(left(top(stack(s)))) + lv(right(top(stack(s))))$.

This completes the proof of V.

Exercises

1. [B] Use the deductive system s.IA* to prove the correctness of statement Lf with respect to the I-specification (S,R), where R is {(s,s')| count(s) = 0 ∧ stack(s) = ⟨tree0⟩ ∧ count(s') = lv(tree0)}. Comment on the appropriateness of the invariant assertion method and the intermittent assertion method to prove the correctness of this statement.

2. [B] Determine the functional abstraction of statement Lf and prove its correctness with respect to the specification given above using the symbolic execution method. Comment on how the symbolic execution method and the intermittent assertion method compare on this example. Comment on the irrelevance of current([Lf](s)), which the symbolic execution method will compute anyway.

3. [A] Finish the last details of the proof of V' in Example 1.

2 Example 2: Preorder Traversal of a Binary Tree

Let:

$$S =$$
set
    current: treetype;
    stack: stacktype
end,

where treetype and stacktype are the sets defined in the previous example, except that we shall only consider non-empty trees. Let Pr be the following statement whose P-space is S and whose output space is OS = L*(**char**).

```
Pr =
1: while not stack.empty do
   begin
   stack.pop(current);
   write(current↑ .content);
   if not current↑ .leaf then
      begin
      stack.push(current↑ .right);
      stack.push(current↑ .left)
      end
   end.
```

Because the statement does not involve any **read** statement, its extended space can merely be defined as $ES = S \times OS$. Let es $= (s,os)$ be an element of ES. We will abuse the notation by referring to the first and second component of (es) as (respectively) s(es) and os(es). The reader will find this notation convenient. We denote the loop body of Pr by lb. Let pt be the E-function from treetype to L*(**char**) defined by:

$$pt(t) = \text{preorder traversal of tree t.}$$

We want to prove the following property about statement Pr:

$$V: \quad (\forall es, os(es) = (\ ) \wedge stack(s(es)) = \langle tree0 \rangle$$
$$\Rightarrow os([Pr](es)) = pt(tree0)).$$

Again, in order to prove V, we shall prove a lemma first. The formulation of this lemma requires that we introduce an auxiliary I-function on ES that we call l and that we define as follows:

domain: the set of E-states attainable at label 1, while stack(s(es)) is not empty.

expression: the E-state reached subsequently when the top of stack(s(es)) has been *pop*-ed and processed. More precisely, E(es) can be characterized by
— E(es) is a state reached at label 1 after es,
— stack(s(E(es))) = pp(stack(s(es))).

The lemma is:

$$V': \quad (\forall es, \tilde{\ }empty(stack(s(es)))$$
$$\Rightarrow os(l(es)) = \textbf{cont}(os(es), \ pt(top(stack(s(es))))) \ ).$$

Let es be an E-state such that os(es) = () and stack(s(es)) = $\langle tree0 \rangle$. If V' is valid, then

$$os(l(es)) = \textbf{cont}((\ ), pt(top(stack(s(es)))))$$
$$= pt(top(stack(s(es))))$$
$$= pt(top(\langle tree0 \rangle))$$
$$= pt(tree0).$$

On the other hand, because stack(s(es)) = $\langle tree0 \rangle$, we can say that

$$l(es) = [Pr](es).$$

Replacing in the equation above, we get

$$os([Pr](es)) = pt(tree0).$$

Hence in order to prove V it suffices to prove V'.

We write V' as ($\forall es$, v(es)), where v(es) is defined as

v(es): ~empty(stack(s(es)))
$\Rightarrow$ os(l(es)) = **cont**(os(es), pt(top(stack(s(es)))))),

and we invoke the Noetherian Induction Theorem with the following well-founded relation on ES:

$<$ = {(es',es)| ~empty(stack(s(es'))) $\wedge$ ~empty(stack(s(es))) $\wedge$
top(stack(s(es'))) is a subtree of top(stack(s(es))))}.

Basis of induction: es is minimal; hence either empty(stack(s(es))), in which case v(s) is vacuously true, or ~empty(stack(s(es))) and top(stack(s(es))) is a leaf, in which case l(es) = [lb](es). Hence,

$$\begin{aligned} os(l(es)) &= os([lb](es)) \\ &= \textbf{app}(os(es), content(top(stack(s(es))))) \\ &= \textbf{app}(os(es), pt(top(stack(s(es))))), \end{aligned}$$

because if t (in treetype) is a leaf then pt(t) = content(t).

Induction step: es is not minimal; hence

~empty(stack(s(es))) $\wedge$ top(stack(s(es))) is an internal node.

Because ~empty(stack(s(es))), the loop body executes at least once on es and yields

[lb](es) = ((top(stack(s(es))),
psh(psh(pp(stack(s(es))),
right(top(stack(s(es))))),
left(top(stack(s(es)))))),
app(os(es), content(top(stack(s(es)))))).

From this formula, we deduce the following:

— [lb](es)$<$es, hence v holds for [lb](es) by induction hypothesis.
— l([lb](es))$<$es, hence v holds for l([lb](es)).

— $l(l([lb](es))) = l(es)$ by definition of l.
— **cont**(**cont**(**app**(os(es),
content(top(stack(s(es))))))
pt(left(top(stack(s(es)))))),
pt(right(top(stack(s(es))))))
= **cont**(os(es), pt(top(stack(s(es)))))).

It is left to the reader to verify that these conditions yield v(es).

Exercises

1. [B] Use the deductive system s.IA* to prove the correctness of Pr with respect to (ES,R), where

$$R = \{(es,es')|\ os(es) = ()\ \wedge\ stack(s(es)) = \langle tree0 \rangle\ \wedge\ os(es') = pt(tree0)\}.$$

   Compare the invariant assertion method and the intermittent assertion method on this example.

2. [B] Determine the functional abstraction of statement Pr and prove the correctness of Pr with respect to (ES,R) (given in exercise 1) using the symbolic execution method. Compare the appropriateness of the symbolic execution and the intermittent assertion method vis-a-vis this particular example.

3. [B] Complete the proof of V' in the example above.

3 Example 3: Ackermann Function (due to Manna et al, [4])

The Ackermann function is defined for non negative integers by

$$Ak(x,y) = \mathbf{ite}(x=0,\ y+1,$$
$$\mathbf{ite}(y=0,\ Ak(x-1,1),$$
$$Ak(x-1,Ak(x,y-1)))).$$

Let S be the following set

$$S = \mathbf{set}$$
$$\mathbf{crt}$$
$$\quad k: \mathbf{integer};$$
$$\quad a: \mathbf{array}\ [1..k]\ \mathbf{of\ integer};$$
$$\quad i: 0..k;$$

```
        sub
         1≤i≤k ⟹ a[i]≥0 (*and k large enough*)
        end.
```

and let Ac be the following statement on P-space S:

```
                    Ac=
                    1: while i≠1 do
                       begin
                       if a[i−1] =0 then
                          begin
                          a[i−1]:= a[i]+1;
                          i:=i−1
                          end
                       else
                          if a[i]=0 then
                             begin
                             a[i−1]:= a[i−1]−1;
                             a[i]:=1
                             end
                          else
                             begin
                             a[i+1]:= a[i]−1;
                             a[i]:= a[i−1];
                             a[i−1]:= a[i−1]−1;
                             i:= i+1
                             end
                       end.
```

We want to prove the following:

$$V: \quad (\forall s, i(s)=2 \Rightarrow a([Ac](s))[1] = Ak(a(s)[1], a(s)[2])).$$

Before we prove V, we prove a lemma; this lemma requires that we define an auxiliary function l on S:

    domain: the states reached at label 1 while i>1,
    expression: the state reached after s, such that $i(E(s))=i(s)-1$.

The lemma is

$$V': \quad (\forall s, i(s)\geq 2 \Rightarrow a(l(s))[i(l(s))] = Ak(a(s)[i(s)-1], a(s)[i(s)])).$$

Henceforth, we abbreviate $Ak(a(s)[i(s)-1], a(s)[i(s)])$ by $ack(s)$. By the very definition of l, if s is such that $i(s) = 2$ then $[Ac](s) = l(s)$; hence V' implies V. We now concentrate on proving V'. We define:

$$v(s): i(s) \geqslant 2 \implies a(l(s))[i(l(s))] = ack(s),$$

and we invoke the Noetherian Induction Theorem. The well-founded relation we choose on set S is:

$$< \; = \; \{(s',s) \mid \; i(s') \geqslant 2 \; \wedge \; i(s) \geqslant 2 \; \wedge \; (a(s')[i(s')-1] < a(s)[i(s)-1] \; \vee$$
$$a(s')[i(s')-1] = a(s)[i(s)-1] \; \wedge \; a(s')[i(s')] < a(s)[i(s)])\}.$$

We have to prove:

$$(\forall s, (\forall s', s' < s \implies v(s')) \implies v(s)).$$

Let s be an element of S. We want to deduce $v(s)$ from $(\forall s', s' < s \implies v(s'))$. In other words, we want to deduce $a(l(s))[i(l(s))] = ack(s)$ from $(\forall s', s' < s \implies v(s'))$ and $i(s) \geqslant 2$. We can do so by a case analysis on s which parallels the recursive definition of function Ak (and which does not, by the way, parallel the *s minimal/non-minimal* distinction we usually make for proofs by induction). Because it is very tedious, the proof is not presented here; it is given in detail in [4].

Exercises

1. [B] Use the deductive system s.IA* to prove the total correctness of statement Ac with respect to the I-specification (S,R), where

$$R \; = \; \{(s,s') \mid \; i(s) = 2 \; \wedge \; a(s')[1] = ack(s)\}.$$

Comment on the appropriateness of the invariant assertion method and the intermittent assertion method to prove the correctness of this statement.

2. [C] Determine the functional abstraction of statement Ac and prove its correctness with respect to the specification given above using the symbolic execution method. How does the symbolic execution method and the intermittent assertion method compare on this example?

3. [C] Complete the proof of the example above. (Hint: See [4]).

4 General Characteristics

There seem to be some common features in the examples given above. We are given a while statement w on space S in the form

$$w = \textbf{while } t \textbf{ do } \text{lb}.$$

We want to prove a formula V which has the form

$$V: (\forall s, \text{init}(s) \Rightarrow u([w](s))).$$

In order to prove V, we introduce an auxiliary function l such that:

$$s:\textbf{dom}(l) \Rightarrow s:\textbf{dom}([\text{lb}]),$$
$$\text{init}(s) \Rightarrow [w](s) = l(s),$$
$$s:\textbf{dom}(l) \Rightarrow l(s) = l(l([\text{lb}](s))),$$

and we prove a lemma about function l in the form

$$V': (\forall s, \text{init}'(s) \Rightarrow u'(l(s))),$$

where init' and u' are such that

$$\text{init}(s) \Rightarrow \text{init}'(s),$$
$$\text{init}(s) \ \wedge \ u'(l(s)) \Rightarrow u(l(s)).$$

We introduce a well-founded relation $<$ on S such that

$$s:\textbf{dom}(l) \Rightarrow [\text{lb}](s) < s,$$
$$s:\textbf{dom}(l) \Rightarrow l([\text{lb}](s)) < s.$$

We define predicate v on S by:

$$v(s): \text{init}'(s) \Rightarrow u'(l(s)),$$

which means that V' can be written as $(\forall s, v(s))$ and we invoke the Noetherian Induction Theorem to prove V'.

Perhaps the major difficulty with this method is the elusiveness of defining function l. The intermittent assertion method is the iterative version of a very natural method of proof of recursive programs: the *structural induction method* (see Chapter 11). In the structural induction method, the roles of functions [w] and l are played by the same function (namely that computed by the recursive program) but with different arguments: The difficulty with the intermittent assertion method is that one cannot parameterize a while statement.

A comment is in order regarding the name of the method. The term *intermittent assertion* was first coined by Z Manna and R Waldinger [4] to contrast this method with the invariant assertion method on the grounds that the latter proves that the assertion attached to the top of the loop body (i.e. the loop invariant) holds every time the top of the loop body is reached (see rule r'5 of s.IA or r5 of s.IA*, Chapter 7), whereas the former proves assertions about the top of the loop body across applications of function *l* which may take more than one iteration to compute (see sections 1, 2 and 3 of this chapter).

Exercises

1. [C] Let:

```
treetype = ↑ nodetype;
nodetype = set
crt
    l, r: treetype;
sec
    function leaf: boolean;
    begin leaf: = (l = nil) and (r = nil) end;
sub
    (l = nil) = (r = nil) (*regular*)
end.
```

and let:

```
stacktype = set
crt
    k: integer;
    a: array [1..k] of treetype;
    d: array [1..k] of integer; (*distance to root*)
    i: 0..k;
sec
    function empty: boolean; begin empty: = (i = 0) end;
    function top: treetype; begin top: = a[i] end;
    procedure pop (var x: treetype; var y: integer);
        begin x: = a[i]; y: = d[i]; i: = i − 1 end;
    procedure push (x: treetype; y: integer);
        begin i: = i + 1; a[i]: = x; d[i]: = y end;
sub
    (*k is large enough*)
end.
```

We let ht (height) be the E-function from treetype to **integer** defined by:

$$ht(t) = \text{ite}(\text{leaf}(t),\ 0,\ 1 + \max(ht(l(t)),\ ht(r(t)))),$$

and S be the space defined by:

```
set
crt
    cd: integer; (*current distance*)
    ct: treetype; (*current tree*)
    stack: stacktype;
    h: integer;
sub
    ct ≠ nil
end.
```

Let Hg be the statement defined on space S by:

```
Hg =
while not stack.empty do
   begin
   stack.pop(ct,cd);
   if not ct ↑.leaf then
      begin
      if cd > h then h: = cd;
      stack.push(ct ↑.r, cd + 1);
      stack.push(ct ↑.l, cd + 1)
      end
   end.
```

Let R be the relation on S defined by

$$R = \{(s,s') \mid h(s) = 0 \ \wedge\ \text{stack}(s) = \langle t0 \rangle \ \wedge\ t0 \neq \text{nil} \ \wedge\ h(s') = ht(t0)\}.$$

Prove the total correctness of Hg with respect to (S,R).

2. [B] Let S be the set defined by

```
set
    current: treetype;
    stack: stacktype;
    nodes: integer
end,
```

where treetype and stacktype are the sets presented in section 1; let ns be the E-function from treetype to **integer** defined as

$$ns(t) = \textbf{ite}(leaf(t),\ 1,\ 1 + ns(left(t)) + ns(right(t))).$$

Let Nd be the statement on S defined by

```
Nd =
while not stack.empty do
   begin
   stack.pop(current);
   nodes:= nodes+1;
   if not current ↑.leaf then
      begin
      stack.push(current ↑.left);
      stack.push(current ↑.right);
      end
   end.
```

Use the intermittent assertion method to prove the total correctness of Nd wrt (S,R), where

$$R = \{(s,s') \mid nodes(s) = 0 \ \wedge \ stack(s) = \langle t0 \rangle \ \wedge \ t0 \neq \textbf{nil} \ \wedge \ nodes(s') = ns(t0)\}.$$

5 Problems

1. [B] Characterize as precisely as possible the programs for which the intermittent assertion method is most appropriate. Base your discussions on the following criteria:
   a) Outer control structure.
   b) Structure of the proper space.
   c) Nature of the function computed by the program.

2. [B] Compare the appropriateness of the invariant assertion method and the intermittent assertion method on the basis of:
   a) The types of control structures they can be applied to.
   b) The need for ingenuity (generating inv for the former, l for the latter).
   c) The level of complexity.
   d) The naturalness.

3. [A] Consider formula V given in section 4. Express it as the correctness of w wrt some specification. (Hint: see Remark 3).

4. [B] Read references [4] then [3] and express your opinion regarding the debate invariant assertion vs intermittent assertion.

6 Bibliography

The intermittent assertion method surfaced in [2] as a method for program verification by "hand simulation with a little induction". It was given its name and general format in [4] and was critically evaluated in [3]. Different approaches to its formalization have been attempted in the past, including predicate calculus [6], invariant-assertion-like axiomatization [7], modal logic [5] and the Lucid formalism [1].

1: Ashcroft, E A and W W Wadge. Intermittent Assertion Proofs in Lucid. Information Processing 1977, North-Holland, pp 723-726.
2: Burstall, R M. Program Proving as Hand Simulation with a Little Induction. Information Processing 1974, North-Holland, pp 308-312.
3: Gries, D. Is Sometime Ever Better Than Alway?. ACM-TOPLAS 1(2) (October 1979), pp 258-265.
4: Manna, Z and R Waldinger. Is "Sometime" Sometimes Better Than "Always"?. CACM 21(2) (February 1978), pp 159-172.
5: Pratt, V R. Semantical Considerations on Floyd-Hoare Logic. Proceedings, Seventeenth Symposium on the Foundations of Computer Science. Houston, 1976, pp 109-121.
6: Schwarz, J. Event-based Reasoning: A System for Proving Correct Termination of Programs. Proceedings, Third International Colloquium on Automatas, Languages and Programming. Edinburgh, July 1976, pp 131-146.
7: Wang, A. An Axiomatic Basis for Proving Total Correctness of Go-to Programs. BIT Vol 16 (1976), pp 88-102.

Chapter 9

Induction on the Length of Execution: The Subgoal Induction Method

The *subgoal induction method* proves while statements by induction on their number of iterations: If the while statement iterates n times and works correctly then if it iterates $n+1$ times it will also work correctly. Before we discuss the method itself, we present some results about while statements.

1 Preliminary Results

Let w = (**while** t **do** lb) be a while statement on space S; we shall assume that w does not involve any read or write statements, hence we shall focus our attention on the proper space of w. Furthermore, we shall assume ideal arithmetic on the computer running statement w and that the only exceptional condition we are concerned about is the failure to terminate.

PROPOSITION 1. Let w = (**while** t **do** lb) be a while statement on S. The range of w is a subset of the domain of w.

Proof. Let s be an element of **rng**(w). Then ˜t(s) holds. Clearly w terminates on state s (very promptly, in fact), hence s is an element of **dom**(w).

QED

The proposition above assures us that when some state s in **dom**(w) is submitted to w, the final state computed by w is in **dom**(w). The question that comes to mind is then: How about the intermediate states obtained after some number of iterations? The proposition below provides the answer:

PROPOSITION 2. Let w = (**while** t **do** lb) be a while statement on space S. Let s0 be an element of **dom**(w) and let s1, s2, s3, . . . be the elements obtained after 1, 2, 3, . . . iterations. Then all of s1, s2, s3 . . . belong to **dom**(w).

Proof. Each one of s1, s2, s3, . . . is obtained from its predecessor by application of the I-function on S: [**if** t **then** lb]. Hence we have to prove that if s is in **dom**(w) then so is [**if** t **then** lb](s). This, in conjunction with the hypothesis that s0 belongs to **dom**(w) establishes (by simple induction) the claim of the proposition. Let s be a state in **dom**(w); when w is executed on s, it terminates. Because w is the same as

$$\textbf{if } t \textbf{ then } lb; w ,$$

we can say that when

$$\textbf{if } t \textbf{ then } lb; w$$

is executed on s, it terminates. This is the same as saying: Whenever w is executed on [**if** t **then** lb](s), it terminates. Hence [**if** t **then** lb](s) belongs to **dom**(w).

QED

Note that Proposition 2 implies Proposition 1. The interest of these two propositions is the following: If we are given a while statement w on space S, we can henceforth, without loss of generality, restrict our attention to the study of the while statement on **dom**(w). Let R be a I-relation on S = **dom**(w). The correctness of w with respect to R is expressed by the following predicate:

$$v(s): s:\textbf{dom}(R) \Rightarrow s:\textbf{dom}([w]) \wedge (s,[w](s)):R.$$

Because S equals **dom**(w), which is -by definition- the same as **dom**([w]), the predicate s:**dom**([w]) is a P-tautology on S; hence v(s) becomes:

$$v(s): s:\textbf{dom}(R) \Rightarrow (s,[w](s)):R.$$

If S = **dom**(R), u(s) becomes simply (s,[w](s)):R. We want to prove that we can, without loss of generality, assume that S = **dom**(R). Let R be an I-relation on S; we define relation R' by:

$$R' = \{(s,s') \mid s:\textbf{dom}(R) \Rightarrow (s,s'):R\}.$$

We notice that R' has two desirable properties: First, **dom**(R') = S. Second, the two propositions:

w is correct with respect to R, and
w is correct with respect to R'

are equivalent, since they can both be expressed by:

$$s:\textbf{dom}(R) \Rightarrow (s,[w](s)):R.$$

Hence, it is without loss of generality that we shall, in the remainder of this chapter, discuss while statements on a space S which is equal to their domain, and that we shall discuss their correctness with respect to relations whose domain is S. Under these two hypotheses, the correctness of a while statement w with respect to relation R is equivalent to:

$$(\forall s, (s,[w](s)):R),$$

which -by the way- means that $[w]$ is a subset of R.

Before we close this section, let's mention two more properties of while statements, resulting from Propositions 1 and 2.

COROLLARY 1. Let w = (**while** t **do** lb) be a while statement on space S, and let d and r be its domain and range respectively.

a) if d=r then $[w]=[:d,s]$, i.e. the identity function restricted to d.
b) $[:d,s]$ is the only invertible function that a while statement on domain d can compute.

For an outline of the proof of this corollary, see problems 1 and 2.

2 The Subgoal Induction Theorem

THEOREM 1. (The Subgoal Induction Theorem, due to Morris and Wegbreit, 1977). Let w = (**while** t **do** lb) be a while statement on space S and R be an I-relation on S. We assume that **dom**(w)=S and **dom**(R)=S. If

i)   ~t(s) $\Rightarrow$ (s,s):R,
ii) t(s) $\wedge$ ([lb](s),s*):R $\Rightarrow$ (s,s*):R,

then w is correct with respect to (S,R).

Proof. We shall prove that (i) and (ii) imply (s,[w](s)):R, by induction on the number of iterations it takes w to process s.

a) *Basis of induction.* It takes zero iterations to process s, hence ~t(s) holds. By hypothesis (i) and the modus ponens rule, we deduce (s,s):R. Because of the semantics of while statements, we can say that ~t(s)$\Rightarrow$[w](s)=s. Hence, when s is minimal, (s,[w](s)):R.

b) *Induction step.* Statement w works correctly for any state needing n iterations to process it. Let s be a state needing $n+1$ iterations; then t(s) holds and [lb](s) needs n iterations to process it. By the induction hypothesis,

$$([lb](s), \ [w]([lb](s))){:}R. \tag{0}$$

The conjunction of t(s) and (0), with the modus ponens rule applied to hypothesis (ii) yields

$$(s, \ [w]([lb](s))){:}R. \tag{1}$$

Due to the semantics of while statements, $[w]([lb](s)) = [w](s)$. Hence equation (1) becomes

$$(s,[w](s)){:}R,$$

which is the conclusion of the induction step.

From (a) and (b) we deduce that $(s,[w](s)){:}R$ is a P-tautology on S. Therefore w is correct wrt R.

QED

In order to illustrate the method, we shall apply it on three examples which differ by how *tight* the specification (S,R) is, i.e. how much of the functional aspect of the while statement relation R grasps.

EXAMPLE 1.Let S be the set:

```
S = set
crt   a, b: integer;
sub
   b≥0
end.
```

Let sm (sum) be the following statement on space S:

```
sm =
while b≠0 do
   begin
   a: = a+1;
   b: = b−1
   end,
```

and let R be the I-relation on S defined by:

$$R = \{(s,s') \mid a(s') = a(s) + b(s) \;\wedge\; b(s') = 0\}.$$

Notice that R is a function, i.e. s′ can be determined from s: We say that this specification is *tight*. See problem 3 for a general discussion of this case.

Clearly, **dom**(sm) = S and **dom**(R) = S; hence we may apply the Subgoal Induction Theorem.
(i) $b(s) = 0 \Rightarrow a(s) = a(s) + b(s) \;\wedge\; b(s) = 0 \Rightarrow (s,s):R$.
(ii) Let s and s* be two states such that

$$b(s) \neq 0, \tag{0}$$
$$a(s^*) = a(s) + 1 + b(s) - 1 \;\wedge\; b(s^*) = 0. \tag{1}$$

From (0) we deduce that $(a(s)+1, b(s)-1)$ belongs to S (i.e. application of [lb] to s has not thrown the computed state outside of space S); from (1), we deduce:

$$a(s^*) = a(s) + b(s) \;\wedge\; b(s^*) = 0,$$

which is equivalent to $(s,s^*):R$.
By virtue of the Subgoal Induction Theorem, sm is correct wrt (S,R).

EXAMPLE 2. We consider the following set:

$$
\begin{aligned}
S = \;&\textbf{set} \\
&\text{t: } \textbf{real}; \; (*\text{total}*) \\
&\text{a: } \textbf{array } [1..k] \textbf{ of real}; \\
&\text{i: } 1..k+1 \; (*\text{index}*) \\
&\textbf{end,}
\end{aligned}
$$

where k is some positive integer. We define the E-function sig (stands for sigma) from S to **real** by:

$$\text{ite}(i(s) \leqslant k, \; a(s)[i(s)] + \;\ldots\; + a(s)[k], \; 0).$$

Let Sg (sigma) be the following while statement

$$
\begin{aligned}
\text{Sg} = \;&\\
&\textbf{while } i \leqslant k \textbf{ do} \\
&\quad \textbf{begin} \\
&\quad\quad \text{t:} = t + a[i];
\end{aligned}
$$

$$i := i+1$$
end,

and let R be the I-relation on S defined as:

$$R = \{(s,s') \mid t(s') = t(s) + sig(s) \ \wedge \ a(s) = a(s')\}.$$

This specification is not a function but it is tight enough to carry the interesting functional properties of Sg. Clearly, **dom**(Sg) = S and **dom**(R) = S; hence we may apply the Subgoal Induction Theorem.

(i) ˜(i(s)≤k) ⟹ sig(s) = 0 ⟹ t(s) = t(s) + sig(s) ∧ a(s) = a(s) ⟹ (s,s):R.

(ii) Let s and s* be two states such that:

$$i(s) \leq k, \tag{0}$$
$$\begin{aligned} t(s^*) &= (t(s) + a(s)[\,i(s)\,]) + \\ &\quad \textbf{ite}(i(s) + 1 \leq k, \ a(s)[\,i(s) + 1\,] + \cdots + a(s)[\,k\,], \ 0) \end{aligned}$$
$$\wedge \ a(s) = a(s^*). \tag{1}$$

From equations (0) and (1), we have:

$$\begin{aligned} t(s^*) \\ &= t(s) + \textbf{ite}(i(s) \leq k, \ a(s)[i(s)] + \ldots + a(s)[k], \ 0) \\ &= t(s) + sig(s). \end{aligned}$$

This, in conjunction with a(s*) = a(s) (equation (1)), yields

$$(s,s^*):R.$$

EXAMPLE 3. Let:

$$\begin{aligned} S = \ &\textbf{set} \\ &a, b: \textbf{integer} \\ &\textbf{end.} \end{aligned}$$

Let mx be the following program on space S:

$$mx = \ \textbf{while} \ a \geq b \ \textbf{do} \ b := b+1$$

and let R be the following I-relation on S:

$$R = \{(s,s') \mid b(s') \geq b(s)\}.$$

This relation is only interested in how b may have been changed by mx. Clearly, **dom**(mx) = S and **dom**(R) = S, hence we can apply the Subgoal Induction Theorem.

(i) ˜(a(s) ⩾ b(s)) ⟹ b(s) ⩾ b(s).
(ii) Let s and s* be two states such that

$$b(s^*) \geqslant b(s) + 1 \qquad\qquad (0)$$
$$a(s) \geqslant b(s) \qquad\qquad (1)$$

Clearly, we can deduce b(s*) ⩾ b(s), hence (s,s*):R.

3   Subgoal Induction as an Induction on the Space

So far, subgoal induction has been viewed as a method of proof of while statements which proceeds by induction on the number of iterations. In this section, we attempt to show it under a different perspective: as a particular form of induction on the space of the program.

Let S be a set and let w = (**while** t **do** lb) be a while statement on S such that **dom**(w) = S. Let tl be the transpose of relation (actually function) [t,s]*[lb]. Relation tl can be written as:

$$\begin{aligned}
tl &= \{(s',s) \mid (s,s'):[t,s]^*[lb]\} \\
   &= \{(s',s) \mid s' = [t,s]^*[lb](s)\} \\
   &= \{(s',s) \mid t(s) \wedge s' = [lb](s)\}.
\end{aligned}$$

Note that (s',s) belongs to tl iff it takes one more iteration for w to process s than to process s'. Let < be the transitive closure of tl. The pair (s',s) belongs to < iff it takes more iterations to process s than to process s'. Relation < ranks elements of S according to how many iterations of w it takes to process them.

PROPOSITION 3. (S, <) is a well-founded set.

Proof. Being a transitive closure, relation < is transitive. If there exists an infinite sequence s1, s2, s3, ... such that (s2,s1), (s3,s2), ... are all members of relation <, then w would not terminate when executed on state s1; this contradicts the hypothesis **dom**(w) = S.

QED

Let R be an internal relation on S such that **dom**(R) = S; the correctness of w with respect to R can be written as

$$V: (\forall s, (s,[w](s)):R).$$

In order to prove V, one may invoke the Noetherian Induction Theorem, using the ordering relation $<$. In this case one has to prove

$$V': (\forall s, (\forall s', s'<s \Rightarrow (s',[w](s')):R) \Rightarrow (s,[w](s)):R).$$

We wish to decompose V' into a basis of induction and an induction step. In order to do so, we have to characterize $<$-minimal elements of S. Note that if some s in S is such that t(s) holds, then [lb](s) $<$ s. On the other hand, if ~t(s) holds for some s, then there is no element less than s (by relation $<$). Hence $<$-minimal elements are characterized by ~t(s). The basis of induction is:

$$(j) \quad \tilde{} t(s) \Rightarrow (s,[w](s)):R.$$

From the semantics of while statements, it follows that ~ t(s)$\Rightarrow$[w](s) = s. Hence (j) can be written as:

$$(j'): \tilde{} t(s) \Rightarrow (s,s):R.$$

As for the induction step, it can be written as:

$$(jj): (s',s):< \wedge (s',[w](s')):R \Rightarrow ((s,[w](s)):R.$$

We shall admit without proof (a proof outline can be found in problem 5) that this is equivalent to:

$$(jj'): (s',s):tl \wedge (s',[w](s')):R \Rightarrow ((s,[w](s)):R.$$

Due to the semantics of while statements, we can deduce [w](s) = [w](s') from (s',s):tl. Also, because tl is the transpose of [t,s]*[lb], (s',s):tl can be written as:

$$(s,s'):[t,s]*[lb],$$

or

$$t(s) \wedge s' = [lb](s).$$

Hence (jj') becomes:

$$(jj''): t(s) \land ([lb](s),[w](s)):R \Rightarrow (s,[w](s)):R.$$

Note that (j') is equivalent to condition (i) of the Subgoal Induction Theorem and (jj'') is a logical consequence of condition (ii) of the theorem. Hence, except for the slight difference between (ii) and (jj''), the Subgoal Induction Theorem can be understood as a special case of induction on the space of the while statement: the case when the complexity of a state is equated to the number of iterations required to process it. It is not surprising then that the induction on the space becomes an induction on the number of iterations.

REMARK 1. By ignoring the equation $s^* = [w](s)$, the Subgoal Induction Theorem loses generality because it imposes a condition of correctness (ii) which is unnecessarily strong: The weaker condition (jj'') suffices. In practice, however, it is not possible to exploit a condition such as $s^* = [w](s)$ since [w] is not known (and if it were, the Subgoal Induction Theorem would make no sense since the symbolic execution method can be applied readily). Nevertheless, one can use the condition s^*:**rng**([w]) which is equivalent to ˜t(s^*). The clause then becomes:

$$t(s) \land ([lb](s),s^*):R \land {}^\sim t(s^*) \Rightarrow (s,s^*):R.$$

See problem 6 for an outline of the proof that s^*:**rng**(w) and ˜t(s^*) are equivalent.

For yet another perspective on the Subgoal Induction Theorem, see problem 3.

4 Exercises

1. [A] Use the subgoal induction method to prove the correctness of G (gcd) with respect to R, as defined below.
   The space is:

   $$S = \text{set}$$
   $$\text{crt}$$
   $$\quad a, b: \text{integer};$$
   $$\text{sub}$$
   $$\quad a > 0 \land b > 0$$
   $$\text{end}.$$

   Relation R is: $\{(s,s')\mid a(s') = \gcd(a(s),b(s))\}$
   Statement G is: **while** $a \neq b$ **do if** $a > b$ **then** $a := a - b$ **else** $b := b - a$.

2. [B] Use the subgoal induction method to prove the correctness of L (linear search) with respect to R, as defined below:
The space is:

$$S = \textbf{set}$$
$$\textbf{crt}$$
$$\quad \text{a: } \textbf{array } [1..k+1] \textbf{ of real};$$
$$\quad \text{i: } 1..k+1; \ (*index*)$$
$$\quad \text{c: } \textbf{real};$$
$$\textbf{sub}$$
$$\quad a[k+1] = c$$
$$\textbf{end,}$$

where k is a positive integer.
Relation R is: $\{(s,s') | \ i(s') = k+1 \Rightarrow (\forall j, \ i(s) \leqslant j \leqslant k \Rightarrow a(s)[j] \neq c(s))\}$.
Statement L is: **while** $a[i] \neq c$ **do** $i := i+1$.
(Hint: Don't forget to show that **dom**(R) = S).

3. [C] Use the subgoal induction method to prove the correctness of statement B (binary search) with respect to R, as defined below.
The space is:

$$S = \textbf{set}$$
$$\textbf{crt}$$
$$\quad \text{a: } \textbf{array } [1..k] \textbf{ of real};$$
$$\quad l, h, m: 1..k; \ (*low, high, middle*)$$
$$\quad \text{c: } \textbf{real};$$
$$\textbf{sub}$$
$$\quad l \leqslant h \ \wedge \ (\forall i, \ 1 \leqslant i \leqslant k \Rightarrow a[i] \leqslant a[i+1])$$
$$\textbf{end,}$$

where k is a positive integer.
Relation R is:

$$\{(s,s') | \ (\ c(s') = a(s')[l(s')] \ ) = (\ (\ \exists i, \ l(s) \leqslant i \leqslant h(s) \ \wedge \ c(s) = a(s)[i]) \ )$$
$$\wedge \ a(s) = a(s') \ \wedge \ c(s) = c(s')\}$$

Statement B is:

```
while l ≠ h do
    begin
    m := (l+h)/2;
    if c > a[m] then l := m+1 else h := m
    end.
```

5 Problems

1. [A] Let w = (**while** t **do** lb) be a while statement whose domain d and range r are equal. Let s be an element of d. What can be said of t(s)? Characterize [w].

2. [B] Let w = (**while** t **do** lb) be a while statement on space S and let d be its domain and r its range. We assume that [w] is an invertible function from d to r. One of two conditions may hold:
   i) t is **false** for every element in d,
   ii) there exists s0 in d such that t(s0) holds.
   a) Show that under hypothesis (ii), there exists at least another element s1 such that [w](s0) = [w](s1).
   b) Show that under hypothesis (i), [w] = [:d,s].
   c) Conclude: What is the only invertible function implemented by a while statement?

3. [B] Let w = (**while** t **do** lb) be a while statement on space S such that **dom**(w) = S and let f be a I-function on S such that **dom**(f) = S.
   a) How can you express the correctness of w wrt (S,f)?
   b) Apply the subgoal Induction Theorem to prove the correctness of w with respect to (S,f).
   c) Compare the conditions found with the conditions of the While Statement Theorem given in section 3.5, Chapter 5. Interpret the results of your comparisons.
   d) Consider that in the context of subgoal induction, the relations given can be arbitrarily non-deterministic: Show that the Subgoal Induction Theorem can simply be understood as a generalization of the While Statement Theorem.

4. [B] In order to apply the invariant assertion method to a while statement, one must generate a loop invariant. This endeavor requires some ingenuity and a good understanding of the while statement. Where, in the subgoal induction proof, is ingenuity required?

5. [B] We define a relation tl (see section 3) and we denote its transitive closure by <. Let (jj) and (jj') be two formulas of the form:

$$(jj): (s',s):< \ \wedge \ u(s') \Rightarrow u(s), \text{ and}$$
$$(jj'): (s',s):tl \ \wedge \ u(s') \Rightarrow u(s).$$

We wish to prove that (jj) and (jj') are logically equivalent.
   a) Prove that u(s) is a logical consequence of

$$(s',s):tl \ \wedge \ u(s'),$$
tl is a subset of <, and
(jj).

Deduce that (jj') is a logical consequence of (jj).

b) Let s' and s be two states such that $(s',s){:}< \; \wedge \; u(s')$. Notice that if $(s',s){:}<$, then there exists a positive integer n such that $(s',s){:}(tl{**}n)$. Use (jj') n times to prove that then u(s) stems from u(s'). Deduce that (jj) is a logical consequence of (jj').

6. [A] Let w = (**while** t **do** lb) be a while statement whose space and domain is S.
   a) Prove that ~t(s) $\Rightarrow$ s:**rng**(w).
   b) Prove that t(s) $\Rightarrow$ ~(s:**rng**(w)).
   c) Conclude: How can one characterize the set **rng**(w)?

6 Bibliography

The subgoal induction method was given its name and general format in [5]. Related methods of proof have appeared in [1], [2], [3], [4] and [6]. Consult [5] for more examples of proofs of while statements by the subgoal induction method.

1: Basu, S K and J D Misra. Proving Loop Programs. IEEE-TSE 1(1) (1975), pp 76-86.
2: Manna, Z and A Pnueli. Formalization of Properties of Functional Programs. JACM 17(3) (1970), pp 555-569.
3: Mills, H D. The New Math of Computer Programming. CACM 18(1) (1975), pp 43-48.
4: Moore, J S. Introducing Prog Into the Pure Lisp Prover. CSL-74-3, Xerox Palo Alto Research Center. December 1974.
5: Morris, J H and B Wegbreit. Program Verification by Subgoal Induction. Current Trends in Programming Methodology, (Chapter 8, Vol II). R T Yeh, editor. Prentice-Hall, 1977.
6: Topor, R W. Interactive Program Verification Using Virtual Programs. Doctoral dissertation, University of Edinburgh, 1975.

Chapter 10

Induction on the Trace of Execution:
The Cutpoint Method

The *cutpoint method* proves the correctness of programs by induction on their trace of execution: Labels are attached to statements throughout the statement part of the program and a predicate is attached to each label, characterizing the set of correct states at that label. Let s be a state and te(s) (i.e. *trace of execution* of s) be the sequence of labels reached by the control of the program when it is executed starting at state s. The cutpoint method proves the correctness of the program by proving that as the control of the program transfers from one label to the next, it goes from one correct state to another and progresses (somehow) toward termination.

This method, due to Floyd (1967), was originally designed for flowchart programs. Its most particular feature is that it can be applied to structured as well as unstructured programs. However, its most favorable feature is the simplicity of the concepts it involves: labels, assertions, execution paths, simple induction.

1 Paths and Path Functions

Let st be a statement on space S and let 1, 2, ... k be k labels attached to statements throughout the text of st. We assume that 1 is attached to the beginning of st and k is attached to the end of it, so that each execution of st starts at label 1 and terminates at label k.

DEFINITION 1. Let (i,j) be a pair of labels. The *path* from i to j is defined iff there exists a state s such that if execution is started from label i with state s then it reaches label j and reaches no label before j. The path from i to j, denoted (i→j) is the sequence of statements that are executed between i and j.

Below are examples of paths illustrating Definition 1.

EXAMPLE 1. Let st be

$$\textbf{begin } 1: x := 4; \ 2: x := 2*x + 1; \ 3: \textbf{end}.$$

(Syntactically, 3 is a label for the empty statement preceding **end**).

$$(1\rightarrow2) \text{ is } (1\text{: } x\text{:} = \text{ } 4\text{; } 2\text{:}).$$
$$(2\rightarrow3) \text{ is } (2\text{: } x\text{:} = \text{ } 2\text{*}x + 1\text{; } 3\text{:}).$$

As for $(1\rightarrow3)$, $(2\rightarrow1)$, $(3\rightarrow2)$ and $(3\rightarrow1)$, they are not defined; nor are $(1\rightarrow1)$, $(2\rightarrow2)$ and $(3\rightarrow3)$.

EXAMPLE 2. Let st be

> ◦   **begin** 1: **read**(x); 2: **if** x$<$0 **then** x: $= -$x; 3: **end**.

$(1\rightarrow2)$ is (1: **read**(x); 2:).
$(2\rightarrow3)$ is (2: **if** x $<$0 **then** x: $= -$x; 3:).

All other paths are not defined.

EXAMPLE 3. Let st be

> **begin** 1: **read**(x); **read**(y);
>   2: x: $=$x$+$y; **if** y$>$x **then begin** y: $=$y$-$x; 3: **end**
>   **else** 4: x: $=$x$-$y;
>   5: **end**.

$(1\rightarrow2)$ is (1: **read**(x); **read**(y); 2:).
$(2\rightarrow3)$ is (2: x: $=$x$+$y; (y$>$x?**true**); y: $=$y$-$x; 3:).
$(2\rightarrow4)$ is (2: x: $=$x$+$y; (y$>$x?**false**); 4:).
$(3\rightarrow5)$ is (3:; 5:).
$(4\rightarrow5)$ is (4: x: $=$x$-$y; 5:).
All other paths are not defined. Notice how test reports (e.g. (y$>$x?**true**)) are represented. Notice also that **begin**'s and **end**'s do not appear in path descriptions.

EXAMPLE 4. Let st be

> **begin** 1: **read**(x); **read**(y);
>   2: **while** y$>$x **do** x: $=$x$+$1
>   3: **end**.

$(1\rightarrow2)$ is (1: **read**(x); **read**(y); 2:).
$(2\rightarrow3)$ is (2: (y$>$x?**false**); 3:).
$(2\rightarrow2)$ is (2: (y$>$x?**true**); x: $=$x$+$1; 2:).

All other paths are not defined. Even though it is written before the while statement, label 2 is attached to the test of the loop and is reached before each
execution of the loop body. See the next example for more details.

EXAMPLE 5. Let st be

   begin 1: x:=1; 2:; 3: **while** x≤42 **do** x:=x+1; 4: **end**.

$(1 \to 2)$ is $(1: x:=1; 2:)$.
$(2 \to 3)$ is $(2:; 3:)$.
$(3 \to 3)$ is $(3: (x≤42?\textbf{true}); x:=x+1; 3:)$.
$(3 \to 4)$ is $(3: (x≤42?\textbf{false}); 4:)$.
All other paths are not defined. The purpose of this example is to show how to
distinguish between a label which truly precedes a while statement (label 2)
from a label which, even though written before the while statement, is reached
at every iteration before the test of the loop condition (label 3).

EXAMPLE 6. Let st be

   begin
   1: x:=15; y:=0;
   2: **while** x>0 **do**
      begin
      x:=x-1;
      3: **if** y>0 **then** x:=x-1
         else x:=x+1
      end;
   4: **end**.

$(1 \to 2)$ is $(1: x:=15; y:=0; 2:)$.
$(2 \to 3)$ is $(2: (x>0?\textbf{true}); x:=x-1; 3:)$.
$(3 \to 2)$ is $(3: \textbf{if } y>0 \textbf{ then } x:=x-1 \textbf{ else } x:=x+1; 2:)$.
$(2 \to 4)$ is $(2: (x>0?\textbf{false}); 4:)$.
All other paths are not defined.

EXAMPLE 7. Let st be

   begin
   1: **if** x>y **then**
      2: **begin**
      while x>y **do** 3: x:=x-1;
      y:=-x
      end

```
            else
              begin
              while y>x do x:=x+1;
              4: y:= −x
              end;
        5:
        end.
```

$(1{\rightarrow}2)$ is $(1\colon (x{>}y?\textbf{true}); 2\colon)$.
$(2{\rightarrow}3)$ is $(2\colon (x{>}y?\textbf{true}); 3\colon)$.
$(2{\rightarrow}5)$ is $(2\colon (x{>}y?\textbf{false}); y\colon= −x; 5\colon)$.
$(3{\rightarrow}3)$ is $(3\colon x\colon=x−1; (x{>}y?\textbf{true}); 3\colon)$.
$(3{\rightarrow}5)$ is $(3\colon x\colon=x−1; (x{>}y?\textbf{false}); y\colon= −x; 5\colon)$.
$(1{\rightarrow}4)$ is $(1\colon (x{>}y?\textbf{false}); \textbf{while } y{>}x \textbf{ do } x\colon=x+1; 4\colon)$.
$(4{\rightarrow}5)$ is $(4\colon y\colon= −x; 5\colon)$.
All other paths are not defined.

Paths are represented by a sequence of SM-Pascal statements and test reports of the form (t?**true**) or (t?**false**), where t is a predicate on S. The semantics of SM-Pascal statements are defined in Chapter 5 in function-theoretic terms. Likewise, we define the semantics of test reports in function-theoretic terms, by means of two axioms to be added to system FA.

DEFINITION 2. The semantics of test reports are defined as follows

$$[(t?\textbf{true})] = [t,s].$$ (a9)

$$[(t?\textbf{false})] = [\tilde{\ }t,s].$$ (a10)

Using these axioms, we define the notions of *path function,* i.e. the function computed by a path. Labels do not affect path functions.

DEFINITION 3. The *path function* of path $(i{\rightarrow}j)$ is the functional abstraction of $(i{\rightarrow}j)$. It is denoted $[i{\rightarrow}j]$.

Hence, in Example 1, assuming that the E-space considered is **real** and that no input or output space is considered, we have:

$$[1{\rightarrow}2] = [\textbf{true},4.].$$
$$[2{\rightarrow}3] = [\textbf{true},2{*}x+1].$$

Exercises

1. [A] Determine all the defined paths of the following SM-Pascal statement.
   a) st = **begin** 1: st1; 2: st2; 3: st3; 4: **end**.
   b) st = **begin** 1: st1; st2; 2: **end**.
   c) st = **begin** 1: **if** t **then** 2: st1 **else** 3: st2; 4: **end**.
   d) st = **begin** 1: **if** t **then** st1; 2: **end**.
   e) st = **begin** 1: **if** t **then** 2: st1; 3: **end**.

2. [B] Same as 1.
   a) st = **begin** 1: **if** t **then** 2: st1 **else** st2; 3: **end**.
   b) st = **begin** 1: **if** t **then** st1 **else** 2: st2; 3: **end**.
   c) st = **begin** 1: **if** t **then** 2: st1 **else** **begin** st2; 3: **end**; 4: **end**.
   d) st = **begin** 1: **if** t **then** st1 **else** **begin** st2; 2: **end**; 3: **end**.
   e) st = **begin** 1: **if** t **then** 2: st1 **else** **begin** st2; 3: st3 **end**; 4: **end**.

3. [B] Same as 1.
   a) st = **begin** 1:; **while** t **do** st1; 2: **end**.
   b) st = **begin** 1: **while** t **do** st1; 2: **end**.
   c) st = **begin** 1:; 2: **while** t **do** st1; 3: **end**.
   d) st = **begin** 1:; 2: **while** t **do** 3: st1; 4: **end**.
   e) st = **begin** 1: **while** t **do** **begin** st1; 2: **end**; 3: **end**.

4. [B] Same as 1.
   a) st = **begin** 1:; **while** t **do** **if** u **then** st1; 2: **end**.
   b) st = **begin** 1:; **while** t **do** 2: **if** u **then** st1; 3: **end**.
   c) st = **begin** 1:; **while** t **do** **if** u **then** 2: st1; 3: **end**.
   d) st = **begin** 1:; **while** t **do** 2: **if** u **then**
                              begin 3: st1; 4: **end**; 5: **end**.
   e) st = **begin** 1:; **while** t **do** **if** u **then**
                              begin st1; 2: **end**; 3: **end**.

5. [C] Same as 1.
   a) st = **begin** 1: **while** t **do** **if** u **then** st1 **else** st2; 2: **end**.
   b) st = **begin** 1: **while** t **do** **if** u **then** st1 **else**
                              begin st2; 2: **end**; 3: **end**.
   c) st = **begin** 1: **while** t **do** **if** u **then** 2: st1 **else** st2; 3: **end**.
   d) st = **begin** 1: **while** t **do** **if** u **then** st1 **else** st2; 2: **end**.
   e) st = **begin** 1: **while** t **do** **if** u **then** 2: st1 **else** 3: st2; 4: **end**.

6. [B] Assuming the proper space to be **real** and the input space to be L*(**real**), determine the path functions of the statement given in Example 2.

7. [B] Assuming the proper space to be:

> set
>   x, y: **real**
> **end,**

and the input space to be L*(**real**), determine the path functions of Example 3.

8. [B] Same as exercise 7, for Example 4.

9. [B] Same as exercise 6, for Example 5.

10. [B] Same as exercise 7, for Example 6.

11. [B] Same as exercise 7, for Example 7.

2   The Cutpoint Theorem for Partial Correctness

THEOREM 1 (Cutpoint Theorem for Partial Correctness; due to Floyd, 1967). Let st be a statement on space S and let $1, 2, \ldots k$ be k labels appearing in st such that 1 is attached to the beginning of st and k is attached to the end ι f it. Let $a_1, a_2, \ldots a_k$ be predicates on S (which characterize correct states at labels $1, 2, \ldots k$ respectively). If for any defined path $(i \rightarrow j)$ the formula $c_{ij}(s)$ defined by

$$a_i(s) \; \wedge \; s{:}\textbf{dom}([i \rightarrow j]) \; \Rightarrow \; a_j([i \rightarrow j](s))$$

is a P-tautology on S then st is partially correct wrt the I-specification (S,R), where

$$R = \{(s,s') | \; a_1(s) \; \wedge \; a_k(s')\}.$$

Proof. Let s be a state in **dom**(R). Then $a_1(s)$ holds. We assume that s:**dom**([st]). Then the list of consecutive labels reached by st during execution on state s is finite, say $(l_1(s), l_2(s), \ldots l_h(s))$. Note that, by definition, we have $l_h(s) = k$ for any s. A simple induction (whose basis is $a_1(s)$ and whose induction step is $c_{ij}(s)$) on the list of labels (which is simply ordered and well-founded) yields that a_k holds for the state:

$$([l_1(s) \rightarrow l_2(s)] \; * \; [l_2(s) \rightarrow l_3(s)] \; * \ldots * \; [l_{h-1}(s) \rightarrow l_h(s)]) \, (s),$$

which -by definition of the path functions- is equal to [st](s). We have deduced $a_k([st](s))$ from $a_1(s)$ and $s:\mathbf{dom}([st])$. This can be rewritten:

$$a_1(s) \ \wedge \ s:\mathbf{dom}([st]) \ \Rightarrow \ a_1(s) \ \wedge \ a_k([st](s)),$$

or

$$s:\mathbf{dom}(R) \ \wedge \ s:\mathbf{dom}([st]) \ \Rightarrow \ (s,[st](s)):R.$$

QED

EXAMPLE 8. Let IS and OS be L*(**integer**) and S be

> **set**
> > x, y: **integer**
> **end**.

We define ES = IS×S×OS. An element of ES shall be denoted by (is,s,os) and abbreviated by es. Also, we abbreviate gcd(x(s),y(s)) by gcd(s).

Let Gc be the following statement on space S. The labels appearing on Gc have not been chosen so as to simplify the proof, but rather to make it more challenging. For a discussion on the tradeoffs involved in deciding how many labels to place, see problem 1. For a discussion of where to place labels, see problem 3.

```
Gc =
begin
1: read(x); read(y);
while x ≠ y do
   if x>y then 2: x:=x−y
   else 3: y:=y−x;
write(x);
4:
end.
```

Let R be the I-relation on S defined by

$$R = \{((is,s,os),(is',s',os'))| \ \ \mathbf{lng}(is) = 4 \ \wedge \ \mathbf{car}(is) > 0$$
$$\wedge \ \mathbf{car}{\bullet}\mathbf{cdr}(is) > 0$$
$$\wedge \ \mathbf{car}(os') = \ gcd(\mathbf{car}(is),\mathbf{car}{\bullet}\mathbf{cdr}(is))\}.$$

We want to prove the correctness of Gc wrt (IS,OS,R).

We shall adopt the following abbreviations:

$$is1 = \textbf{car}(is),$$
$$is2 = \textbf{car•cdr}(is),$$
$$s0 = (is1,is2),$$
$$\textbf{cdr2} = \textbf{cdr•cdr}.$$

The predicates attached to labels 1, 2, 3 and 4 are defined as follows.

a_1: $\textbf{lng}(is) = 4 \wedge is1 > 0 \wedge is2 > 0 \wedge os = (\ )$.
a_2: $gcd(s) = gcd(s0) \wedge x(s) > 0 \wedge y(s) > 0 \wedge x(s) > y(s) \wedge os = (\ )$.
a_3: $gcd(s) = gcd(s0) \wedge x(s) > 0 \wedge y(s) > 0 \wedge x(s) < y(s) \wedge os = (\ )$.
a_4: $\textbf{car}(os) = gcd(s0)$.

We study one by one all the defined paths.

$(1 \rightarrow 2)$ is (1: $\textbf{read}(x)$; $\textbf{read}(y)$; $(x \neq y?\textbf{true})$; $(x > y?\textbf{true})$; 2:).
$[1 \rightarrow 2] = [\textbf{read}(x)] * [\textbf{read}(y)] * [(x \neq y?\textbf{true})] * [(x > y?\textbf{true})]$.

It is left to the reader to verify that this is equal to

$$[\textbf{lng}(is) \geqslant 2 \wedge is1 > is2, (\textbf{cdr2}(is),s0,os)].$$

Condition c_{12} is

$\textbf{lng}(is) = 4 \wedge is1 > 0 \wedge is2 > 0 \wedge os = () \wedge \textbf{lng}(is) \geqslant 2 \wedge is1 > is2$
$\Rightarrow gcd(s0) = gcd(s0) \wedge is1 > 0 \wedge is2 > 0 \wedge is1 > is2 \wedge os = (),$

which is valid.

$(1 \rightarrow 3)$ is (1: $\textbf{read}(x)$; $\textbf{read}(y)$; $(x \neq y?\textbf{true})$; $(x > y?\textbf{false})$; 3:).
It is left to the reader to verify that

$$[1 \rightarrow 3] = [\textbf{lng}(is) \geqslant 2 \wedge is1 < is2, (\textbf{cdr2}(is),s0,os)]$$

and that c_{13} is a tautology.

$(1 \rightarrow 4)$ is (1: $\textbf{read}(x)$; $\textbf{read}(y)$; $(x \neq y?\textbf{false})$; $\textbf{write}(x)$; 4:).

$[1 \rightarrow 4] = [\textbf{read}(x)] * [\textbf{read}(y)] * [x(s) = y(s),s] * [\textbf{write}(x)]$.
$= [\textbf{lng}(is) \geqslant 2 \wedge is1 = is2, (\textbf{cdr2}(is),s0,\textbf{app}(os,is1))]$.

Condition c_{14} is

$$\textbf{lng}(is) = 4 \ \wedge \ is1 > 0 \ \wedge \ is2 > 0 \ \wedge \ os = () \ \wedge \ \textbf{lng}(is) \geqslant 2 \ \wedge \ is1 = is2$$
$$\Rightarrow \textbf{car}(\textbf{app}(os, is1)) \ = \ \gcd(s0),$$

which is valid.

$(2 \rightarrow 2)$ is $(2: \ x := x - y; \ (x \neq y? \textbf{true}); \ (x > y? \textbf{true}); \ 2:)$.

$$
\begin{aligned}
[2 \rightarrow 2 \ ] \ &= \ [\textbf{true}, \ (is, (x(s) - y(s), y(s)), os)] \\
&\quad * \ [x(s) \neq y(s), s] \\
&\quad * \ [x(s) > y(s), s] \\
&= \ [x(s) - y(s) > y(s), \ (is, (x(s) - y(s), y(s)), os)] \ .
\end{aligned}
$$

Condition c_{22} is

$$\gcd(s) = \gcd(s0) \ \wedge \ x(s) > 0 \ \wedge \ y(s) > 0 \ \wedge \ x(s) > y(s) \ \wedge \ os = (\ ) \ \wedge$$
$$x(s) - y(s) > y(s)$$
$$\Rightarrow \gcd(x(s) - y(s), y(s)) = \gcd(s0) \ \wedge \ x(s) - y(s) > 0 \ \wedge$$
$$y(s) > 0 \ \wedge \ x(s) - y(s) > y(s),$$

which is valid.

It is left to the reader to treat paths (2,3), (3,3), (3,2), (2,4) and (3,4) as shown on the selected paths above. For simpler ways to prove this statement, see exercises 1 and 2.

Exercises

1. [B] Redo the proof of statement Gc (Example 8) using the following labels.

> **begin**
> 1: **read**(x); **read**(y);
> 2: **while** $x \neq y$ **do**
>   **if** $x > y$ **then** $x := x - y$
>   **else** $y := y - x$;
> 3: **write**(x);
> 4: **end**.

2. [B] Same as exercise 1, with the following labels.

> **begin**
> 1: **read**(x); **read**(y);

```
2: while x ≠ y do
      if x>y then 3: x: = x−y
      else 4: y: = y−x;
   write(x);
5: end.
```

3 The Cutpoint Theorem for Total Correctness

Let st be a statement on space S and let s be an element of S. Let $l_1(s)$, $l_2(s)$ . . . be the sequence of labels reached upon execution of st on s. The non-termination of st on state s may occur in one of two ways: Either the sequence of labels is infinite, or the control of the program leaves a label but does not reach the following label, due to an infinite loop in between. The theorem for total correctness must ensure the freedom from both occurrences.

THEOREM 2 (Cutpoint Theorem for Total Correctness). Let st be a statement on space S and let 1, 2, . . . k be k labels appearing in st such that 1 is attached to the beginning of st and k is attached to the end. Let a_1, a_2, . . . a_k be predicates on S (which characterize correct states at labels 1, 2, . . . k respectively) and let u be an E-function from $S \times \{1..k\}$ to some well-founded set $(W, <)$. For any label i, we define nxt(i) by $\{j | (i \rightarrow j) \text{ is a defined path}\}$. For each label i<k, we define two predicates:

$$t_i(s) = (a_i(s) \Rightarrow (\exists j: nxt(i), s:\mathbf{dom}([i \rightarrow j]))).$$
$$c_i(s) = (\forall j: nxt(i), a_i(s) \wedge s:\mathbf{dom}([i \rightarrow j]))$$
$$\Rightarrow a_j([i \rightarrow j](s)) \wedge u([i \rightarrow j](s),j) < u(s,i)).$$

If, for every label i, $t_i(s)$ and $c_i(s)$ are valid then the statement st is correct wrt the I-specification (S,R), where

$$R = \{(s,s') | a_1(s) \wedge a_k(s')\}.$$

Proof. Let s be an element of S such that $a_1(s)$ holds. From $a_1(s)$ we must deduce that

— s:**dom**([st]), i.e. that execution of st on s terminates,
— (s,[st](s)):R, i.e. that $a_k([st](s))$ holds.

In order to do so, one can prove that te(s) is finite then prove by induction that if execution of st on s reaches some label distinct from k, then the assertion attached to that label holds and the execution reaches another label. The basis of induction follows from $a_1(s)$ and $t_1(s)$; the induction step follows from $t_i(s)$ and $c_i(s)$.

QED

REMARK 1. Let i be a label distinct from k. For any two labels j′ and j″ in nxt(i), we can assert that

$$\mathbf{dom}([i{\to}j']) \cap \mathbf{dom}([i{\to}j'']) = \{\},$$

because SM-Pascal is a deterministic language, and because of the definition of path functions. Condition t_i ensures that the union of $\mathbf{dom}([i{\to}j])$ for all j in nxt(i) is equal to the set of feasible states, i.e. states satisfying predicate a_i.

EXAMPLE 9.

We shall prove the total correctness of program Gc wrt (S,R) (see Example 8). Since its partial correctness has been proven, it suffices to prove its termination wrt (S,R), namely its total correctness wrt R′, where R′ = $\{(s,s')|\ a_1(s)\}$. In this example, we shall simply do the non-trivial part of the proof and leave it to the reader to do the (straightforward) generation and verification of conditions t_i and c_i for each label.

$$a1: \mathbf{lng}(is) = 4 \ \wedge \ is1 > 0 \ \wedge \ is2 > 0.$$
$$a2: x(s) > 0 \ \wedge \ y(s) > 0 \ \wedge \ x(s) > y(s).$$
$$a3: x(s) > 0 \ \wedge \ y(s) > 0 \ \wedge \ x(s) < y(s).$$
$$a4: \mathbf{true}.$$

The well-founded set chosen for this proof is $(W, <)$, where

$$W = \mathbf{set}$$
$$\mathbf{crt}$$
$$a, b: \mathbf{integer};$$
$$\mathbf{sub}$$
$$a > 0 \ \wedge \ b > 0$$
$$\mathbf{end},$$

and

$$< \ = \ \{(w,w')|\ a(w) < a(w') \ \vee \ a(w) = a(w') \wedge b(w) < b(w')\}.$$

In other words, W is the set of pairs of non-negative integers and $<$ is the lexicographic ordering on W.

Function u from $S \times \{1,2,3,4\}$ to W is:

$$u((is,s,os),4) = (1,0).$$
$$u((is,s,os),3) = (2, x(s)+y(s)).$$
$$u((is,s,os),2) = (2, x(s)+y(s)).$$
$$u((is,s,os),1) = (3,0).$$

Exercises

1. [B] Prove the total correctness of the following statement wrt the specification given, using the labels shown.
Space:

```
S = set
crt
    dr, dd, qt: integer; (*divisor, dividend, quotient*)
sub
    dr>0 ∧ dd>0
end.
```

Specification: (S,R), where

$$R = \{(s,s') \mid dd(s) = dr(s)*qt(s') + dd(s') \ \wedge \ dd(s') < dr(s)\}.$$

Statement: st =

```
          begin
        1: qt: = 0;
        2: while dd≥dr do
             begin
             qt: = qt+1;
             dd: = dd − dr
             end;
        3:
          end.
```

2. [C] (Due to Manna, 1974) Same as 1.
Space:

```
S = set
    a, b, c, d: integer
end.
```

Specification: (S,R), where

$$R = \{(s,s') \mid d(s) \geq 0 \ \wedge \ a(s')**2 \leq d(s) < (a(s')+1)**2\}.$$

This specification expresses that a(s′) must be the floor of the square root of d(s). Statement, st =

```
begin
1: a: = 0; b: = 1; c: = 1;
2: while d⩾b do
   begin
   a: = a + 1;
   c: = c + 2;
   b: = b + c
   end;
3: end.
```

This method for computing the floor of the square root of a positive integer is based on the identity:

$$(n+1)**2 = 1+3+5+ \ldots +(2n+1).$$

(Hint: In order to write R as $\{(s,s′)|\ a_1(s) \wedge a_3(s′)\}$, you must introduce a constant, say s0).

3. [C] (Due to Manna, 1974). Same as 1.
   Space:

```
S = set
   a, b, c: integer
end.
```

Specification: (S,R), where

$$R = \{(s,s′)|\ b(s)\geq 0 \ \wedge \ c(s′) = a(s)**b(s)\}.$$

This specification expresses that c(s′) must equal a(s) raised to the power b(s).

Statement: st =

```
begin
1: c: = 1;
2: while b ≠ 0 do
   if b mod 2 = 0 then
      begin
      a: = a*a; b: = b/2
      end
   else
      begin
      b: = b − 1; c: = a*c
      end;
3: end.
```

4. [B] Same as 1.
   Space:

$$S = \textbf{set}$$
$$\textbf{crt}$$
$$\quad a, b: \textbf{integer};$$
$$\textbf{sub}$$
$$\quad a > 0 \ \wedge \ b > 0$$
$$\textbf{end}.$$

Specification: (S,R), where

$$R = \{(s,s') \mid a(s') = gcd(a(s), b(s))\}.$$

Statement:

```
st =
begin
1:; while a ≠ b do
    if a > b then begin a: = a − b; 2: end
    else begin b: = b − a; 3: end;
4:
end.
```

Note: This program is identical to that of Example 8; the labeling is not.

5. [B] Same as 1.
   Space:

$$S = \textbf{set}$$
$$\quad a, b, p: \textbf{integer}$$
$$\textbf{end}.$$

Specification: (S,R), where

$$R = \{(s,s') \mid b(s) \geqslant 0 \ \wedge \ p(s') = a(s) * b(s)\}.$$

Statement:

```
st =
begin
1: p: = 0;
while b > 0 do
    begin
    b: = b − 1;
    2: p: = p + a
    end;
3: end.
```

6. [B] Same space and statement as exercise 5; specification (S,R′), where R′ = {(s,s′) | b(s) ⩾ 0}.
What is the significance of this specification?

4 Problems

1. [B] Discuss the tradeoffs involved in deciding how many labels to put on a given statement st. In particular, tell what becomes of the Cutpoint Method Theorem of total correctness when only two labels are attached to statement st. Also, consider the case where you put enough labels to make conditions (t_i) in Theorem 2 vacuously true (This was a requirement in the original version of the method).

2. [C] Consider function u defined in Example 9. Note that, for a state s and a label i, a(u(s,i)) is a constant depending on i and not depending on s. We call this constant the *level* of label i.
   a) What is the purpose of the level of a label?
   b) What property does the level of a label have to meet?
   c) Is it always possible to assign levels to labels which meet this property?
   d) When it is possible, how should one do it? (Use the notion of *connected component* in graph theory).

3. [B] Redo the proof of Example 8 with the following set of labels.

```
begin
1: read(x);  read(y);
2: while x ≠ y do
   if x > y then x := x − y
   else y := y − x;
   write(x);
3:
end.
```

Give general guidelines regarding where to put labels on a while statement.

4. [B] Complete the details of the proof of Theorem 2.

5 Bibliography

The cutpoint method was proposed in 1967 by Floyd [2]. For a textbook-like presentation of the method and for more examples of proofs, consult [1], [3] and [4].

1: Anderson, R B. Proving Programs Correct. John Wiley, 1979.
2: Floyd, R W. Assigning Meanings to Programs. Proceedings, American Mathematical Society Symposium in Applied Mathematics. 1967, pp 19-31.
3: Livercy, C. Théorie des Programmes. Dunod, 1978.
4: Manna, Z. Mathematical Theory of Computation. McGraw-Hill, 1974.

Chapter 11

Proof of Recursive Functions

In this chapter we shall discuss proof methods for recursive functions. The first section is concerned with the semantics of recursion and the generation of functional abstractions for recursive functions. Section 2 introduces the computational induction method, which proves properties of recursive functions by induction on the depth of the recursion, and section 3 introduces the structural induction method, which proves properties of recursive functions by induction on the structural complexity of their arguments.

1 The Semantics of Recursion

In order to be consistent with the spirit of Chapter 5, we must define the semantics of a recursive **function** (in the SM-Pascal sense of the term) in terms of an internal function (in the mathematical sense of the term). A SM-Pascal **function** whose function heading reads as

$$\text{function } f(s:A):B$$

computes an E-function from set A to set B (see problem 2, Chapter 5). Without loss of generality, we can redefine function f so that the type of its argument coincides with its result type. Hence, without loss of generality, we shall only consider SM-Pascal **function**'s whose function heading reads as:

$$\text{function } f(s:S):S.$$

This SM-Pascal **function** computes an internal function on set S.

1.1 Recursive Declaration and Functional Abstraction

We consider the following SM-Pascal recursive **function** declaration which we call, for short, a recursive declaration:

```
function f (s: integer): integer;
begin
if s>100 then f:=s-10 else f:=f(f(s+11))
end.
```

We are interested in defining the functional abstraction of this **function**. Let's follow its execution on the argument 99:

$$f(99)$$
$$= [\textbf{if } s > 100 \textbf{ then } f := s - 10 \textbf{ else } f := f(f(s+11))] \ (99)$$
$$= f(f(110)).$$

From this step on, one may envisage many possible expansions of this expression:

a) Substituting both occurrences of f:
f(f(110))
= **if** (**if** $110 > 100$ **then** $110 - 10$ **else** f(f(121))) > 100
   then (**if** $110 > 100$ **then** $110 - 10$ **else** f(f(121))) $- 10$
   else f(f((**if** $110 > 100$ **then** $110 - 10$ **else** f(f(121))) $+ 11$)).

b) Substituting the inner occurrence of f:
f(f(110))
= f(**if** $110 > 100$ **then** $110 - 10$ **else** f(f(110+11)))

c) Substituting the outer occurrence of f:
f(f(110))
= **if** f(110) > 100 **then** f(110) $- 10$ **else** f(f(f(110)+11)).

Each one of these substitutions results from some *computation rule*. Manna ([5], 1974) lists six such rules:

1. Leftmost-Innermost (Call by Value) Rule: Replace only the leftmost innermost occurrence of f, that is the leftmost occurrence of f which has all its arguments free of f.
2. Parallel-Innermost Rule: Replace all the innermost occurrences of f simultaneously, that is the occurrences of f with all their arguments free of f.
3. Leftmost (Call by Name) Rule: Replace only the leftmost occurrence of f.
4. Parallel-Outermost Rule: Replace all the outermost occurrences of f simultaneously, that is all the occurrences of f which do not occur as arguments of other occurrences of f.
5. Free-Argument Rule: Replace simultaneously all occurrences of f which have at least one argument free of f.
6. Full-Substitution Rule: Replace all occurrences of f simultaneously.

Let f be a recursive **function** and C1 and C2 two computation rules. For any s in S, if execution of f on s following rules C1 and C2 converges in both cases then the value returned in both cases is the same. However, one rule may lead to an infinite execution whereas the other terminates.

Among the substitutions of f(f(110)) shown above, (a) can be interpreted as an instance of the full-substitution rule; (b) can be interpreted as an instance of the leftmost-innermost rule, the parallel-innermost rule or the free-argument rule; (c) can be interpreted as an instance of the leftmost rule or the parallel-outermost rule.

Clearly, one can only define the functional abstraction of a recursive **function** with respect to a computation rule.

DEFINITION 1. Let f be a SM-Pascal recursive declaration on space S. The *functional abstraction of f wrt computation rule C* is the I-function on S defined by

{(s,s')| if **function** f is invoked with argument s and executed following rule C then it terminates and returns s'}.

The interest of this definition is solely theoretical. It is usually difficult to determine the functional abstraction of a recursive **function** on the basis of this definition.

1.2 Recursive Equations and Least Fixpoints

We consider the following recursive declaration:

function f(s:S):S;   (0)
begin
if t(s) **then** f: = a(s)
else f: = b(s, f(h₁(s)), f(h₂(s)), ... f(hₙ(s)))
end.

We wish to abstract all the syntactic details of this recursive declaration and interpret it in purely function-theoretic terms. In order to do so, we need to define a new concept.

DEFINITION 2. A *functional* on set S is an I-function on the set of I-functions on S.

EXAMPLE 1. Let S be a set, let f0 be an internal function on S, and let t be a predicate on S. Then

$$\{(f,f')|\ f' = f0*f\},\ \text{and}$$
$$\{(f,f')|\ f' = [t,s]*f\}$$

are two functionals on S.

We consider the recursive declaration (0) above and we abbreviate the expression

$$b(s, f(h_1(s)), \; f(h_2(s)), \; \ldots \; f(h_n(s)))$$

by $E(f)(s)$, where E is defined in terms of b, h_1, h_2, . . . h_n. Let k be the function defined by expression E and let T, A and NT be the I-functions on S defined by:

$$T = [t,s],$$
$$A = [:\mathbf{def}(a),a],$$
$$NT = [\tilde{}t,s],$$

where s is an element of S.

We leave it to the reader to convince himself that by abstracting the recursive declaration (0) above into the equation

$$f = T*A \; \cup \; NT*k(f), \tag{1}$$

we remain faithful to the semantics of:

— Alternative statements (see section 3, Chapter 5),
— **Function** declarations (see problem 2, Chapter 5).

Equation (1) is said to be a *recursive equation*. If we wish to highlight the relationship of equation (1) with the recursive declaration (0), we say that equation (1) is the recursive equation *derived from* the recursive declaration (0).

If we define functional K by

$$\{(f,f') \mid \; f' = T*A \; \cup \; NT*k(f)\},$$

then we can write the recursive equation (1) as:

$$f = K(f). \tag{1'}$$

DEFINITION 3. Function f0 is said to be a *fixpoint* of the recursive equation $f = K(f)$ (or, equivalently, a fixpoint of functional K) iff f0 is equal to K(f0).

A recursive equation may have more than one fixpoint: Consider, for example, $f = f$. If we are to define a unique solution to the equation $f = K(f)$, we must introduce a criterion for selection among the fixpoints of the equation.

DEFINITION 4. The solution of equation $f = K(f)$ is (if it exists) the smallest (with respect to inclusion) fixpoint of the equation. It is called the *least fixpoint* of equation $f = K(f)$ (or: of functional K).

Because of the antisymmetry of the relation of inclusion, a recursive equation may not have more than one least fixpoint. However, a recursive equation may fail to have a least fixpoint or even a fixpoint at all.

Theorem 1 provides a sufficient condition for a functional to have a least fixpoint. Before we give the theorem, we need to introduce some preliminary concepts.

DEFINITION 5. A functional K on S is said to be *monotonic* iff

$$f \subseteq g \Rightarrow K(f) \subseteq K(g).$$

EXAMPLE 2. Let

$$K1 = \{(f,f')| \ f' = [t,s]*f\}, \text{ for some predicate t on S,}$$
$$K2 = \{(f,f')|f' = f0 \cup f\}, \text{ for some I-function f0 on S, and}$$
$$K3 = \{(f,f')| \ f' = I - f\}.$$

It is left to the reader to verify that K1 and K2 are monotonic whereas K3 is not.

DEFINITION 6. Let $c = (f_1, f_2, \dots)$ be an infinite sequence of I-functions on S. We say that c is a *chain* iff for all i, f_i is a subset of f_{i+1}. The *least upper bound* of chain c is the union of all f_i's. We denote it by $lub(f_i)$.

EXAMPLE 3.
If S = **integer** and $f_i = \{(s,s')| \ s < i \ \wedge \ s = s'\}$, then (f_i) is indeed a chain and $lub(f_i)$ is the identity function on S.

DEFINITION 7. A functional K on S is said to be *continuous* iff
a) It is monotonic,
b) For any chain (f_i), $lub(K(f_i)) = K(lub(f_i))$.

EXAMPLE 4. We consider the chain (f_i) given above and the functional K defined by $K = \{(f,f')| \ f' = [s \geqslant 0,s]*f\}$. Clearly, K is monotonic and $lub(K(f_i)) = K(lub(f_i))$, for the particular chain (f_i) given above. It is left to the reader to prove that K is actually continuous.

THEOREM 1 (due to Kleene, 1952). Every continuous functional has a least fixpoint, which is $lub(K**i(\{\}))$.

Proof. Because K is monotonic, the sequence $(K^{**}i(\{\}))$ is a chain. We denote the least upper bound of $(K^{**}i(\{\}))$ by f. We shall show that f is a least fixpoint of functional K in two steps.

Step 1: We must show that f is a fixpoint of K.

$$
\begin{aligned}
& K(f) \\
& = K(\text{lub}(K^{**}i(\{\}))) && \text{by definition,} \\
& = \text{lub}(K^{**}i+1(\{\})) && \text{K is continuous,} \\
& = \text{lub}(K^{**}i(\{\})) && K^{**}i(\{\}) \text{ is a chain,} \\
& = f && \text{by definition.}
\end{aligned}
$$

Step 2: We must show that if g is a fixpoint of K then f is a subset of g. In order to do so, it suffices to prove that for any non-negative integer i, $K^{**}i(\{\})$ is a subset of g. We do a proof by simple induction:

i) $K^{**}0(\{\}) = \{\}$ is a subset of g,
ii) $K^{**}i-1(\{\}) \subseteq g$
$$
\begin{aligned}
& \Rightarrow K(K^{**}i-1(\{\})) \subseteq K(g) && \text{K is monotonic,} \\
& \Rightarrow K^{**}i(\{\}) \subseteq g && \text{g is a fixpoint.}
\end{aligned}
$$

QED

In order for Kleene's Theorem to be used in practice, we need a simple condition for the continuity of functionals. This is given by a theorem due to Manna, 1974.

THEOREM 2. Any functional whose expression is made up of the relative product of some constant functions with the function variable is continuous.

Hence f0*f, f*f1 and f0*f*f1 are all expressions of continuous functionals of the variable f.

1.3 Functional Abstraction and Least Fixpoint

Given a recursive declaration written in SM-Pascal, one can:

— determine its functional abstraction fc with respect to some computation rule, or
— determine the least fixpoint fl of the recursive equation derived from it.

One may be tempted to define the semantics of the recursive declaration by either fc or fl. Hence it is important that we investigate the relationship between the functional abstraction of a recursive declaration with respect to some computation rule and the least fixpoint of the recursive equation derived from it. For the sake of simplicity, the least fixpoint of the recursive equation (e) derived from a recursive declaration (d) will be called the least fixpoint of the recursive declaration (d).

The two theorems below shed some light on this relationship. We shall give both of them without proof. (Their proof is given in Chapter 5 of Manna, 1974).

THEOREM 3 (due to J M Cadiou, 1972). For any computation rule, the functional abstraction fc of a recursive declaration is a subset of its least fixpoint fl.

For any s in **dom**(fc) and **dom**(fl), fc(s) = fl(s). However, there may be elements in the domain of fl for which execution of the recursive **function** following some computation rule fails to terminate.

THEOREM 4 (due to Manna, 1974). For the Parallel-Outermost Rule, the Free-Argument Rule and the Full-Substitution Rule, the functional abstraction of a recursive declaration equals its least fixpoint.

In the remainder of this chapter, we shall always use the Full-Substitution Rule, unless specified otherwise. Hence we can talk about the functional abstraction of a recursive declaration without specifying the computation rule; the Full-Substitution Rule is implied.

1.4 Examples

Below are some examples to help the reader see the relationship between the functional abstraction of a recursive declaration and its least fixpoint. The examples are ordered in increasing level of difficulty.

EXAMPLE 5. Let:

> **function** f(s:S):S;
> **begin**
> **if false then** f: = s0 **else** f: = f(s)
> **end.**

We derive the following recursive equation:

$$f = [\textbf{false},s]*[\textbf{true},s0] \cup [\textbf{true},s]*f,$$

which can be simplified to:

$$f = f.$$

Any I-function on S is a fixpoint of this recursive equation. The least fixpoint is: {}. Clearly, the functional abstraction of the recursive **function** declared above is empty since the function fails to terminate for every input.

EXAMPLE 6. Let:

> **function** f(s:integer):integer;
> **begin**
> **if** s = 0 **then** f: = 1 **else** f: = f(s)
> **end**.

We derive the following recursive equation:

$$f = [s = 0,s]*[\text{true},1] \cup [s \neq 0,s]*f,$$

which we can simplify to:

$$f = [s = 0,1] \cup [s \neq 0,s]*f.$$

Any function which contains the pair (0,1) is a fixpoint of this recursive equation. Hence the least fixpoint is {(0,1)}. Clearly, the recursive **function** declared above is defined only for 0, and it returns 1.

EXAMPLE 7. Let:

> **function** f(s: integer): integer;
> **begin**
> **if** s = 0 **then** f: = 1 **else** f: = f(s−1)
> **end**.

We derive the following recursive equation:

$$f = [s = 0,s]*[\text{true},1] \cup [s \neq 0,s]*[\text{true},s−1]*f,$$

which we transform into:

$$f = [s = 0,1] \cup [s \neq 0,s−1]*f. \tag{1}$$

Claim: [s⩾0,1] is a fixpoint of recursive equation (1).
Proof: [s=0,1] ∪ [s≠0,s−1]*[s⩾0,1]
    = [s=0,1] ∪ [s≠0 ∧ s−1⩾0, 1]
    = [s=0 ∨ s>0 , 1]
    = [s⩾0,1].

QED

We have not shown that [s⩾0,1] is the least fixpoint of equation (1), even though it is (one can prove so by simple induction). Clearly, function f computes [s⩾0,1]: It is defined for non-negative integers only, and it always returns 1.

EXAMPLE 8. Let:

> **function** f(s: **integer**): **integer**;
> **begin**
> **if** s=0 **then** f:=1 **else** f:=s*f(s−1)
> **end**.

We derive from it the following recursive equation:

$$f = [s=0,1] \ \cup \ [s≠0,s] * ([\textbf{true},s] \ \textbf{times} \ ([\textbf{true},s−1]*f)) \tag{1}$$

where

$$[p,E] \ \textbf{times} \ [p',E'] \ = \ [p \wedge p', E(s) * E'(s)].$$

(In this particular formula, "*" represents integer multiplication).

Claim: [s⩾0,s!] is a fixpoint of equation (1).

Proof: (In the proof below, "*" will be used to represent integer multiplication and relative product of functions. The context easily tells which meaning is implied).

> [**true**,s−1]*f
> = [**true**,s−1]*[s⩾0,s!]
> = [s>0,(s−1)!].
> [**true**,s] **times** ([**true**,s−1]*f)
> = [s>0, s * (s−1)!]
> = [s>0,s!].

$$[s \neq 0,s] * ([\text{true},s] \text{ times } ([\text{true},s-1]*f))$$
$$= [s \neq 0,s]*[s>0,s!]$$
$$= [s>0,s!].$$
$$[s=0,1] \cup [s \neq 0,s] * ([\text{true},s] \text{ times } ([\text{true},s-1]*f))$$
$$= [s=0,1] \cup [s>0,s!]$$
$$= [s \geqslant 0,s!].$$

Using Kleene's Theorem and assuming the functional of equation (1) to be continuous, one can actually prove that $[s \geqslant 0,s!]$ is the least fixpoint of (1) by showing:

— first that $K^{**}i(\langle\rangle) = [s \geqslant 0 \wedge s<i, s!]$,
— second that $\text{lub}([s \geqslant 0 \wedge s<i, s!]) = [s \geqslant 0,s!]$.

EXAMPLE 9. Let

$$S = \textbf{set}$$
$$a, b: \textbf{integer}$$
$$\textbf{end}.$$

We consider the following recursive declaration:

> **function** f(s:S):S;
> **begin**
> **if** b=0 **then** f: = (a,0) **else** f: = f(a+1,b−1)
> **end**.

We derive the following recursive equation:

$$f = [b(s)=0,(a(s),0)] \cup [b(s) \neq 0,s]*(a*\text{inc},b*\text{dec})*f, \tag{1}$$

where

> inc is the I-function on **integer**: $[\text{true},x+1]$,
> dec is the I-function on **integer**: $[\text{true},x-1]$,

and

> (g,h) is the I-function on S $[:\textbf{dom}(g) \wedge :\textbf{dom}(h), (g(s),h(s))]$,
> (g and h are E-functions from S to **integer**).

One may prove that $f = [b(s) \geq 0, (a(s) + b(s), 0)]$ is a fixpoint for recursive equation (1). In order to prove that this is the least fixpoint of the recursive equation, one may:

— prove that the functional K of the recursive equation is continuous,
— show that $K^{**}i(\{\}) = [b(s) \geq 0 \wedge b(s) < i, (a(s) + b(s), 0)]$,
— show that $lub(K^{**}i(\{\})) = [b(s) \geq 0, (a(s) + b(s), 0)]$.

Clearly, $[b(s) \geq 0, (a(s) + b(s), 0)]$ is the function computed by the SM-Pascal **function** given in the recursive declaration above.

Determining the least fixpoint of a recursive equation has three major drawbacks:

— It requires a great deal of ingenuity.
— It is very difficult to prove even when the guess is right.
— It is often unnecessary because the property one is interested in proving about the recursive function may require little knowledge about the functional properties of the least fixpoint. For example, imagine that we are only interested in proving that the "final" value of a in Example 9 is a+b but we are not interested in the "final" value of b.

For all these reasons, we shall, in sections 2 and 3, turn our attention to inductive methods of proof. Notice that the drawbacks listed above sound very similar to those mentioned regarding symbolic execution.

1.5 Exercises

1. [A] From the recursive declaration below, derive a recursive equation and find its least fixpoint. Prove formally that the function you have guessed is a fixpoint and give at least an informal argument to support your belief that it is the least fixpoint.

```
function f (s: integer): integer;
begin
if s = 0 then f: = 0 else f: = 1 + f(s − 1)
end.
```

2. [A] Same as exercise 1.

```
function f (s: integer): integer;
begin
if s ≤ 0 then f: = 1 else f: = 1 + f(s − 1)
end.
```

3. [A] Same as exercise 1.

```
function f (s: integer): integer;
begin
if s = 0 then f: = 1 else f: = 2*f(s−1)
end.
```

4. [B] Same as exercise 1.

```
function f(s: integer): integer;
begin
if s = 1 then f: = 1 else f: = s+f(s−1)
end.
```

5. [B] Same as exercise 1.

```
function f(s: integer): integer;
begin
if s ≤ 1 then f: = s else f: = f(s−2)
end.
```

6. [B] Same as exercise 1.

```
function f(s: integer): integer;
begin
if s ≤ 2 then f: = s else f: = f(s−3)
end.
```

7. [C] Same as exercise 1.

```
function f(s: integer): integer;
begin
if s > 100 then f: = s−10 else f: = f(f(s+11))
end.
```

8. [B] Consider the recursive declaration of exercise 7. Compute f(99) following each one of the six computation rules.

9. [B] We consider the following recursive declaration.

```
function f(s: integer): integer;
begin
if s = 0 then f: = 0 else f: = f(f(s−1))
end.
```

a) Compute f(3) using the full substitution computational rule, then the leftmost rule.

b) Derive the recursive equation corresponding to this recursive declaration.

c) Find the least fixpoint of the equation.

2 Proof of Recursive functions by Computational Induction

2.1 The Computational Induction Theorem

We consider the recursive equation

$$f = K(f)$$

where K is a continuous functional on S and f is an I-function on S. By Kleene's Theorem, K has a unique least fixpoint (say: lf) which equals

$$lub(K**i(\{\})).$$

Let q be a predicate that we wish to prove about function lf. In order to prove q(lf), the computational induction method proves by induction that q holds for all $K**i(\{\})$. This cannot be done for every predicate q:

DEFINITION 8. Let q be a predicate on the set of I-functions on S. Predicate q is said to be an *admissible predicate* iff for any continuous functional K on S, if $q(K**i(\{\}))$ holds for all i then it holds for $lub(K**i(\{\}))$.

EXAMPLE 10.
    We consider the functional K on S = **integer** defined by

$$K(f) = [s=0,1] \ \cup \ [s \neq 0,s]*([\textbf{true},s] \ \textbf{times} \ ([\textbf{true},s-1]*f)),$$

where **times** is defined as shown in Example 8 of section 1.4. It is left to the reader to prove that:

$$K**i(\{\}) = [0 \leqslant s < i,s!]$$

and that:

$$lub(K**i(\{\})) = [s \geqslant 0,s!].$$

We define two predicates on the set of I-functions on S:

$$q(f) = (\exists s, s \geqslant 0 \land {}^\sim(s\text{:}\mathbf{dom}(f)))$$
$$r(f) = f \subseteq lf,$$

where lf is $lub(K^{**}i(\{\}))$. Clearly, predicate q holds for every $K^{**}i(\{\})$ but does not hold for lf: It is not admissible. As for r, it holds for every element in the chain $(K^{**}i(\{\}))$ and for its least upper bound, lf. So far we have not proved that r is an admissible predicate but the theorem below provides that it is in fact.

THEOREM 5 (due to Manna, 1974). Let q be a predicate on the set of I-functions on S. If q can be written as the finite conjunction of predicates of the form

$$A(f) \subseteq B(f),$$

where A and B are continuous functionals then q is an admissible predicate.

Proof. We shall prove the theorem for the case when q(f) has the form $A(f) \subseteq B(f)$ and leave it to the reader to generalize the result. We assume that

$$(\forall i, A(K^{**}i(\{ \})) \subseteq B(K^{**}i(\{ \}))). \tag{0}$$

Because B is monotonic, we have:

$$B(K^{**}i(\{ \})) \subseteq B(lub(K^{**}i(\{ \}))). \tag{1}$$

Now, $B(lub(K^{**}i(\{\})))$ is an upper bound of $B(K^{**}i(\{\}))$. Because of (0), it is also an upper bound of $A(K^{**}i(\{\}))$. Hence

$$lub(A(K^{**}i(\{ \}))) \subseteq B(lub(K^{**}i(\{ \}))). \tag{2}$$

Because A is continuous, (2) can be transformed into

$$A(lub(K^{**}i(\{ \}))) \subseteq B(lub(K^{**}i(\{ \}))). \tag{3}$$

QED

Theorem 5 is useful because a large class of predicates can be written as a conjunction of predicates of the form $A(f) \subseteq B(f)$.

Theorem 6 follows immediately from Definition 8 and the Strong Induction Principle (Proposition 6,Chapter 3).

THEOREM 6 (Computational Induction Theorem, due to Morris, 1971). Let K be a continuous functional whose least fixpoint is lf; let q be an admissible predicate. If

$$(\forall i, (\forall j, j < i \Rightarrow q(K^{**}j(\{\}))) \Rightarrow q(K^{**}i(\{\})))$$

then q(lf) holds.

2.2 Examples

EXAMPLE 11. We consider the functional K defined in Example 10. We denote by fl the least fixpoint of K. We define the predicate q on the set of I-functions on S by

$$q(f) = (\forall s, s{:}\mathbf{dom}(f) \Rightarrow (s,s!){:}f).$$

Even though we cannot apply Theorem 5 to predicate q, we can convince ourselves that q is an admissible predicate because, as we recall, the least upper bound of a chain of functions is nothing but their (infinite) union. The details of the proof are left to the reader. Clearly, q({}) holds. On the other hand,

$$K^{**}i(\{\}) = \{(i-1,(i-1)!)\} \ \cup \ K^{**}(i-1)(\{\}),$$

hence q(K**i − 1({})) logically implies q(K**i({})).

By virtue of Theorem 6, we conclude that q(lf) holds. This proof does not tell us what function lf is, but does tell us that:

$$(\forall s, s{:}\mathbf{dom}(lf) \Rightarrow (s,s!){:}lf).$$

Example 12. We consider the following recursive equation:

$$f = [t,s] \ \cup \ [\tilde{\ }t,s]^*h^*f^*f,$$

and we call K its functional and lf its least fixpoint. We wish to prove the following property about lf:

$$lf^*lf = lf.$$

In order to do so, we introduce predicate q defined by

$$q(f) = (f^*lf = f).$$

Clearly, q(f) is an admissible predicate, for it can be written as:

$$f*lf \subseteq f \land f \subseteq f*lf$$

and both of functionals k and k′ defined by k(f)=f and k(f)=f*lf are continuous.

Basis of induction: $\{\}*lf = \{\}$, hence q($\{\}$) holds.

Induction step: Let $f_i = K**i(\{\})$. We assume that q(f_j) holds for any $j \leq i$. Then $f_{i+1}*lf$

$$
\begin{aligned}
&= K(f_i)*lf \\
&= [t,s]*lf \cup [\tilde{}t,s]*h*f_i*f_i*lf &&\text{by definition of K} \\
&= [t,s]*lf \cup [\tilde{}t,s]*h*f_i*f_i &&\text{by induction hypothesis.}
\end{aligned}
$$

We must prove that $[t,s]*lf = [t,s]$. If we observe the execution of the following recursive declaration:

```
function f(s:S):S;
begin
if t then f:=s else f(f(h(s)))
end
```

on some argument s such that t(s) holds, following the full-substitution computation rule, we see that the execution terminates and returns s. By virtue of Theorem 4, this means lf(s)=s. Hence lf can be written as:

$$[t,s] \cup [\tilde{}t,E]$$

for some expression E on S. It is left to the reader to verify that:

$$[t,s] * ([t,s] \cup [\tilde{}t,E]) = [t,s].$$

Once $[t,s]*lf = lf$ is established, one concludes:

$$
\begin{aligned}
&f_{i+1}*lf \\
&= [t,s] \cup [\tilde{}t,s]*h*f_i*f_i \\
&= f_{i+1}.
\end{aligned}
$$

2.3 Exercises

1. [B] We consider the recursive declaration:

> **function** f(s: **integer**): **integer**;
> **begin**
> **if** s = 1 **then** f: = 1 **else** f: = −f(s−1)
> **end**.

   a) Derive the corresponding recursive equation and functional.
   b) Let lf be the least fixpoint of the recursive equation. Prove by computational induction that $(\forall s,\ s{:}\mathbf{dom}(\mathrm{lf}) \Rightarrow s \geqslant 1)$.
   c) Prove by computational induction that $(\forall s,\ s \geqslant 1 \wedge \mathrm{odd}(s) \Rightarrow (s,1){:}\mathrm{lf})$.
   d) Prove by computational induction that $(\forall s,\ s \geqslant 1 \wedge \mathrm{even}(s) \Rightarrow (s,-1){:}\mathrm{lf})$.

2. [B] We consider the recursive declaration

> **function** f(s: **integer**): **integer**;
> **begin**
> **if** s = 0 **then** f: = 1 **else** f: = 2*f(s−1)
> **end**.

   a) Let q be the predicate $q(f) = (\ (s,s'){:}f \Rightarrow s' \geqslant 0\ )$. Write q in the form $A(f) \subseteq B(f)$ where A and B are continuous functionals and show that q is an admissible predicate.
   b) Use the Computational Induction Theorem to show that q holds for lf.

3. [C] Consider the recursive declaration given in Example 9.
   a) Derive its corresponding recursive equation and functional.
   b) Let lf be the least fixpoint of the recursive equation. Prove that

$$f*a*inc = (a,b*inc)*f,$$

where inc is the I-function on **integer** [**true**, x + 1].

4. [B] Prove that predicate q given in Example 11 is admissible.

3 Proof of Recursive Programs by Structural Induction

3.1 The Structural Induction Theorem

For the sake of simplicity, we shall, in this section, use a simplified pattern of recursive declarations, namely:

```
function f(s:S):S;
begin
if t then f: = a(s) else f: = b(s,f(h(s)))
end.
```

Let lf be the least fixpoint of declaration f (or, equivalently, its functional abstraction: See section 1.3). We shall assume that **dom**(lf)=S. Due to this hypothesis, the correctness of f wrt a specification (S,R) is equivalent to:

$$(\forall s,\ s{:}\textbf{dom}(R) \implies (s,lf(s)){:}R).$$

We have shown in section 1 of Chapter 9 that we can, without loss of generality, assume **dom**(R)=S. Hence the correctness of f wrt (S,R) is equivalent to:

$$(\forall s,\ (s,lf(s)){:}R),$$

which means:

$$lf \subseteq R.$$

The crux of the Structural Induction Theorem is to prove the correctness of f wrt (S,R) by Noetherian induction on space S.

THEOREM 7. Let f be the following recursive declaration:

```
function f(s:S):S;
begin   if t then f: = a(s) else f: = b(s,f(h(s)))
end,
```

and let lf be its least fixpoint. We assume that **dom**(lf)=S and we let R be a relation on S such that **dom**(R)=S. If

i) $t(s) \implies (s,a(s)){:}R$,
ii) $\tilde{}t(s) \land (h(s),s^*){:}R \implies (s,b(s,s^*)){:}R$,
then f is correct wrt (S,R).

Proof. Let $<$ be the transitive closure of the transpose of relation $[\tilde{}t,s]^*h$. Because **dom**(lf)=S, the recursive function above terminates for any s in S. Hence there are no infinite sequences of the form (s, h(s), h**2(s), h**3(s),

...); this in turn implies that $<$ is a well-founded relation. We use relation $<$ to prove by induction on S that:

$$(\forall s, (s,lf(s)):R).$$

Basis of induction: State s is $<$-minimal, hence t(s) holds. Condition (i) provides that (s,a(s)):R which can be written (s,lf(s)):R due to the semantics of the recursive declaration.

Induction step: State s is not $<$-minimal, hence ˜t(s) holds. State h(s) is less than s by relation $<$, hence, by induction hypothesis, (h(s),lf(h(s))):R. Due to condition (ii), we have (s,b(s,lf(h(s)))):R. Due to the semantics of the recursive declaration, b(s,lf(h(s))) = lf(s); hence (s,lf(s)):R.

QED

Because of its definition, relation $<$ used in the proof above equates the complexity of any element in S to the depth of the recursive call needed to process it. Hence the induction on S can also be understood as an induction on the depth of recursion. This double interpretation of the Structural Induction Theorem is reminiscent of the Subgoal Induction Theorem, given in section 2 of Chapter 9. See problem 4.

3.2 Examples

EXAMPLE 13. We consider the following recursive declaration:

```
function f(s:natural):natural;
begin
if s = 0 then f: = 1 else f: = s*f(s−1)
end,
```

and the relation R on **natural**:

$$\{(s,s')|\ s'=s!\ \}.$$

Let lf be the least fixpoint of f; clearly, we do have **dom**(lf) = S since the function above terminates for any initial state in S. Also, we verify easily **dom**(R) = S. The Structural Induction Theorem provides that in order to prove the correctness of f wrt (S,R), one must verify the following two conditions:

i) $s = 0 \Rightarrow (s,1):R$.
ii) $s \neq 0 \land (s-1,s''):R \Rightarrow (s,s''*s):R$.

Both of these conditions can be verified quite easily. Because R is a function, we have actually proved that lf = R.

EXAMPLE 14. We consider the recursive declaration:

> **function** f(s:**natural**):**natural**;
> **begin**
> **if** s = 0 **then** f: = 2 **else** f: = 2*f(s − 1)
> **end**,

and let R be the relation on **natural** defined by:

$$\{(s,s') \mid \log(s'):\textbf{natural}\},$$

where log is the base 2 logarithm. Clearly, **dom**(lf) = S and **dom**(R) = S. The conditions generated by the Structural Induction Theorem are:

> i) s = 0 ⟹ log(2):**natural**.
> ii) s ≠ 0 ∧ log(s″):**natural** ⟹ log(2*s″):**natural**.

Both of these conditions are satisfied; hence we have proved that lf is a subset of R, hence that f is correct wrt (S,R).

3.3 Exercises

1. [A] We consider the recursive declaration:

> **function** f(s: **natural**): **natural**;
> **begin**
> **if** s = 0 **then** f: = 1 **else** f: = 2*f(s − 1)
> **end**.

Let R be the relation defined by:

$$R = \{(s,s') \mid s' = 2**s\}.$$

Prove the correctness of f with respect to Sp = (S,R).

2. [A] Prove that f (defined in Example 13) is correct wrt the following relation:

$$R' = \{(s,s') \mid s \leqslant s'\}.$$

3. [A] Prove that f (defined in Example 13) is correct wrt the following relation:

$$R'' = \{(s,s') \mid s \geqslant 4 \Rightarrow s' > 2**n\}.$$

4. [B] Let S be the set

> **set**
> > a: **array** [1..n] **of integer**;
> > i: 0..n−1;
> > b: **boolean**
> **end**,

for some positive integer n.

We consider the recursive declaration

> **function** f(s:S):S;
> **begin**
> **if** i = 0 **then** f: = (a,i,**true**) **else** f: = f(a,i−1, b ∧ a[i] = a[n])
> **end**.

Prove that f is correct wrt the following relation:

$$R = \{(s,s')|\ b(s) \wedge b(s') = (a(s)[1] = a(s)[2] = \ \ldots\ = a(s)[n])\}.$$

5. [A] Prove the correctness of f (defined in exercise 4) wrt the following relation:

$$R' = \{(s,s')|\ a(s) = a(s')\}.$$

6. [B] Prove the correctness of f (defined in exercise 4) wrt the following relation:

$$R'' = \{(s,s')|\ i(s') = 0\}.$$

4 Problems

1. [B] Find an example of recursive declaration on some set S and an element s0 of S such that
   — The execution on s0 following the call-by-value rule terminates,
   — The execution on s0 following the full-substitution rule fails to terminate.
   Can you find an example where the first rule fails to terminate whereas the second does terminate? Prove your claim.

2. [C] Prove Theorem 2.

3. [B] Consider Theorem 5. Discuss the generality of the characterization given, i.e. find forms of predicates which are amenable to the form specified in the theorem. Give alternate characterizations of admissible predicates on the basis that a least upper bound of a chain is the union of the elements of the chain. Compare the generality of your characterizations with that of Theorem 5.

4. [C] Consider the recursive declaration on S:

> **function** f(s:S):S;
> **begin**
> **if** t **then** f: = a(s) **else** f: = b(s,f(h(s)))
> **end**.

a) Transform this recursive declaration into an "equivalent" while statement w and formally define "equivalent".
b) Apply the Subgoal Induction Theorem (Chapter 9) to w and the Structural Induction Theorem to f.
c) Conclude.

5 Bibliography

Chapter 5 of [5] thoroughly covers the semantics of recursion as well as a great many inductive methods for proving recursive functions. For more examples of proofs of recursive functions, consult [1], [5] or [6]. For more on the formal semantics of recursive programs, consult [4].

1: Anderson, R B. Proving Programs Correct. John Wiley, 1979.
2: Cadiou, J M. Recursive Definition of Partial Functions and their Computations. PhD thesis, Computer Science Department, Stanford University, March 1972.
3: Kleene, S C. Introduction to Meta-Mathematics. D Van Nostrand, 1952.
4: Livercy, C. Theorie des Programmes. Dunod, 1978.
5: Manna, Z. Mathematical Theory of Computation. McGraw-Hill, 1974.
6: McGettric, A D. Program Verification Using Ada. Cambridge Computer Science Texts-13. Cambridge University Press, 1982.

Part IV: Formal Program Design

There is an old myth about programming today, and there is a new reality. The old myth is that programming must be an error-prone, cut-and-try process of frustration and anxiety. The new reality is that you can learn to consistently design and write programs that are correct from the beginning and that prove to be error-free in their testing and subsequent use.

Linger, Mills and Witt
Structured Programming: Theory and Practice, *1979*

So far we have been concerned with program analysis; we have addressed the questions: What is a specification? What is a program? When can we say that a program is correct wrt a specification? etc ... The logical conclusion of program analysis is, of course, program synthesis; in Part IV, we shall address the question: How do we design a correct program from a specification? Three chapters will be devoted to answering this question; they differ by the way in which they represent specifications. With some exceptions, the design rules that we discuss in the following chapters are essentially paraphrases of correctness rules. Because of the emphasis of this book on program analysis, program design will not be treated in depth.

Chapter 12

Predicate Decomposition

We are given a predicate-based specification in the form $Sp = (S,p,q)$ where p and q are predicates on S. We are to generate a SM-Pascal statement which is correct wrt Sp. Recall (Chapter 4) that the predicate-based specification (S,p,q) is semantically equivalent to the I-specification $(S,\{(s,s') \mid p(s) \wedge q(s')\})$. The system of design rules given in this chapter will be called system PD (stands for: *Predicate Decomposition*).

1 The Design Rules

The context of the rules below is the following: We are given a predicate-based specification $Sp = (S,p,q)$ and we are to derive a statement st whose space is S and which is correct wrt Sp. If the specification is so simple that it is possible to derive st immediately then we do so; otherwise we decompose specification Sp into simpler specifications, say Sp_1, Sp_2, ... Sp_K, find statements correct wrt Sp_1, Sp_2, ... Sp_K, say st_1, st_2, ... st_K, then combine these statements to construct a solution for Sp. There are many ways to decompose a specification, each resulting in a distinct *design rule*. The convergence of a design process is subject to the derived specifications Sp_1, Sp_2, ... Sp_K being *simpler* (in some sense) than Sp. We shall not define formally the term *simpler*, but we give two easy examples to illustrate the notion:

If $p' \Rightarrow p$ then (S,p',q) is simpler than (S,p,q).
If $q \Rightarrow q'$ then (S,p,q') is simpler than (S,p,q).

A. The Assignment Rule

Input:

$$Sp = (S,p,q).$$

Output:

$$st = (s := E(s)).$$

Condition: E is an expression on S such that:

$$p(s) \Rightarrow s:\textbf{def}(E) \ \wedge \ q(E(s)).$$

PROPOSITION 1: Statement st is correct wrt Sp.

Proof:

The result follows immediately from the semantic definition of the assignment statement (given in Chapter 5, section 3) and from the condition listed above.

QED

EXAMPLE 1:

$$S = \textbf{integer}; \ p(s) = \ (s = s0 \wedge s > 1); \ q(s) = \ (s = s0 + 1 \wedge s \geqslant 2).$$

We consider the expression $E(s) = s + 1$. Clearly, $\textbf{def}(E) = S$. The condition of this rule can then be written as:

$$s = s0 \ \wedge \ s > 1 \Rightarrow s + 1 = s0 + 1 \ \wedge \ s + 1 \geqslant 2,$$

which is a P-tautology.

REMARK 1: This is the only rule which generates no new specifications.

B. The Sequence Rule

Input:

$$Sp = (S,p,q).$$

Output:

$$Sp1 = (S,p,r).$$
$$Sp2 = (S,r,q).$$

Conditions:

None, except that Sp1 and Sp2 must be simpler than Sp. Note: This condition is not as critical to the validity of the design rule as much as it is to its convergence. For Example, the decomposition of Sp = (**real,**

$s = s0 \land s > 0$, $s = \log(s0)$) into $Sp1 = (\textbf{real}, s = s0 \land s > 0, s = s0)$ and $Sp2 = (\textbf{real}, s = s0, s = \log(s0))$ is semantically valid. But such a decomposition leads to a dead end in the design process since Sp2 has no solution. Yet Sp does have a solution.

PROPOSITION 2:

If st1 is correct wrt Sp1 and st2 is correct wrt Sp2 then st = (st1;st2) is correct wrt Sp.

Proof:

If st1 is correct wrt Sp1 then:

$$\{p\} \text{ st1 } \{r\}.$$

If st2 is correct wrt Sp2 then:

$$\{r\} \text{ st2 } \{q\}.$$

By rule r2 of system s.IA* (Chapter 7), we deduce: (st1;st2) is correct wrt Sp.

QED

EXAMPLE 2:

$$Sp = (\textbf{real}, s = s0 \land s > -1, s = \log(s0 + 1)).$$

We derive:

$$Sp1 = (\textbf{real}, s = s0 \land s > -1, s = s0 + 1 \land s > 0).$$
$$Sp2 = (\textbf{real}, s = s0 + 1 \land s > 0, s = \log(s0 + 1)).$$

REMARK 2:

Because of the freedom in choosing the intermediate predicate, this rule is awkward: It can be arbitrarily misused. It compares unfavorably with the corresponding rules of Chapters 13 and 14, which are more structured.

One may conceive an improvement of this rule whereby the spaces of Sp1 and Sp2 are distinct from S, thereby allowing for the possibility to introduce new intermediate variables. See problem 2.

C. The Conditional Rule

Input:

$$Sp = (S,p,q).$$

Output:

    — A predicate t on S.
    — Tc $= (S, p \wedge t, q).$

Condition:

$$p \wedge {}^\sim t \Rightarrow q.$$

PROPOSITION 3:

If tc is correct wrt Tc then st $=$ (**if** t **then** tc) is correct wrt Sp.

Proof:

Because tc is correct wrt Tc:

$$\{p \wedge t\} \text{ tc } \{q\}.$$

By hypothesis:

$$p \wedge {}^\sim t \Rightarrow q.$$

By rule r3 of system s.IA*, we deduce that st is correct wrt Sp.

                                                 QED

EXAMPLE 3:

Sp $= (S,p,q)$, where

$$\begin{aligned} S = \ &\textbf{set} \\ &a, b: \textbf{integer} \\ \textbf{end}&, \end{aligned}$$

$p(s) = (s = s0)$, and
$q(s) = (a(s) = \max(a(s0), b(s0)))$.

Notation: $\max(a(s),b(s)) = \max(s)$.
We choose: $t(s) = (a(s) < b(s))$. Then

$$Tc = (S,\ s = s0 \ \wedge \ a(s) < b(s),\ a(s) = \max(s0)),$$

which can be written as

$$(S,\ s = s0 \ \wedge \ a(s) < b(s),\ a(s) = b(s0)).$$

Clearly,

$$s = s0 \ \wedge \ \tilde{}(a(s) < b(s)) \ \Rightarrow \ a(s) = \max(s0).$$

REMARK 3:

Notice that Tc is simpler than Sp; it matches the first pattern shown at the beginning of this chapter.

D. The Alternative Rule

Input:

$$Sp = (S,p,q).$$

Output:

— A predicate t on S.
— $Tc = (S,p \wedge t,q)$.
— $Ec = (S,p \wedge \tilde{}t,q)$.

Conditions:

None.

PROPOSITION 4:

If tc is correct wrt Tc and ec is correct wrt Ec then

$$st = (\textbf{if } t \ \textbf{then } tc \ \textbf{else } ec)$$

is correct wrt Sp.

Proof:

Because tc is correct wrt Tc:

$$\{p \wedge t\} \text{ tc } \{q\}.$$

Because ec is correct wrt Ec:

$$\{p \wedge {}^{\sim}t\} \text{ ec } \{q\}.$$

By rule r4 of system s.IA*, we deduce that st is correct wrt Sp.

QED

EXAMPLE 4:

Sp = (S,p,q), where

$$
\begin{aligned}
&S= \textbf{ set}\\
&\quad \text{a, b, c: } \textbf{boolean}\\
&\textbf{end,}\\
&p(s) = \textbf{true,}\\
&q(s) = (c(s) = (a(s) \Rightarrow b(s))).
\end{aligned}
$$

We choose

$$t(s) = a(s).$$

Then

$$
\begin{aligned}
Tc &= (S, a(s), c(s) = (a(s) \Rightarrow b(s)))\\
&= (S, a(s), c(s) = b(s)),
\end{aligned}
$$

because a(s) holds, and

$$
\begin{aligned}
Ec &= (S, {}^{\sim}a(s), c(s) = (a(s) \Rightarrow b(s)))\\
&= (S, {}^{\sim}a(s), c(s) = \textbf{true})
\end{aligned}
$$

because ${}^{\sim}a(s)$ holds.

REMARK 4:

Clearly, Tc and Ec are simpler than Sp.

E. The Iteration Rule

Input:

$$Sp = (S,p,q).$$

Output:

Specification B = $(S, t \land p \land s=s1, p \land s<s1)$,
where
       t is a predicate on S,
      $<$ is a well-founded relation on S.

Conditions:

$$q = p \land \sim t.$$

This condition can be expressed in terms which depend on p and q alone, hence on specification Sp alone: q must be the conjunction of p with some other predicate, say u (i.e. $q = p \land u$). This can then be understood as a condition of feasibility of the Iteration Rule: One can apply the Iteration Rule only to those specifications which meet this condition. In generating specification B, one then takes $t = \sim u$.

PROPOSITION 5:

If lb is correct wrt B then (**while** t **do** lb) is correct wrt Sp.

Proof: If lb is correct wrt B then:

$$\{t \land p \land s=s1\} \text{ lb } \{p \land s<s1\}.$$

This equation, plus the conditions

$$p \Rightarrow p,$$
$$p \land \sim t \Rightarrow q$$

and the hypothesis that $(S,<)$ is well-founded constitute the four premises of rule r5 of system s.IA* (section 2.2 of Chapter 7). The conclusion of this rule is precisely the result we seek to prove.

QED

EXAMPLE 5:

Sp = (S,p,q), where

$$S = \textbf{set}$$
$$\textbf{crt}$$
$$\quad x, y: \textbf{integer};$$
$$\textbf{sub } x > 0 \ \wedge \ y > 0$$
$$\textbf{end},$$
$$p(s) = (\text{gcd}(s) = \text{gcd}(s0)),$$
$$q(s) = (x(s) = y(s) \ \wedge \ \text{gcd}(s) = \text{gcd}(s0)),$$

where gcd(s) is an abbreviation for gcd(x(s),y(s)). Predicate q is the conjunction of predicate p with

$$u(s) = (x(s) = y(s)).$$

Hence, we choose

$$- \ t(s) = (x(s) \neq y(s)),$$
$$- \ < \ = \{(s,s') \mid x(s) + y(s) < x(s') + y(s')\}.$$

Then B is defined as:

$$B = (S, \ x(s) \neq y(s) \ \wedge \ \text{gcd}(s) = \text{gcd}(s0) \ \wedge \ s = s1,$$
$$\text{gcd}(s) = \text{gcd}(s0) \ \wedge \ x(s) + y(s) < x(s1) + y(s1) \ ).$$

REMARK 5:

Let's consider the specification Sp' = (S,p',q') where S is the set defined above and

$$p'(s) = (s = s0),$$
$$q'(s) = (x(s) = \text{gcd}(s0)).$$

Statement w is correct wrt Sp'; yet, one cannot apply the Iteration Rule to Sp' because q' is not the conjunction of p' with some other predicate. The rule given below shows how to transform Sp' so as to make it meet the condition of feasibility of the Iteration Rule.

PREDICATE DECOMPOSITION 223

F. The Consequence Rule

Input:

$$Sp = (S, p, q).$$

Output:

$$Sp' = (S, p', q').$$

Conditions:

i) $p \Rightarrow p'$.
ii) $q' \Rightarrow q$.

PROPOSITION 6:

If st is correct wrt Sp' then it is correct wrt Sp.

Proof:

The result follows immediately from the definition of correctness wrt a predicate-based specification.

EXAMPLE 6:

$$Sp = (S, s = s0, x(s) = gcd(s0)),$$

where S is the set defined in Example 5. We transform Sp into:

$$Sp' = (S, gcd(s) = gcd(s0), x(s) = y(s) \land gcd(s) = gcd(s0)).$$

We verify that:

$$s = s0 \Rightarrow gcd(s) = gcd(s0), \text{ and}$$
$$x(s) = y(s) \land gcd(s) = gcd(s0) \Rightarrow x(s) = gcd(s0).$$

REMARK 6:

Notice that, although the Consequence Rule transforms a simple specification into a more complex one (by the criteria we have introduced in the beginning of the chapter), it is justified, by the need to prepare specifications for the Iteration Rule. See problem 4 for a discussion of how a specification can be prepared by the Consequence Rule for the purpose of the Iteration Rule.

2 Discussions

System PD shows how to develop programs by predicate decomposition. Its design rules are derived from the correctness rules of the deductive system s.IA* given in Chapter 7. With the exception of the Iteration Rule, the system does not provide means to select the rule that may be chosen at each step; rather, once the designer has chosen a rule, the system ensures the semantic validity of the decomposition. In the case of the Iteration Rule, one can interpret the condition $(q = p \wedge u)$ as a condition of feasibility.

Also, the rules of system PD give little guidance in determining the parameters of each design decision, such as: predicate r in the Sequence Rule; predicate t in the Conditional and Alternative Rules; predicate t and relation $<$ in the Iteration Rule. In pratice one decides on the design rule as well as its parameters solely on the basis of experience and intuition.

This system and variations of it are fairly widely used, even for (rather) complex applications.

3 Exercises

1. [A] Apply system PD to design a solution for the following specification:

   $Sp = (S,p,q)$.
   $S =$ **set**
      a, b, c: **integer**
   end,
   $p(s) = (b(s) \geq 0 \wedge s = s0)$,
   $q(s) = (c(s) = c(s0) + a(s0)*b(s0))$.

2. [B] Same question as exercise 1, with the same S and q;

   $$p(s) = (s = s0).$$

3. [B] Same question as exercise 1, with the same S and p;

   $$q(s) = (c(s) = a(s0)*b(s0)).$$

4. [B] Consider the following set

$$S = \textbf{set}$$
$$\text{a, b: } \textbf{integer}$$
$$\textbf{end}.$$

Let Sp be (S, s=s0 $\wedge$ b(s)$\geqslant$0, a(s)=a(s0)+b(s0)), and Sp' be (S, s=s0, a(s)= a(s0)+b(s0)).

a) Which of Sp and Sp' is simpler? Use the criteria of section 1.

b) Design a solution for Sp and a solution for Sp' following the design rules of system PD.

c) Compare the complexity of st and st' and conclude (non-assertively).

5. [B] Consider the set

$$S = \textbf{set}$$
$$\text{a, b: } \textbf{integer}$$
$$\textbf{end}.$$

Let

$$Sp = (S, s=s0, a(s)=max(s0)).$$
$$Sp' = (S, s=s0, a(s)=max(s0) \wedge b(s)=min(s0)).$$

Note: max(s) and min(s) are abbreviations for max(a(s),b(s)) and min(a(s),b(s)).

a) Which of Sp and Sp' is simpler?

b) Design a statement st for Sp and a statement st' for Sp' following the rules of system PD.

c) Compare the complexity of st and st' and conclude (non-assertively).

6. [B] Consider Example 5. Apply the Alternative Rule then the Assignment Rule to specification B and generate a solution for specification Sp.

7. [C] Consider the specification Sp=(S,p,q), where

$$S = \textbf{set}$$
$$\textbf{crt}$$
$$\text{a: } \textbf{array } [1..n] \textbf{ of real};$$
$$\text{i: } \textbf{integer};$$
$$\textbf{sub}$$
$$0 \leqslant i \leqslant n+1$$
$$\textbf{end},$$

for some positive integer n,

$$p(s) = (s = s0)$$
$$q(s) = (ord(s) \land perm(s0,s)),$$

where ord(s) means a(s) is ordered and perm(s0,s) means a(s) is a permutation of a(s0).

a) Let i-ord(s) be the predicate

$$a(s)[1] \leqslant a(s)[2] \leqslant \ldots \leqslant a(s)[i(s)-1] \leqslant a(s)[i(s)].$$

Write ord(s) as a conjunction of i-ord(s) and some other predicate.

b) Deduce a strategy for applying the Consequence Rule then the Iteration Rule to Sp.

c) Let lt be the relation:

$$\{(s,s') \mid i(s) > i(s')\}.$$

Prove that lt is a well-founded relation on S.

d) Using the parameters determined in questions (b) and (c) derive a program which is correct wrt Sp. This is the *insertion sort program*.

8. [C] Consider the same specification as exercise 7.

a) Let s-ord(s) be the predicate

$$a(s)[1] \leqslant a(s)[2] \leqslant \ldots \leqslant a(s)[i(s)-2] \leqslant a(s)[i(s)-1]$$
$$\land (\forall j, (\forall k, 1 \leqslant k \leqslant i(s)-1 \land i(s) \leqslant j \leqslant n \Rightarrow a(s)[k] \leqslant a(s)[j])).$$

Write ord(s) as a conjunction of s-ord(s) and some other predicate.

b) Deduce from this decomposition of ord(s) a strategy for applying the Consequence Rule then the Iteration Rule to Sp.

c) Let lt be the relation:

$$\{(s,s') \mid i(s) > i(s')\}.$$

Prove that lt is a well-founded relation on S.

d) Using the parameters determined in questions (b) and (c) derive a program which is correct wrt Sp. This is the *selection sort program*.

4 Problems

1. [A] Prove Proposition 1 using the Consequence Rule of system PD and axiom a2 of system s.IA*.

2. [B] In this problem we are concerned with enriching system PD to make it handle variable introduction.

a) Among the six rules of system PD, which ones must be altered?

b) How does one model variable introduction in set-theoretic terms?

c) Identify the problems posed by the change in the space of the specification: What happens to predicates and functions defined on the previous space?

d) Generate a new system of design rules to support variable introduction: system PD′.

3. [B] Enhance system PD to include a Write Rule and a Read Rule. (Hint: Consider **write** and **read** statements as assignment statements on the extended space of the program).

4. [B] This problem is concerned with how to apply the Consequence Rule to a specification in order to prepare it for the Iteration Rule. Let (S,p,q) be a specification to which we intend to apply the Iteration Rule.

a) We want to transform $Sp = (S,p,q)$ into $Sp' = (S,p',p' \wedge u)$. Write the equations that p, q, p′ and u must verify.

b) Consider the following specifications:

$$Sr = \quad (\textbf{set}$$
$$\qquad a: \textbf{array } [1 \mathrel{..} n] \textbf{ of real}$$
$$\qquad \textbf{end,}$$
$$\qquad s = s0,$$
$$\qquad ord(s) \wedge perm(s0,s) \ ).$$

$$Gc = \quad (\textbf{set}$$
$$\qquad \textbf{crt}$$
$$\qquad\quad x, y: \textbf{integer;}$$
$$\qquad \textbf{sub}$$
$$\qquad\quad x{>}0 \wedge y{>}0$$
$$\qquad \textbf{end,}$$
$$\qquad s = s0,$$
$$\qquad x(s) = y(s) \wedge gcd(s) = gcd(s0) \ ).$$

$$Rm = \quad (\textbf{natural,}$$
$$\qquad s = s0,$$
$$\qquad s < 5 \wedge s \textbf{ mod } 5 = s0 \textbf{ mod } 5).$$

In each one of the examples, predicate q is written as the conjunction of two predicates: say $q' \wedge q''$, in this order. Give a brief characterization of predicates q′ and q″. Can the roles of q′ and q″ be interchanged?

c) Use the Consequence Rule to modify the input predicate of these specifications so as to make them meet the condition of the Iteration Rule.

d) In light of the examples given in question (b), give general guidelines for decomposing the output predicate.

e) Derive a global algorithm for this transformation and apply it to a specification of your choice.

5 Bibliography

For more examples of program design by predicate decomposition along the lines of system PD, consult [3]. For alternative models of program design by predicate decomposition, consult [1] and [2].

1: Dijkstra, E W. A Discipline of Programming. Prentice-Hall, 1976.
2: Gries, D. The Science of Programming. Springer-Verlag, 1980.
3: Manna, Z and R Waldinger. The Logic of Computer Programming. IEEE-TSE SE-6(3) (May 1978), pp 199-229.

Chapter 13

Functional Decomposition

We are given an I-specification $Sp = (S,R)$, where R is an I-function on S and we are to generate a solution for this specification, i.e. a statement on space S which is correct wrt Sp. Because R is a function, we shall represent it by the letter f. Note that the correctness of statement st wrt (S,f) can be expressed as:

$$(\forall s, s:\textbf{dom}(f) \Rightarrow s:\textbf{dom}([st]) \wedge f(s) = [st](s)),$$

which is equivalent to:

$$f \subseteq [st].$$

The system of design rules given in this chapter will be called system FD (for *Functional Decomposition*).

1 The Design Rules

The context of the rules below is the following: We are given an I-specification (S,f) where f is a function and we are to generate a statement st correct wrt (S,f). If f is so simple that it is possible to derive st immediately then we do so; otherwise we decompose f into *simpler* functions, say $f_1, f_2, \ldots f_K$ and generate statements $st_1, st_2, \ldots st_K$ which are correct wrt $(S,f_1), (S,f_2), \ldots (S,f_K)$ respectively, then combine $st_1, st_2, \ldots st_K$ to obtain a statement st which is correct wrt (S,f). There are many ways to decompose a function, each resulting in a separate design rule. The convergence of the design process is subject to the derived specifications $(S,f_1), (S,f_2), \ldots (S,f_K)$ being simpler than the original specification (S,f). The simplicity of a function-based specification is a difficult notion to grasp, let alone define formally. The view we shall take is that complex functions can be built from simpler functions by relative product, union or transitive closure. Hence complex functions can be decomposed by expressing them as the relative product, the union or the transitive closure of simpler functions. This description suffers from some paradoxes: Problem 1 shows examples of functions whose union or relative product is intuitively thought of as being *simpler*.

A. The Assignment Rule

Input:

$$Sp = (S,f).$$

Output:

$$st = (s: = E(s)).$$

Condition:

$$s:\mathbf{dom}(f) \Rightarrow s:\mathbf{def}(E) \wedge f(s) = E(s).$$

PROPOSITION 1:

Statement st is correct wrt (S,f).

Proof:

The result follows immediately from the condition above, the definition of correctness and the semantic definition of the assignment statement. QED

EXAMPLE 1:

$$Sp = (\mathbf{real}, [s>9, \log(s)]).$$

We choose $E(s) = \log(s)$; hence $\mathbf{def}(E) = \{s \mid s > 0\}$. The condition is readily checked and $(s: = \log(s))$ is indeed a solution for specification Sp.

B. The Sequence Rule

Input:

$$Sp = (S,f).$$

Output:

$$Sp1 = (S,f1).$$
$$Sp2 = (S,f2).$$

Condition:

$$f = f1*f2.$$

PROPOSITION 2:

If st1 is correct wrt Sp1 and st2 is correct wrt Sp2 then

$$st = (st1; st2)$$

is correct wrt Sp.

Proof:

f
= f1*f2   by virtue of the condition of the rule,
⊆: [st1]*[st2] by virtue of the correctness of st1 and st2,
= [st1; st2]   by the semantic definition of (;),
= st.

Hence st is correct wrt (S,f).

QED

EXAMPLE 2:

$$Sp = (\textbf{real}, [s>e, \log(\log(s)-1)]),$$

where e is the real whose logarithm is 1. We choose:

$$f1 = [s>0, \log(s)],$$
$$f2 = [s>1, \log(s- 1)].$$

We compute

f1*f2
= [s>0, \log(s)] * [s>1, \log(s-1)]
= [s>0 ∧ \log(s)>1, \log(\log(s)-1)]
= [s>e, \log(\log(s)-1)] .

REMARK 2:

Notice how this rule is much more structured than its counterpart in system
PD.

C. The Conditional Rule

Input:

$$Sp = (S,f).$$

Output:

$$Tc = (S,g).$$

Condition:

$$f = g \cup [\tilde{\ }:\mathbf{dom}(g),s]. \tag{0}$$

PROPOSITION 3:

If tc is correct wrt Tc then

$$st = (\mathbf{if}\ t\ \mathbf{then}\ tc)$$

is correct wrt Sp, where t is :**dom**(g).

Proof:

Statement tc is correct wrt (S,g), hence:

$g \subseteq [tc]$
$\Rightarrow [:\mathbf{dom}(g),s]*[tc] = g$ by the definition of relative product,
$\Rightarrow [t,s]*[tc] = g$ by definition of t,
$\Rightarrow [t,s]*[tc] \cup [\tilde{\ }t,s] = g \cup [\tilde{\ }t,s]$
$\Rightarrow [t,s]*[tc] \cup [\tilde{\ }t,s] = f$ by the condition of the rule,
$\Rightarrow [st] = f$ by the semantics of the conditional statement,
$\Rightarrow$ st is correct wrt (S,f).   QED

EXAMPLE 3:

$$Sp = (\mathbf{real},\ [\mathbf{true},\ \mathrm{abs}(s)]).$$

We choose

$$Tc = (\mathbf{real},\ [s<0,-s]).$$

Clearly,

$$[\textbf{true}, \text{abs}(s)] = [s{<}0, -s] \cup [s{\geqslant}0, s].$$

D. The Alternative Rule

Input:

$$Sp = (S,f).$$

Output:

$$Tc = (S,g).$$
$$Ec = (S,h).$$

Conditions:

$$\text{a) } f = g \cup h.$$
$$\text{b) } g \cap h = \{\}.$$

Proposition 4:

If tc is correct wrt Tc and ec is correct wrt Ec then

$$st = (\textbf{if } t \textbf{ then } tc \textbf{ else } ec)$$

is correct wrt Sp, where t is :**dom**(g).

Proof:

$g \subseteq [tc]$
$\Rightarrow g = [:\textbf{dom}(g), s]*[tc]$ by definition of the relative product,
$\quad\ = [t,s]*[tc]$ by definition of t.
$h \subseteq [ec]$
$\Rightarrow h = [:\textbf{dom}(h), s]*[ec]$ by definition of the relative product,
$\quad\ = [\tilde{}t,s]*[ec]$ due to condition (b) and the definition of t.
Now,
$\quad f = g \cup h$ due to condition (a),
$\quad\ = [t,s]*[tc] \cup [\tilde{}t,s]*[ec]$ as established above,
$\quad\ = [st]$ by the semantic definition of alternative.
Hence st is correct wrt (S,f).

QED

EXAMPLE 4:

$$Sp = (S,f), \text{ where}$$
$$S = \textbf{set}$$
$$\text{a, b: } \textbf{integer}$$
$$\textbf{end,}$$
$$f = [\textbf{true}, (max(s),max(s))],$$

where max(s) is an abbreviation for max(a(s),b(s)). We choose

$$Tc = (S, [a(s)>b(s), (a(s),a(s))]),$$
$$Ec = (S, [a(s)\leqslant b(s), (b(s),b(s))]).$$

Conditions (a) and (b) are obvious and can easily be verified:

a) $[a(s)>b(s),(a(s),a(s))] \cup [a(s)\leqslant b(s),(b(s),b(s))]$
   $= [a(s)>b(s) \vee a(s)\leqslant b(s), \textbf{ite}(a(s)>b(s), (a(s),a(s)), (b(s),b(s)))]$.
   $= [\textbf{true}, (max(s),max(s))]$.
b) $[a(s)>b(s), (a(s),a(s))] \cap [a(s)\leqslant b(s),(b(s),b(s))]$
   $= [a(s)>b(s) \wedge a(s)\leqslant b(s) \wedge (a(s),a(s))=(b(s),b(s)), (a(s),a(s))]$.
   $= [\textbf{false}, (a(s),a(s))]$
   $= \{ \}$.

E. The Iteration Rule

Input:

$$Sp = (S,f), \text{ where } \textbf{dom}(f) = S.$$

Output:

$$B = (S,g).$$

Conditions:

a) Condition of feasibility:

$$1) \ [:\textbf{rng}(f),s]*f = [:\textbf{rng}(f),s].$$

b) Equations on g:

1) $\mathbf{dom}(g) = S - \mathbf{rng}(f)$.
2) g^+ is a well-founded relation on S.
3) $[:\mathbf{dom}(g),s]*f = g*f$.

PROPOSITION 5:

If lb is correct wrt B then $w = (\textbf{while } t \textbf{ do } lb)$ is correct wrt Sp, where t is :$\mathbf{dom}(g)$.

Proof:

For this proof, we shall use the *Modified While Statement Rule* given in Remark 2 of Chapter 5.

If lb is correct wrt B then:

$$g \subseteq [lb],$$

which can be written:

$$g = [:\mathbf{dom}(g),s]*[lb],$$

or, due to the definition of predicate t,

$$g = [t,s]*[lb].$$

This, combined with condition (b2) and the hypothesis $\mathbf{dom}(f) = S$ yields premise p2 of rule r'1 of system FA.

From condition (b1) and the hypothesis $t = (:\mathbf{dom}(g))$, we deduce:

$$:\mathbf{rng}(f) = \tilde{\ }t.$$

Hence condition (a1) can be written as:

$$[\tilde{\ }t,s]*f = [\tilde{\ }t,s],$$

which is precisely premise p0 of rule r'1 in system FA.

Finally, from $g = [t,s]*[lb]$ and $t = (:\mathbf{dom}(g))$ we can rewrite condition (b3) as:

$$[t,s]*f = [t,s]*[lb]*f,$$

which is precisely premise p′1 of rule r′1 in system FA. The conclusion of rule r′1 is [w] = f, which implies that w is correct wrt (S,f).

QED

EXAMPLE 5:

$$S = \textbf{set}$$
$$\textbf{crt}$$
$$\quad a, b: \textbf{integer;}$$
$$\textbf{sub}$$
$$\quad b \geqslant 0$$
$$\textbf{end,}$$
$$f = [\textbf{true}, (a(s)+b(s),0)].$$

Clearly, we have:

$$\textbf{dom}(f) = S.$$

a) The condition of feasibility is:

$$[:\textbf{rng}(f),s]*f = [:\textbf{rng}(f),s].$$

Clearly, $:\textbf{rng}(f) = (b(s)=0)$, and:

$$[b(s)=0,s]*[\textbf{true},(a(s)+b(s),0)]$$
$$= [b(s)=0,(a(s),b(s))]$$
$$= [b(s)=0,s].$$

b) Equations on g:

$$1)\ \textbf{dom}(g) = \{s|\ b(s)>0\}. \tag{1}$$

Notice that the condition above actually gives us the first argument of function g's pE-formula: namely its p-domain. In other words, we now know that g can be written as

$$g = [b(s)>0, G]$$

for some expression G on S. We must use equations (b2) and (b3) of the iteration rule in order to determine G.

2) Relation g^+ must be a well-founded relation on S. Because this condition is too vague to be useful, we take a stronger one: Relation g^+ must be equal to:

$$\{(s,s')|\ b(s)<b(s')\}. \tag{2}$$

It is left to the reader to verify that this is indeed a well-founded relation on S. Also, the condition that g^+ be equal to this relation can be described by the following inequation in G:

$$b(G(s))<b(s).$$

3) Condition (b3) is:

$$[b(s)>0,s]*[\mathbf{true},(a(s)+b(s),0)]\ =\ [b(s)>0,G]*[\mathbf{true},(a(s)+b(s),0)].$$

This equation can be simplified to become:

$$[b(s)>0,(a(s)+b(s),0)]\ =\ [b(s)>0,\ (a(G(s))+b(G(s)),0)].$$

We interpret this condition as:

$$a(s)+b(s)\ =\ a(G(s))+b(G(s)). \tag{3}$$

Expression G must decrease b, but without making it negative (see definition of S). Hence we pose: $b(G(s))=b(s)-1$.
According to equation (3), G must keep the sum $a(s)+b(s)$ invariant. Hence we choose: $a(G(s))=a(s)+1$.

Function g is:

$$g\ =\ [b(s)>0,\ (a(s)+1,b(s)-1)].$$

REMARK 5:

Some remarks are in order regarding this rule.

1) Condition a1 involves f alone. It is a necessary condition for the Iteration Rule to be applicable. Hence, before deciding to implement a function with a while statement, a programmer is normally required to verify that the function he has in mind verifies property a1. Example 6 shows a function

which does not meet condition a1 and which must be transformed by the Consequence Rule before the Iteration Rule is applied to it.

2) Condition b1 determines **dom**(g) from **rng**(f) without leaving any latitude to the programmer. Notice that :**dom**(g) is precisely the condition of the while statement. This means that the condition of a loop is fully determined from function f! Does this mean that if an instructor gives a programming assignment to a class of, say, forty students he may expect forty identical loop conditions? The answer is "yes", if:

— The specification is totally unambiguous,
— The specification given is a function,
— All the students use the iteration as the outermost control structure of their programs,
— All the students use the same space (e.g. they all use the space provided by the instructor and introduce no additional variables).

Of course, any one of these conditions is difficult to realize, let alone all of them simultaneously.

3) Notice that condition a1 logically implies $rng(f) \subseteq dom(f)$. Let s be an element of **rng**(f); (s,s) belongs to [:**rng**(f),s]; by condition a1, (s,s) belongs to [:**rng**(f),s]*f; by definition of the relative product, we deduce (s,s) belongs to f; hence s:**dom**(f).

4) Let (S,f) be a specification which many algorithms are known to solve. A question which is both interesting and challenging in formal program design is: When a design process is started with a given specification, how does it get routed toward one algorithm or another? In other words, at what step is the algorithm decided? We shall attempt to use the Iteration Rule in order to provide some insight into this question. It seems that, once a designer has considered conditions (b1), (b2) and (b3), he is left with very little latitude in choosing an appropriate function g. Furthermore, the formulation of conditions (b1) and (b3) is straightforward, i.e. totally determined by the specification (S,f). The formulation of condition (b2) offers the program designer significant manoeuvring room; it is equivalent to saying: Choose a well-founded relation $<$ on S then impose the condition $g^+ = <$. If a function can be computed by many different iterative algorithms, then the choice of the algorithm is determined by the choice of the well-founded relation. The intuitive feeling is that underlying every algorithm is the idea of a well-founded relation on the space of the specification: The result of the program on large (i.e. complex) states is computed using the result of the program on

smaller (i.e. less complex) states. On the basis of this relationship one may venture to define the elusive notion of algorithm simply as a well-founded relation on the space of the program.

F. The Consequence Rule

Input:

$$Sp = (S,f).$$

Output:

$$Sp' = (S,f').$$

Conditions:

$$a)\ f \subseteq f'.$$

Implicit in this condition is the fact that f′ is also a function; from (a), one can deduce the following:

a″) $(\forall s, s:\mathbf{dom}(f) \Rightarrow f(s) = f'(s))$.

PROPOSITION 6:

If statement st is correct wrt Sp′, then it is correct wrt Sp.

Proof:

$$f' \subseteq [st] \qquad \text{because st is correct wrt } (S,f'),$$
$$f \subseteq f' \qquad \text{by condition (a).}$$

Hence $f \subseteq [st]$, i.e. st is correct wrt (S,f).

QED

EXAMPLE 6:

$$Sp = (S,f),$$

where:

$$S = \{0,1,2,3,4,5,6\}.$$
$$R = \{(6,0),(5,1),(4,0),(3,1)\}.$$

We choose:

$$Sp' = (S, \{(6,0),(5,1),(4,0),(3,1),(2,0),(1,1),(0,0)\})$$
$$= (S,f').$$

One may -justifiably- wonder what advantage could one have in transforming specification Sp into Sp'. Clearly, the while statement:

$$w = (\textbf{while } s \geqslant 2 \textbf{ do } s := s - 2)$$

is correct wrt (S,f). Yet, function f does not meet condition a1 of the Iteration Rule. Function f', on the other hand, does meet the condition. Hence in order to find a solution to specification (S,f) one must apply the Consequence Rule to find (S,f') then apply the Iteration Rule to find statement w.

REMARK 6:

Three comments are of interest regarding this rule:

1. One might ask why this rule is called the Consequence Rule and what is its connection to system PD's Consequence Rule. Let's convert specification Sp = (S,f) into a predicate-based form:

$$Sp1 = (S, s:\textbf{dom}(f) \wedge s = s0, s = f(s0))$$
$$= (S,p,q).$$

We convert specification Sp' = (S,f') into the same form:

$$Sp1' = (S, s:\textbf{dom}(f') \wedge s = s0, s = f'(s0))$$
$$= (S,p',q').$$

Because of condition (a'), we have

$$p \Rightarrow p'.$$

Because of conditions (a') and (a''), we have, under hypothesis p,

$$q' \Rightarrow q.$$

Hence Sp1' is derived from Sp1 by PD's Consequence Rule.

2. Like its counterpart in system PD, the Consequence Rule of system FD transforms simpler specifications into more complex ones: f⊆f'.

3. Like its counterpart in system PD, the Consequence Rule of system FD is used to prepare specifications to undergo the Iteration Rule.

2 Discussions

The rules of system FD are derived from the deductive system FA (Chapter 5) and can be proved and understood in terms of it.

An interesting feature of system FD is the relationship it highlights between the usual operations defined on functions (such as relative product, union, and transitive closure) and the usual programming language constructs (sequence, alternative and iteration). Also, the crisp representation of specifications by a function f (the space S being implicit) gives system FD an edge with regard to the simplicity of the rules: Each rule is presented as the resolution of a system of equations whose unknowns are functions. The determination of the unknown functions can further be simplified when the domains of these functions and their expressions arc subject to separate equations, hence can be determined independently; see the determination of function g in Example 5. Like system PD, system FD makes little provisions for guiding a designer in his choice of a design rule: The condition of feasibility (a1) of the Iteration Rule determines whether a specification Sp = (S,f) can be solved by an iteration or not. The Iteration Rule is the only rule to have such a provision.

System FD and variations of it have been used successfully in practical applications.

The main weakness of system FD is its representing specifications by functions whereas they can be arbitrarily non-deterministic relations. It is rather seldom that one is interested in the final values of all the variables of his program, or that he is interested in their exact values (vs. relations between them). The system presented in the next chapter attempts to generalize the rules of system FD by using relations instead of functions. It does, of course, have weaknesses of its own that we will discuss in section 2 of the next chapter.

3 Exercises

1. [B] Find a solution to the specification Sp = (S,f), where

$$S = \textbf{integer},$$
$$f = \{(1,1),(2,2),(3,3),(4,4),(5,1),(6,2),(7,3),(8,4),(9,5)\}.$$

2. [B] Let Sp be the specification (S,f), where

$$S = \textbf{natural},$$
$$f = \{(9,0),(8,1),(7,0),(6,1),(5,0),(4,1),(3,0)\}.$$

a) Let $g=\{(0,1),(1,0)\}$. Find f' such that $f=f'*g$.
b) Apply the Consequence then Iteration Rule to (S,f') and deduce a statement which is correct wrt (S,f).
c) Let $h = [3\leqslant s\leqslant 9, s+1]$. Find f'' such that $f=h*f''$.
d) Apply the Consequence then Iteration Rule to (S,f'') and deduce a statement which is correct wrt (S,f).

3. [B] Let Sp be the specification (S,f) where

       S = **set**
         a, b: **integer**
       end,
       $f = [\textbf{true}, (\max(s),\max(s))]$,
       max(s) being an abbreviation of max(a(s),b(s)).

   a) Characterize **rng**(f) and [:**rng**(f),s]. Verify condition a1 of the Iteration Rule.
   b) Show that function

   $$g = [a(s)\neq b(s),\ \textbf{ite}(a(s)>b(s),\ (a(s),b(s)+1),\ (a(s)+1,b(s)))]$$

   verifies conditions b1, b2 and b3 of the Iteration Rule.
   c) Write g as the union of two functions, say g' and g''. Apply the Alternative Rule to (S,g).
   d) Deduce a solution for specification (S,f).
   e) Comment on the solution found, and on system FD.

4. [A] Consider the specification (S,f) given in exercise 3.
   a) Write f as the union of two functions.
   b) Apply the Alternative Rule.
   c) Deduce a solution for specification (S,f).

5. [A] Consider the specification (S,f) where

           S = **set**
             a, b, t: **integer**
           end

   and

   $$f = [\textbf{true}, (\max(s),\min(s),\min(s))].$$

   Find a solution for (S,f) using the Conditional Rule.

6. [C] Consider the specification (S,f) where S is defined as follows:

$$S = set$$
$$crt$$
$$a, b: integer;$$
$$sub$$
$$a > 0 \land b > 0$$
$$end,$$

and

$$f = [a(s) > 0 \land b(s) > 0, (gcd(s), gcd(s))].$$

a) Determine $rng(f)$ and verify condition a1 of the Iteration Rule. What can you deduce?

b) Write the equation (b1) and deduce the domain of the (unknown) function g.

c) Write equations (b2) and (b3). Propose a solution and deduce from it the pE-formula of g.

d) Decompose g as the union of two functions and apply to (S,g) the Alternative then the Iteration Rules.

e) Deduce a solution to (S,f). Deduce a solution for (S,f'), where

$$f' = [a(s) > 5 \land b(s) > 5, (gcd(s), gcd(s))].$$

7. [C] Consider the specification (S,f), where

$$S = set$$
$$a, b, p: integer;$$
$$sub$$
$$b \geqslant 0$$
$$end,$$
$$f = [true, (a(s), 0, a(s)*b(s))].$$

a) Does function f verify condition a1 of the Iteration Rule?

b) Find function f' such that $f = [true, (a(s), b(s), 0)] * f'$ and that f' meets condition a1.

c) Determine the domain of function g using equation (b1).

d) Determine the expression of function g and deduce a solution to (S,f).

e) Find a statement correct wrt (S,g) and deduce a solution for (S,f).

4 Problems

1. [A] On the elusiveness of defining a measure of simplicity for functions:

a) Consider functions $[s \geqslant 5, s + 1]$ and $[s < 5, s + 1]$ on the space **integer**. What can you say about their union?

b) Consider functions $[0 \leqslant s \leqslant 4, s + 5]$ and $[5 \leqslant s \leqslant 9, s - 5]$ on the space **integer**.

Compute their two relative products and compare them to the individual functions in terms of intuitive simplicity.

c) Observe that nearly all design rules decompose functions along the union or the relative product strategies.

d) Comment.

2. [B] Show the equivalence of the four conditions below:

b2: g^+ is a well-founded relation on S.

b2': There exists a well-founded relation on S, say $<$, such that g is a subset of $<$.

b2": There exists a well-founded set $(W, <)$ and a function u from S to W such that $(\forall s, s{:}\mathbf{dom}(g) \Rightarrow u(g(s)) < u(s))$.

b2''': There exists a well-founded relation $<$ on S such that $< \; = g^+$.

Compare the merits of each one of these characterizations on the basis of

a) Conceptual elegance,

b) Practical use.

3. [C]

a) Read chapters 12 and 13 and compare systems PD and FD: Give comments of the same type as section 2 in these chapters.

b) Looking back at your programming experience, which of systems PD of FD is your way of thought closest to?

c) Note that predicates (PD) describe *states* whereas functions (FD) describe *processes*; in your view, what approach to programming is most appropriate (i.e. that emphasizing states or that emphasizing processes)?

5 Bibliography

For other informations of systems FD, see [1] and [2].

1: Linger, RC, HD Mills and BI Wilt. Structured Programming: Theory and Practice. Addison-Wesley, 1979.

2: Mills, H D, V R Basili, J D Gannon, R G Hamlet, B Schneidermann, R J Austing and J E Kohl. The Calculus of Programming. To appear with Allyn & Bacon.

Chapter 14

Relational Decomposition

We are given an I-specification $Sp = (S,R)$ where R is an I-relation on S, and we are to generate a statement st which is correct wrt Sp. In the context of this chapter, R is not necessarily a function; it can be arbitrarily non-deterministic. The correctness of st wrt R can be expressed, as we recall, by

$$s:\mathbf{dom}(R) \implies s:\mathbf{dom}([st]) \; \wedge \; (s,[st](s)):R.$$

The system of design rules given in this chapter will be called system RD (for *Relational Decomposition*).

1 The Design Rules

The context of the rules below is the following: We are given an I-specification (S,R) and we are to generate a statement st correct wrt (S,R). If R is so simple that it is possible to generate st immediately then we do so; otherwise we decompose R into simpler relations, say $R_1, R_2 \ldots R_K$, and generate statements $st_1, st_2, \ldots st_K$ which are correct wrt $(S,R_1), (S,R_2) \ldots (S,R_K)$ respectively, then combine $st_1, st_2, \ldots st_K$ to obtain a statement st correct wrt (S,R). There are many ways to decompose a relation, each resulting in a different design rule. The convergence of the design process is subject to the derived relations $R_1, R_2, \ldots R_K$ being *simpler* than the original relation R. The intuitive notion of simplicity of a relation evades formal grasp but it may be reasonably fair to say that in general,

> Relations R1 and R2 are simpler than the relative product R1*R2.
> Relations R1 and R2 are simpler than the union R1 $\cup$ R2.
> Relation R is simpler than its transitive closure R^+.

Each one of these assertions suffers from some counter examples (see problem 1, Chapter 13 and problems 5 and 6 of this chapter). It is instructive to see, however, that these decomposition policies correspond to SM-Pascal's constructs of sequence, alternative and iteration.

A. The Assignment Rule

Input:

$$Sp = (S,R).$$

Output:

$$st = (s := E(s)).$$

Condition:

$$s:\textbf{dom}(R) \Rightarrow s:\textbf{def}(E) \wedge (s,E(s)):R.$$

PROPOSITION 1: st is correct wrt (S,R).

Proof:
This result follows readily from the condition above and from the identity

$$[s := E(s)] = [:\textbf{def}(E), E].$$

EXAMPLE 1:

$Sp = (\textbf{integer}, \{(0,1), (5,6), (5,8), (9,1), (9,2), (9,10), (8,8), (8,9), (9,8)\}).$
We choose: $E(s) = s+1$.
We have: $\textbf{def}(E) = \textbf{integer}$,
$\qquad \textbf{dom}(R) = \{0, 5, 8, 9\}$.

Clearly the condition above is met since $(0,1)$, $(5,6)$, $(8,9)$ and $(9,10)$ all belong to R. Hence

$$s := s+1$$

is a correct statement for Sp.

B. The Sequence Rule

Input:

$$Sp = (S,R).$$

Output:

$$Sp1 = (S,R1).$$
$$Sp2 = (S,R2).$$

Conditions:

a) R = R1*R2.
b) **rng**(R1) ⊆ **dom**(R2).

PROPOSITION 2:

If st1 is correct wrt Sp1 and st2 is correct wrt Sp2 then

$$st = (st1; st2)$$

is correct wrt Sp.

Proof:
Let s be an element of **dom**(R). Because of condition (a), we deduce
dom(R)⊆**dom**(R1). Hence s:**dom**(R1). Because st1 is correct wrt Sp1,

$$s:\textbf{dom}([st1]) \tag{1}$$
$$\wedge$$
$$(s,[st1](s)):R1 . \tag{1'}$$

From equation (1') we deduce [st1](s):**rng**(R1). Due to condition (b), we
deduce [st1](s):**dom**(R2). Because st2 is correct wrt Sp2,

$$[st1](s):\textbf{dom}([st2]) \tag{2}$$
$$\wedge$$
$$([st1](s), [st2]([st1](s))):R2. \tag{2'}$$

From (1) and (2) we deduce

$$s:\textbf{dom}([st1]*[st2]). \tag{3}$$

From (1') and (2') we deduce

$$(s, [st1]*[st2](s)):R1*R2. \tag{3'}$$

Because of condition (a) and the semantics of the sequence statement, we
can write:

$$s:\textbf{dom}([st1; st2]) \tag{4}$$
$$\wedge$$
$$(s,[st1; st2](s)):R. \tag{4'}$$

We have deduced (4) and (4′) from the hypothesis s:**dom**(R). Hence st is correct wrt (S,R).

QED

EXAMPLE 2:

$$Sp = (S,R),$$

where

$$S = \textbf{real}$$

and

$$R = \{(s,s')\mid (a/s)-u \leqslant s' \leqslant (a/s)+u\},$$

for some positive constants a and u. This relation expresses that s′ is an approximation of a/s within a precision of u.

Let u1 and u2 be two positive constants such that:

$$u = a*u1 + u2. \tag{0}$$

We define relations R1 and R2 as follows:

$$R1 = \{(s,s')\mid 1-u1 \leqslant s' \leqslant 1+u1\}.$$
$$R2 = \{(s,s')\mid a*s-u2 \leqslant s' \leqslant a*s+u2\}.$$

Clearly, **dom**(R2) = **real**. Hence condition (b) is verified. As for condition (a), it follows from (0). This example shows that in order to compute a/s with precision u, one may compute 1/s with precision u1 and a*s with precision u2, subject to equation (0).

C. The Conditional Rule

Input:

$$Sp = (S,R).$$

Output:

$$Tc = (S,R').$$

Conditions:

a) $R' \subseteq R$.
b) $s{:}(\mathbf{dom}(R) - \mathbf{dom}(R')) \Rightarrow (s,s){:}R$.

PROPOSITION 3:

If tc ic correct wrt Tc then st = (**if** t **then** tc) is correct wrt Sp, where t is (:$\mathbf{dom}(R')$).

Proof:

Let s be an element of $\mathbf{dom}(R)$. We consider two cases.

Case 1: $s{:}(\mathbf{dom}(R) - \mathbf{dom}(R'))$. Clearly, $s{:}\mathbf{dom}([st])$ and $[st](s) = s$.

Hence, by condition (b),

$$s{:}\mathbf{dom}([st]) \wedge (s,[st](s)){:}R.$$

Case 2: $s{:}\mathbf{dom}(R')$. Because tc is correct wrt Tc, we have:

$$s{:}\mathbf{dom}([tc]) \wedge (s,[tc](s)){:}R'.$$

Because of condition (a) and due to the semantics of the conditional statement, we have:

$$s{:}\mathbf{dom}([st]) \wedge (s,[st](s)){:}R.$$

QED

EXAMPLE 3:

$$Sp = (S,R),$$

where

S = **integer**,
R = {(1,1),(1,2),(2,4),(2,6),(3,1),(3,3),(3,6),(4,7),(4,8),(4,9),
    (5,1),(5,5),(5,9)}.

We choose

$$R' = \{(2,4),(2,6),(4,7),(4,8),(4,9)\}.$$

REMARK 1:

In order to facilitate the subsequent design of (S,R'), **dom**(R') must be chosen as small as possible, so as to reduce the number of input states. In order to make the subsequent design optimal, R' must be chosen as non-deterministic as possible (i.e. many outputs for each input), so as to keep the largest range of options possible. The example above meets both criteria. See section 2.

D. The Alternative Rule

Input:

$$Sp = (S,R).$$

Output:

$$Tc = (S,R').$$
$$Ec = (S,R'').$$

Conditions:

a) $R = R' \cup R''$.
b) **dom**(R') $\cap$ **dom**(R'') = { }.

PROPOSITION 4:

If tc is correct wrt Tc and ec is correct wrt Ec then

$$st = (\textbf{if } t \textbf{ then } tc \textbf{ else } ec)$$

is correct wrt Sp, where t is (:**dom**(R')).

Proof:

Let s be an element of **dom**(R). Because of condition (b), two cases are possible.

Case 1: s:**dom**(R'). Because tc is correct wrt Tc we deduce

$$s:\textbf{dom}([tc]) \wedge (s,[tc](s)):R'.$$

Because of the semantics of the alternative statement, and because of condition (a), we have

$$s: \mathbf{dom}([st]) \land (s, [st](s)):R.$$

Case 2: $s:\mathbf{dom}(R'')$. A similar argument leads to the same conclusion.

QED

EXAMPLE 4:

$$Sp = (S,R),$$

where

$$S = \mathbf{real}, \text{ and}$$
$$R = \{(s,s')| \ s>0 \land s'=\log(s) \lor s<0 \land s'=\log(-s)\}.$$

We choose, naturally:

$$R' = \{(s,s')| \ s>0 \land s'=\log(s)\}.$$
$$R'' = \{(s,s')| \ s<0 \land s'=\log(-s)\}.$$

Conditions (a) and (b) are both satisfied.

REMARK 2:

Notice that condition (b): $\mathbf{dom}(R') \cap \mathbf{dom}(R'') = \{\}$ logically implies (b'): $R' \cap R'' = \{\}$. However, condition (b') does not imply (b).

E. The Iteration Rule

Input:

$$Sp = (S,R), \text{ where } S=\mathbf{dom}(R).$$

Output:

$$B = (S,G).$$

Conditions:

a) $\mathbf{dom}(G) = S - \mathbf{rng}(R)$,
b) G^+ is a well-founded relation on S.
c) $R = (G^+ \cup I) * NT$,

where I and NT are defined as follows:

$$I = [\mathbf{true},s],$$
$$NT = [:\mathbf{rng}(R), s].$$

PROPOSITION 5:

If lb is correct wrt B then $w = (\mathbf{while}\ t\ \mathbf{do}\ lb)$ is correct wrt Sp, where t is $:\mathbf{dom}(G)$.

Proof:

We use the Subgoal Induction Theorem (Theorem 1, Chapter 9). First, we have taken the hypothesis that $S = \mathbf{dom}(R)$. We must prove that we also have $S = \mathbf{dom}(w)$. For this, it suffices to prove that any element s of S belongs to $\mathbf{dom}(w)$, i.e. that w terminates for any element s in S. The validity of this claim is due to the correctness of lb wrt B, the semantics of while statements and to condition (b). The details of the proof are left to the reader.

Now, we must prove conditions (i) and (ii) of the Subgoal Induction Theorem.

(i): $\tilde{\ }t(s)$
$\Rightarrow \tilde{\ }(s:\mathbf{dom}(G))$ by definition of t,
$\Rightarrow s:\mathbf{rng}(R)$ by condition (a),
$\Rightarrow (s,s):(G^+ \cup I)$
$\land\ (s,s):NT$ by definition of I and NT,
$\Rightarrow (s,s) : (G^+ \cup I) * NT$ by definition of *,
$\Rightarrow (s,s):R$ by condition (c).

(ii): $t(s)\ \land\ ([lb](s),s^*):R$
$\Rightarrow s:\mathbf{dom}(G)\ \land\ ([lb](s),s^*):R$ by definition of t,
$\Rightarrow (s,[lb](s)):G\ \land\ ([lb](s),s^*):R$ by the correctness of lb,
$\Rightarrow (s,s^*):G*R$ by definition of *.

Now,

G*R

$= G * (G^+ \cup I) * NT$ by condition (c),

$= G^+ * NT$ by definition of G^+,

$\subseteq (G^+ \cup I) * NT$ by condition (c),

$= R$.

From (s,s*):G*R and G*R$\subseteq$R we deduce (s,s*):R. Hence, by the Subgoal Induction Theorem, w is correct wrt Sp.

QED

REMARK 3:

One may justifiably wonder why the Iteration Rule of system RD does not have a condition of feasibility, like that of systems PD and FD. There is a similar condition, which is implicit in the formula of R (c): In order for R to be written as

$$(G^+ \cup I) * NT,$$

R has to meet the following condition:

$$[:\mathbf{rng}(R),s]*R = [:\mathbf{rng}(R),s].$$

Notice that this requires that the restriction of R to $\mathbf{rng}(R)$ be a function.

EXAMPLE 5:

We treat two specifications. The first is:

$$Sp = (S,R),$$

where

S = **natural**,

$R = \{(s,s')|\ s>4 \wedge s'\leqslant 4\} \cup \{(s,s')|\ s=s' \wedge s'\leqslant 4\}$.

We have $\mathbf{dom}(R)=S$. Notice that we also have s:$\mathbf{rng}(R)\Longrightarrow$(s,s):R.

We choose

$G = \{(s,s')|\ s>4 \wedge (s'=s-1 \vee s'=s-2 \vee s'=s-3 \vee s'=s-4)\}$.

a) $\mathbf{dom}(G) = \{s| \ s>4\} = S - \{s| \ s\leqslant4\} = S - \mathbf{rng}(R)$.
b) $G^+ = \{(s,s')| \ s>4 \wedge s'<s\}$ is a well-founded relation on S.
c) $(G^+ \cup I) * NT$
$= \{(s,s')| \ s>4 \wedge s'<s \vee s=s'\} * \{(s,s')| \ s=s' \wedge s\leqslant4\}$
$= \{(s,s')| \ \exists s'', (s>4 \wedge s''<s \vee s=s'') \wedge s''=s' \wedge s''\leqslant4\}$
$= \{(s,s')| \ \exists s'', s>4 \wedge s''<s \wedge s''=s' \wedge s''\leqslant4\}$
$\quad \cup \ \{(s,s')| \ \exists s'', s=s'' \wedge s''=s' \wedge s''\leqslant4\}$
$= \{(s,s')| \ s>4 \wedge s'\leqslant4\} \cup \{(s,s')| \ s=s' \wedge s'\leqslant4\}$.

It is left to the reader to verify that if some statement lb is correct wrt B (e.g. s:=s−1 or s:=s−2 or **if** even(s) **then** s:=s−1 **else** s:=s−3) then (**while** s>4 **do** lb) is correct wrt Sp. Relation R picks an element s greater than 4 and maps it into an element s′ less than or equal to 4. Relation G expresses that this can be done by iteratively decreasing the original value of s by leaps of 1, 2, 3 or 4.

The second specification is:

$$S = \{0,1,2,3,4,5,6\},$$
$$R = \{(6,0),(5,1),(4,0),(3,1),(2,0),(1,1),(0,0)\}.$$

We choose:

$$G = \{(6,4),(5,3),(4,2),(3,1),(2,0)\}.$$

We have:

$$G^+ = \{(6,4),(6,2),(6,0),(5,3),(5,1),(4,2),(4,0),(3,1),(2,0)\}.$$
$$G^+ \cup I$$
$$= \{(6,6),(6,4),(6,2),(6,0),$$
$$(5,5),(5,3),(5,1),$$
$$(4,4),(4,2),(4,0),$$
$$(3,3),(3,1),$$
$$(2,2),(2,0),$$
$$(1,1),$$
$$(0,0)\}.$$

Now,

$$(G^+ \cup I) * NT = \{(6,0),(5,1),(4,0),(3,1),(2,0),(1,1),(0,0)\},$$

which is precisely equal to R. Hence (S,G) is a valid specification for the loop body. Relation (function) R maps 0 to even numbers and 1 to odd numbers. Relation G expresses that this can be done by iteratively subtracting 2.

F. The Consequence Rule

Input:

$$Sp = (S,R).$$

Output:

$$Sp' = (S,R').$$

Conditions:

> a) **dom**$(R) \subset$ **dom**(R'),
> b) For any s in **dom**(R), (s,s'):$R' \Rightarrow (s,s')$:R.

PROPOSITION 6.

If st is correct wrt Sp' then it is correct wrt Sp.

Proof:

Let s be an element of **dom**(R). By condition (a), it is an element of **dom**(R'), whence, by correctness of st wrt Sp',

$$s:\textbf{dom}([st]) \wedge (s,[st](s)):R'.$$

Because of condition (b),

$$s:\textbf{dom}([st]) \wedge (s,[st](s)):R.$$

$$QED$$

Example 6: Sp = (S,R), where

$$S = \{a, b, c, d, e, f, g\},$$
$$R = \{(a,b), (a,c), (a,d), (b,c), (b,d), (b,e), (c,d), (c,e),$$
$$(c,f), (d,e), (d,f), (d,g)\}.$$

We choose Sp' = (S,R'), where

R' {(a,b), (a,c), (b,c), (b,d), (c,d), (c,e), (d,e), (d,f), (e,f), (e,g)}.

Clearly, conditions (a) and (b) are satisfied.

2 Discussions

System RD formalizes a design decision as the resolution of a relational equation, i.e. an equation involving relational operators, constant relations and variable (unknown) relations.

A relation can be arbitrarily non-deterministic (vague) in its assignment of correct outputs to legal inputs. The more non-deterministic a relation, the more choices the designer is given to pick a solution to the specification and the more optimal the design. Hence it is preferable that the designer propagate the non-determinacy of his relation through each design decision (i.e. through the application of each design rule). This means that instead of reading:

"Determine the object relations . . . under the conditions . . .",

the design rules should read:

"Maximize the non-determinacy of the object relations . . . under the conditions . . . ".

Of course, the current development in the algebra of relations does not afford a way to solve either system in any systematic way. This is the most serious weakness of system RD. The algebra of functions being more structured than the algebra of relations, system FD allows a more structured decision-making since the resolution of its functional equations can be divided into determining the domain of the function *then* its expression.

Like the two other systems, system RD fails to guide the designer in choosing what design rule must be applied at each step. The condition of feasibility of the Iteration Rule,

$$[:\mathbf{rng}(R),s]*R = [:\mathbf{rng}(R),s]$$

is a step in this direction. More such guidelines would be helpful.

To date, system RD has not been used in practical programming contexts.

3 Exercises

1. [A] Apply the Alternative Rule followed by the Assignment Rule to solve the following specification:

   S = {0, 1, 2, 3, 4, 5, 6, 7, 8},
   R = {(0,1), (0,2), (1,2), (1,3), (2,3), (2,4), (3,2), (3,5), (4,3), (4,2), (5,4), (5,3), (6,5), (6,4), (7,6), (7,5), (8,7), (8,6)}.

2. [B] We consider the specification Sp = (S,R), where

   S = {0, 1, 2, 3, 4, 5, 6, 7, 8},
   R = {(0,0), (0,1), (1,0), (1,1), (2,0), (3,1), (4,0), (5,1), (6,0), (7,1), (8,0)}

   a) Can you apply the Iteration Rule to Sp?
   b) Apply the Consequence Rule followed by the Iteration Rule.

3. [C] Give three solutions to the following specification. Show the sequence of your design rules.

   S = {0, 1, 2, 3, 4, 5, 6, 7, 8},
   R = {(0,0), (0,1), (1,0), (1,1), (2,1), (3,0), (4,1), (5,0), (6,1), (7,0), (8,1)}.

4. [B] Apply the Sequence Rule then the Assignment Rule to the following specification.

   S = natural,
   R = {(0,1), (0,2), (1,2), (1,3), (2,5), (2,6), (3,10), (3,11), (4,17), (4,18), (5,26), (5,27), (6,37), (6,38), (7,50), (7,51)}.

4 Problems

1. [B] Justify condition (b) of the Sequence Rule: Give an example where condition (a) only is verified and the resulting design step is not valid. Why doesn't this condition appear in the Sequence Rule of system FD?

2. [B] Consider the conditions of the Alternative Rule in systems RD and FD. Justify their differences.

3. [B] Consider the proof of Proposition 5. Show in detail why the assertion $S =$ **dom**(w) holds.

4. [B] Consider Remark 3 given under the Iteration Rule. Show that if R can be written as $(G^+ \cup ID) * NT$, then:

$$[:\mathbf{rng}(R),s]*R = [:\mathbf{rng}(R),s].$$

(Hint: Note that **dom**(G) = **dom**(G^+)).

5. [B] Consider the following I-relation on S = **integer**:

$$R = \{(s,s') \mid s' = s + 1\}.$$

Compute the transitive closure T of R. Intuitively, which one of T or R is simpler?

6. [B] Same question as 5, for:

$S = \{a,b,c,d,c,f,g\}$,
$R = \{(a,b),(a,c),(b,c),(b,d),(c,d),(c,e),(d,e),(d,f),(e,f),(e,g),(f,g),(f,a),(g,a),(g,b)\}$.

5 Bibliography

For more background on the algebra of relations, consult [3], [4] and [7]. The reader is referred to [1], [2], [5] and [6] for further study on program design with non-determinism and the use of relations in this study.

1: Dijkstra, E W. A Discipline of Programming. Prentice-Hall, 1976.
2: Livercy, C. Theorie des Programmes. Dunod (Paris), 1978.
3: Lyndon, R C. The Representation of Relational Algebra. Annals of Mathematics Vol 51 (1951), pp 705-729.
4: Lyndon, R C. The Representation of Relational Algebra, II. Annals of Mathematics Vol 63 (1956), pp 294-307.
5: Schmidt, G. Programs as Partial Graphs, I: Flow Equivalence and Correctness. Theoretical Computer Science Vol 15 (1981), pp 1-25.
6: Schmidt, G. Programs as Flow Graphs, II: Recursion. Theoretical Computer Science Vol 15 (1981), pp 159-179.
7: Tarski, A. On the Calculus of Relations. Journal of Symbolic Logic Vol 6 (1941), pp 73-89.

Part V: Appendices

Une Science a l'âge de ses instruments de mesure.

Louis Pasteur

The first appendix describes the syntax of SM-Pascal. Appendix B discusses *strongest invariant functions* of while statements and their usefulness in determining the functional abstraction of while statements. Appendix C investigates the *self-stabilizing effect of while statements,* i.e. their capability to smooth out damages done to their states.

Appendix A
The Syntax of SM-Pascal

The metasymbols of this BNF are: ::=, |, } and {. The braces denote possible repetitions of the enclosed symbols zero or more times. Non-terminal symbols are enclosed in angle brackets, ⟩ and ⟨.

⟨SM-Pascal program⟩ ::= ⟨program heading⟩ ⟨block⟩ .

⟨program heading⟩ ::= **program** ⟨identifier⟩ **(input, output)**;

⟨identifier⟩ ::= ⟨letter⟩ { ⟨letter or digit⟩}

⟨letter or digit⟩ ::= ⟨letter⟩ | ⟨digit⟩

⟨block⟩ ::= ⟨label declaration part⟩ |
        ⟨constant definition part⟩ |
        ⟨type definition part⟩ |
        ⟨variable declaration part⟩ |
        ⟨procedure and function declaration part⟩ |
        ⟨statement part⟩

⟨label declaration part⟩ ::= ⟨empty⟩ | **label** ⟨label⟩ {,⟨label⟩} ;

⟨label⟩ ::= ⟨unsigned integer⟩

⟨constant definition part⟩ ::= ⟨empty⟩ |
        const ⟨constant definition⟩ {; ⟨constant definition⟩} ;

⟨constant definition⟩ ::= ⟨identifier⟩ = ⟨constant⟩

⟨constant⟩ ::= ⟨unsigned number⟩ |
        ⟨sign⟩ ⟨unsigned number⟩ |
        ⟨constant identifier⟩ |
        ⟨sign⟩ ⟨constant identifier⟩ |
        ⟨string⟩

⟨unsigned number⟩ :: = ⟨unsigned integer⟩ | ⟨unsigned real⟩

⟨unsigned integer⟩ :: = ⟨digit⟩ { ⟨digit⟩ }

⟨unsigned real⟩ :: = ⟨unsigned integer⟩.⟨digit⟩{⟨digit⟩}|
                    ⟨unsigned integer⟩.⟨digit⟩{⟨digit⟩} E ⟨scale factor⟩ |
                    ⟨unsigned integer⟩ E ⟨scale factor⟩

⟨scale factor⟩ :: = ⟨unsigned integer⟩ |
                    ⟨sign⟩ ⟨unsigned integer⟩

⟨sign⟩ :: = + | −

⟨constant identifier⟩ :: = ⟨identifier⟩

⟨string⟩ :: = '⟨character⟩{⟨character⟩}'

⟨type definition part⟩ :: = ⟨empty⟩ |
                    type ⟨type definition⟩ {;⟨type definition⟩};

⟨type definition⟩ :: = ⟨identifier⟩ = ⟨type⟩

⟨type⟩ :: = ⟨simple type⟩ |
           ⟨structured type⟩ |
           ⟨pointer type⟩

⟨simple type⟩ :: = ⟨scalar type⟩ |
                  ⟨subrange type⟩ |
                  ⟨type identifier⟩

⟨scalar type⟩ :: = (⟨identifier⟩ {, ⟨identifier⟩})

⟨subrange type⟩ :: = ⟨constant⟩ .. ⟨constant⟩

⟨type identifier⟩ :: = ⟨identifier⟩

⟨structured type⟩ :: = ⟨array type⟩ |
                  ⟨set type⟩ |
                  ⟨collection type⟩ |
                  ⟨file type⟩

⟨array type⟩ :: = **array** [⟨index type⟩ {,⟨index type⟩}] **of** ⟨component type⟩

⟨index type⟩ ∷= ⟨simple type⟩

⟨component type⟩ ∷= ⟨type⟩

⟨set type⟩ ∷= **set** ⟨set body⟩ **end**

⟨set body⟩ ∷= ⟨cartesian product⟩ | ⟨subset of cartesian product⟩

⟨subset of cartesian product⟩ ∷= **crt** ⟨cartesian product⟩;
                         sub ⟨subset⟩

⟨cartesian product⟩ ∷= ⟨variable declaration⟩ {;⟨variable declaration⟩}

⟨subset⟩ ∷= ⟨expression⟩

⟨collection type⟩ ∷= **collection of** ⟨base type⟩

⟨base type⟩ ∷= ⟨simple type⟩

⟨file type⟩ ∷= **file of** ⟨type⟩

⟨pointer type⟩ ∷= ↑ ⟨type identifier⟩

⟨variable declaration part⟩ ∷= ⟨empty⟩ |
           var ⟨variable declaration⟩ {;⟨variable declaration⟩} ;

⟨variable declaration⟩ ∷= ⟨identifier⟩ {,⟨identifier⟩} : ⟨type⟩

⟨procedure and function declaration part⟩ ∷=
                {⟨procedure or function declaration⟩;}

⟨procedure or function declaration⟩ ∷=
         ⟨procedure declaration⟩ |
         ⟨function declaration⟩

⟨procedure declaration⟩ ∷= ⟨procedure heading⟩ ⟨block⟩

⟨procedure heading⟩ ∷= **procedure** ⟨identifier⟩ ; |
            procedure⟨identifier⟩
            (⟨formal parameter section⟩ {;⟨formal parameter section⟩});

⟨formal parameter section⟩ ∷= ⟨parameter group⟩ |
              var ⟨parameter group⟩

⟨parameter group⟩ ∷ = ⟨identifier⟩ {,⟨identifier⟩} :
⟨type identifier⟩

⟨function declaration⟩ ∷ = ⟨function heading⟩ ⟨block⟩

⟨function heading⟩ ∷ = **function** ⟨identifier⟩ : ⟨result type⟩ ; |
function⟨identifier⟩ (⟨formal parameter section⟩
{;⟨formal parameter section⟩}) : ⟨result type⟩;

⟨result type⟩ ∷ = ⟨type⟩

⟨statement part⟩ ∷ = **begin** ⟨statement⟩ **end**

⟨statement⟩ ∷ = ⟨unlabelled statement⟩ |
⟨label⟩ : ⟨unlabelled statement⟩

⟨unlabelled statement⟩ ∷ = ⟨simple statement⟩ |
⟨structured statement⟩

⟨simple statement⟩ ∷ = ⟨assignment statement⟩ |
⟨procedure statement⟩ |
⟨empty statement⟩

⟨assignment statement⟩ ∷ = ⟨variable⟩ : = ⟨expression⟩ |
⟨function identifier⟩ : = ⟨expression⟩

⟨variable⟩ ∷ = ⟨entire variable⟩ | ⟨component variable⟩ |
⟨referenced variable⟩

⟨entire variable⟩ : = ⟨variable identifier⟩

⟨variable identifier⟩ ∷ = ⟨identifier⟩

⟨component varible⟩ ∷ = ⟨indexed variable⟩ |
⟨elementary function designator⟩ |
⟨file buffer⟩

⟨indexed variable⟩ ∷ = ⟨array variable⟩ [⟨expression⟩ {,⟨expression⟩}]

⟨array variable⟩ ∷ = ⟨variable⟩

⟨elementary function designator⟩ ∷ =
⟨set variable⟩ . ⟨elementary function identifier⟩

⟨set variable⟩ ::= ⟨variable⟩

⟨elementary function identifier⟩ ::= ⟨identifier⟩

⟨file buffer⟩ ::= ⟨file variable⟩ ^

⟨file variable⟩ ::= ⟨variable⟩

⟨referenced variable⟩ ::= ⟨pointer variable⟩ ^

⟨pointer variable⟩ ::= ⟨variable⟩

⟨expression ⟩ ::= ⟨simple expression⟩ |
        ⟨simple expression⟩ ⟨relational operator⟩ ⟨simple expression⟩

⟨relational operator⟩ ::= = | ≠ | < | > | ≤ | ≥ | **in**

⟨simple expression⟩ ::= ⟨term⟩ | ⟨sign⟩ ⟨term⟩ |
        ⟨simple expression⟩ ⟨adding operator⟩ ⟨term⟩

⟨adding operator⟩ ::= + | − | **or**

⟨term⟩ ::= ⟨factor⟩ | ⟨term⟩ ⟨multiplying operator⟩ ⟨factor⟩

⟨multiplying operator⟩ ::= * | / | **div** | **mod** | **and**

⟨factor⟩ ::= ⟨variable⟩ | ⟨unsigned constant⟩ |
      (⟨expression⟩) | ⟨function designator⟩ | ⟨collection⟩ |
      not ⟨factor⟩

⟨unsigned constant⟩ ::= ⟨unsigned number⟩ | ⟨string⟩ |
        ⟨constant identifier⟩ | **nil**

⟨function designator⟩ ::= ⟨function identifier⟩ |
      ⟨function identifier⟩ (⟨actual parameter⟩ {,⟨actual parameter⟩})

⟨function identifier⟩ ::= ⟨identifier⟩

⟨collection⟩ ::= [⟨element list⟩]

⟨element list⟩ ::= ⟨element⟩ { , ⟨element⟩ } |
        ⟨empty⟩

⟨element⟩ ::= ⟨expression⟩ |
              ⟨expression⟩ .. ⟨expression⟩

⟨procedure statement⟩ ::= ⟨procedure identifier⟩ |
        ⟨procedure identifier⟩ (⟨actual parameter⟩ {,⟨actual parameter⟩})

⟨procedure identifier⟩ ::= ⟨identifier⟩

⟨actual parameter⟩ ::= ⟨expression⟩ | ⟨variable⟩

⟨empty statement⟩ ::= ⟨empty⟩

⟨empty⟩ ::=

⟨structured statement⟩ ::= ⟨begin-end statement⟩ |
                           ⟨sequence statement⟩ |
                           ⟨conditional statement⟩ | ⟨alternative statement⟩ |
                           ⟨while statement⟩ | ⟨with statement⟩

⟨begin-end statement⟩ ::= **begin** ⟨statement⟩ **end**

⟨sequence statement⟩ ::= ⟨statement⟩ {; ⟨statement⟩}

⟨conditional statement⟩ ::= **if** ⟨expression⟩ **then** ⟨statement⟩

⟨alternative statement⟩ ::= **if** ⟨expression⟩ **then** ⟨statement⟩
                                       else ⟨statement⟩

⟨while statement⟩ ::= **while** ⟨expression⟩ **do** ⟨statement⟩

⟨with statement⟩ ::= **with** ⟨set variable list⟩ **do** ⟨statement⟩

⟨set variable list⟩ ::= ⟨set variable⟩ {,⟨set variable⟩}

This BNF description is based on *Pascal User Manual and Report,* by Jensen and Wirth (Springer-Verlag, 1974).

Appendix B
Strongest Invariant Functions

In Chapter 7 we introduced an object which is quite important in the study of while statements: the loop invariant. In this appendix we introduce another object which serves as a useful tool in this study: the *strongest invariant function*.

1 Preliminary Definitions

Let w = (**while** t **do** lb) be a while statement on space S. We assume that **dom**(w) = S, i.e. w terminates for any initial state in S. Proposition 2 of Chapter 9 explains why this hypothesis does not affect the generality of our study. Also, we assume that **dom**(lb) = S.

DEFINITION 1. An *invariant function* of w = (**while** t **do** lb) is an I-function on S whose domain is S and such that:

$$t(s) \implies f(s) = f([lb](s)).$$

An equivalent characterization of invariant functions is

$$[t,s]*f = [t,s]*[lb]*f.$$

Finding an invariant function for a while statement is not interesting per se: A constant function on S is an invariant function for any while statement on S!

DEFINITION 2. Let f and f' be two functions on S such that **dom**(f) = **dom**(f'). We say that f is *stronger than* f' iff

$$f(s) = f(s') \implies f'(s) = f'(s').$$

An equivalent characterization of *f is stronger than f* is:

$$f'(s) \neq f'(s') \implies f(s) \neq f(s').$$

The identity function (or any invertible function whose domain is S) is stronger than any function on S; any function on S is stronger than any constant function. The relation *stronger than* on the set of functions on S is reflexive and transitive. The example below shows that this relation is not symmetric.

EXAMPLE 1.

$$S = \{a,b,c\}; f = \{(a,c), (b,c), (c,a)\};$$
$$f' = \{(a,a), (b,a), (c,c)\}.$$

Clearly, f is stronger than f' and f' is stronger than f; yet, they are not equal.

We shall admit without proof, however, that when f is stronger than f' and f' is stronger than f, there exists an invertible function k from **rng**(f) to **rng**(f') such that

$$f*k = f'.$$

We then say that f and f' are *equally strong* (see problem 1).

More interesting than the determination of just any invariant function is the determination of an invariant function that is stronger than all other invariant functions.

DEFINITION 3. Function f on S is said to be a *strongest invariant function* for while statement w iff:

a) f is an invariant function for w,
b) if f' is an invariant function for w then [t,s]* f is stronger than [t,s]* f'.

Notice that a while statement may have more than one strongest invariant function; if f is a strongest invariant function for w and k is an invertible function from **rng**(f) to some subset of S then f*k is also a strongest invariant function for w.

2 Generation of Strongest Invariant Functions

In this section we will derive formulas for the automatic generation of strongest invariant functions from a systematic analysis of the parameters of the while statement at hand: its space (S), its condition (t) and its loop body (lb). All of the cases studied in this section involve the group properties of **real** (namely: addition and multiplication) and its homomorphisms (log and exp). Hence these formulas can conceivably be generalized to spaces which have isomorphic group structures.

All the strongest invariant functions derived in this section will have their domain equal to S, the space of the while statement; hence their pE-formulas have the form [**true**,E]. For the sake of simplicity, we shall represent these I-functions by their expression only.

2.1 Adding a Constant

S = **real**; t = (s<a), where a is some real constant; lb = (s: = s+c), where c is some positive constant. Clearly, **dom**(lb) = S and if w = (**while** t **do** lb) then **dom**(w) = S.

PROPOSITION 1. Function Fr(s/c) is a strongest invariant function for w, where Fr(x) is the fractional part of x.

Proof. It is quite simple to prove that Fr(s/c) is an invariant function for w. We prove that it is also the strongest invariant function. Let f′ be an invariant function of w, whence f′(s) = f′(s+c) if s<a. Let s and s′ be two elements of S less than a, such that Fr(s/c) = Fr(s′/c); then

$$s/c = s'/c + k$$
$$\Rightarrow s = s' + k*c,$$
$$\text{for some integer k.}$$

Because f′ is an invariant function for w, we deduce that f′(s) = f′(s′).

QED

2.2 Multiplying by a Constant

S = positive real numbers; t = (s<a), for some positive constant; lb = (s: = *l**s), for some constant *l* greater than 1. Clearly, **dom**(lb) = S and if w = (**while** t **do** lb) then **dom**(w) = S.

PROPOSITION 2. fl(s) = Fr(log(s)/log(*l*)) is a strongest invariant function for w.

2.3 Raising to some power

S = real numbers greater than 1; t = (s<a), for some positive constant a; lb = (s: = s**p), for some constant p greater than 1. Clearly, **dom**(lb) and **dom**(w) are both equal to S.

PROPOSITION 3. fp(s) = Fr(log(log(s)) / log(p)) is a strongest invariant function for w.

2.4 Linear Form

S = positive real numbers; t = (s<a), for some positive constant a; lb = (s:= l*s+c), for some positive constant c and some constant l greater than 1. Clearly, **dom**(lb)=S; it is left to the reader to prove that if c⩾0 and l>1 then:

$$w = (\textbf{while } s<a \textbf{ do } s:=l\text{*}s+c)$$

terminates for any initial state s in S, whence one can deduce **dom**(w)=S.

PROPOSITION 4. f(s) = Fr(log(s+c/(l−1)) / log(l)) is a strongest invariant function for w.

EXAMPLE 2. We consider the while statement:

$$w = (\textbf{while } s<120 \textbf{ do } s:=2\text{*}s+1).$$

We use the base 2 logarithms. The proposition provides that

$$f(s) = Fr(log(s+1))$$

is a strongest invariant function. We content ourselves with verifying that it is an invariant function.

$$
\begin{aligned}
&Fr(log(2\text{*}s+1+1))\\
&= Fr(log(2\text{*}(s+1)))\\
&= Fr(1+log(s+1))\\
&= Fr(log(s+1)).
\end{aligned}
$$

2.5 Monomial Form

S = real numbers greater than 1; t = (s<a), for some constant a; lb = (s:= l*s**p), where l and p are greater than 1. Clearly, **dom**(lb)=S; also one may verify that **dom**(w)=S.

PROPOSITION 5. f(s) = Fr(log(log(s)+log(l)/(p−1)) / log(p)) is a strongest invariant function for w.

EXAMPLE 3. We take p=2 and l=4 and we use base 2 logarithms. Hence

$$f(s) = Fr(log(log(s)+2)).$$

We shall only prove that f is an invariant function.

$$f([lb](s))$$
$$= Fr(\log(\log(4*s**2)+2))$$
$$= Fr(\log(\log(s**2)+4))$$
$$= Fr(\log(2*(\log(s)+2)))$$
$$= Fr(1+\log(\log(s)+2))$$
$$= Fr(\log(\log(s)+2))$$
$$= f(s).$$

2.6 Linear Diagonal

We now consider higher cartesian powers of the set **real**. More precisely, S is the set of n-tuples of positive real numbers; $t = (s_1 < a)$, for some constant a;

$$lb =$$
begin
$$s_1 := l_1 * s_1 ;$$
$$s_2 := l_2 * s_2 ;$$
$$\ldots \quad \ldots \quad \ldots$$
$$s_k := l_k * s_k$$
end,

where $l_1, l_2, \ldots l_k$ are constants greater than 1. We do have **dom**(lb) = S and **dom**(w) = S.

PROPOSITION 6. Function f defined by

$$f((s_1, s_2, \ldots s_k))$$
$$= (\ Fr(\ \log(s_1) / \log(l_1)\ )\ ,$$
$$s_1**\log(l_2) / s_2**\log(l_1)\ ,$$
$$s_2**\log(l_3) / s_3**\log(l_2)\ ,$$
$$\ldots \quad \ldots \quad \ldots$$
$$s_{k-1} ** \log(l_k) / s_k ** \log(l_{k-1})\ )$$

is a strongest invariant function for w = (**while** t **do** lb).

One must notice that statements of the form:

$$s_i := s_i + c_i ,$$
$$s_i := s_i ** p_i ,$$
$$s_i := l_i * s_i ** p_i ,$$
$$s_i := l_i * s_i + c_i$$

are all amenable to the form

$$s_i := l_i * s_i$$

by a proper change of variables. Hence the formula of Proposition 6 is actually more general than it seems.

EXAMPLE 4. We take lb =

```
begin
s1 := 2*s1;
s2 := 4*s2
end.
```

The strongest invariant function is

$$f((s1,s2)) = (Fr(\log(s1)), s1**2/s2).$$

We leave it to the reader to verify that f is an invariant function.

2.7 Linear Diagonalizable Forms

If the loop body of the while statement can be written as

$$s := L * s,$$

where $s = (s_1, s_2, \ldots s_k)$ and L is diagonalizable and its eigenvalues are greater than 1, then one may perform the change of variable

$$x = M * s,$$

where M is the diagonalization matrix and apply Proposition 6 to the program derived by the change of variable.

3 Use of Strongest Invariant Functions

3.1 Strongest Invariant Functions and Loop Invariants

Strongest invariant functions can be used to derive loop invariants.

PROPOSITION 7. If f is an invariant function for w and s0 is some element of **dom**(f) then

$$f(s) = f(s0)$$

is a loop invariant for w.

Proof.

$$f(s) = f(s0) \ \wedge \ t(s) \ \Rightarrow f(s) = f(s0) \ \wedge \ s:\textbf{dom}(lb)$$
$$\Rightarrow f(s) = f(s0) \ \wedge \ f(s) = f([lb](s))$$
$$\Rightarrow f([lb](s)) = f(s0).$$

Using the IA notation (see Chapter 7), one can write the assertion:

$$f(s) = f(s0) \ \wedge \ t(s) \ \Rightarrow f([lb](s)) = f(s0)$$

as

$$f(s) = f(s0) \ \wedge \ t(s) \ \{lb\} \ f(s) = f(s0).$$

QED.

Of particular interest is the loop invariant derived from the strongest invariant function (see problem 8). A clear distinction must be made between a loop invariant and an invariant function which happens to be a predicate: See problem 9.

3.2 Strongest Invariant Functions and Functional Abstraction

We consider the while statement $w = (\textbf{while} \ t \ \textbf{do} \ lb)$ on space S such that $S = \textbf{dom}(lb) = \textbf{dom}(w)$. Invariant functions are characterized by:

$$[t,s]*f \ = \ [t,s]*[lb]*f.$$

Now, Theorem 1 and Remark 2 of Chapter 5 together provide that [w], the functional abstraction of w, satisfies the equation above; hence [w] is an invariant function for w. Is it a strongest invariant function?

PROPOSITION 8 (Due to Jules Desharnais, Laval University). The functional abstraction of a while statement is its own strongest invariant function.

Proof. Let f′ be an invariant function of w. We wish to show that [w] is stronger than f′.

$$[w](s) = [w](s')$$
$$\Rightarrow (\ \exists \ m,n \ in \ \textbf{natural}, \ ([lb]**m)(s) = ([lb]**n)(s'))$$
$$\Rightarrow (\ \exists \ m,n \ in \ \textbf{natural}, \ f'(([lb]**m)(s)) \ = \ f'((([lb]**n)(s')).$$

Because f' is an invariant function of w, we can decrement the exponents m and n progressively until both become zero, yielding:

$$(\ \exists \ m,n \ in \ \textbf{natural}, \ f'(s) = f'(s')),$$

which is equivalent to $f'(s) = f'(s')$ since m and n no longer appear.

QED

REMARK 1. Proposition 8 ensures the existence of the strongest invariant function.

This proposition is of prime importance. It provides that once we have found a strongest invariant function f of a while statement w, we are only one invertible function away from [w]! (i.e [w] = f*k or f = [w]*k, for some invertible function k). In particular, we know how the equivalence relation

$$Rw \ = \ \{(s,s') | \ [w](s) = [w](s')\}$$

partitions $S | t$; i.e. we know what elements of $S | t$ have the same image by [w]. Indeed, because [w] and f are equally strong, the restrictions to $S | t$ of relations Rw, defined above, and Rf, defined as follows:

$$Rf \ = \ \{(s,s') | \ f(s) = f(s')\}$$

are identical.

Let's consider the intersection of an equivalence class modulo Rf with $S | t$. We know that all the elements of this intersection have the same image by [w]. What is this image? Let s'' be an element of this intersection such that $[lb](s''):S | \ ̃t$. Then $[lb](s'')$ is precisely this common image.

PROPOSITION 9. Let f be a strongest invariant function of a while statement w; then

$$W \ = \ \{(s,s') | \ ̃t(s) \ \land \ s = s'\}$$
$$\cup$$
$$\{(s,s') | \ t(s) \ \land \ f(s) = f(s') \ \land \ ̃t(s') \ \land \ (\ \exists s'', \ t(s'') \ \land \ s' = [lb](s''))\}$$

is the functional abstraction of w, i.e. $W = [w]$.

Proof. The discussions above constitute an informal proof. For a formal proof, one may use Theorem 1 and Remark 2 of Chapter 5, and prove the three following premises about W.

$$p0: \ [̃t,s]*W \ = \ [̃t,s],$$

$$\text{p1: } [t,s]*W = [t,s]*[lb]*W,$$
$$\text{p2: } \textbf{dom}(W) = \textbf{dom}(w).$$

Note that clauses p0 and p2 are very straightforward.

Clause p0 stems from the definition of W. Clause p2 stems from the hypothesis $\textbf{dom}(w) = S$ and the definition of W.

QED

EXAMPLE 5. $S = \textbf{integer}$; $t = (s < 21)$; $lb = (s: = s+5)$. We do have $\textbf{dom}(lb) = S$ and $\textbf{dom}(w) = S$. The strongest invariant function of w is

$$Fr(s/5)$$

which we can also write $(s \bmod 5)$. Proposition 9 provides

$$
\begin{aligned}
[w] &= \{(s,s') \mid s \geqslant 21 \ \wedge \ s = s'\} \\
&\quad \cup \\
&\quad \{(s,s') \mid s < 21 \ \wedge \ s \bmod 5 = s' \bmod 5 \ \wedge \ s' \geqslant 21 \\
&\qquad\qquad \wedge \ (\exists s'', s'' < 21 \ \wedge \ s' = s'' + 5)\} \\
&= \{(s,s') \mid s \geqslant 21 \ \wedge \ s = s'\} \\
&\quad \cup \\
&\quad \{(s,s') \mid s < 21 \ \wedge \ s \bmod 5 = s' \bmod 5 \ \wedge \ 21 \leqslant s' \leqslant 26\}.
\end{aligned}
$$

4 Exercises

1. [A] Determine the domain of the following while statements (where s is a positive real variable) then find a strongest invariant function for them.
   a) **while** $s < 100$ **do begin** $s: = 2*s$ **end**.
   b) **while** $s < 110$ **do begin** $s: = s**4$ **end**.
   c) **while** $s < 120$ **do begin** $s: = 2*s + 8$ **end**.
   d) **while** $s < 100$ **do begin** $s: = 16*s**4$ **end**.

2. [B] Same as exercise 1, the space being a subset of $real \times \times 2$.
   a) **while** $s1 < 100$ **do begin** $s1: = 2*s1$; $s2: = 2*s2$ **end**.
   b) **while** $s1 < 110$ **do begin** $s1: = 2*s1$; $s2: = 8*s2$ **end**.
   c) **while** $s2 < 120$ **do begin** $s1: = 3*s1$; $s2: = 27*s2$ **end**.
   d) **while** $s1 < s2$ **do begin** $s1: = 9*s1$ **end**

3. [C] Consider the two while statements on the real variables s1 and s2:

$$w = \textbf{while } s1 < 100 \textbf{ do begin } s1: = 2*s1; s2: = 4*s2 \textbf{ end}.$$
$$w' = \textbf{while } s1 < 140 \textbf{ do begin } s1: = 4*s1; s2: = 16*s2 \textbf{ end}.$$

a) Determine the domains of w and w.'
b) Find the strongest invariant function of w.
c) Find the strongest invariant function of w'.
d) Find the strongest function which is an invariant function for both w and w'.
e) Conclude.

4. [B] Consider the following while statement:

$$w = \textbf{while } s2 \geqslant 0 \textbf{ do begin } s1:=s1+3; \ s2:=s2-1 \textbf{ end},$$

where s1 and s2 are integer variables.
a) Determine the domain of w.
b) Determine a strongest invariant function of w.
c) Deduce the functional abstraction of w.

5. [B] Same as exercise 4, for the following statement:

$$w = \textbf{while } s2 \geqslant 6 \textbf{ do begin } s1:=s1+1; \ s2:=s2-6 \textbf{ end}.$$

5 Problems

1. [B] Prove that if functions f and f' are equally strong then there exists an invertible function k such that f*k=f'. (Hint: Prove that if f is stronger than f' then there exists a function h such that f'=f*h).

2. [A] Prove Proposition 2. (Hint: Make the change of variables $x=\log(s)$, $c=\log(1)$).

3. [B] Prove Proposition 3. (Hint: Make the change of variables $x=\log(s)$, $l=\log(p)$).

4. [B] Prove Proposition 4. (Hint: Make the change of variables $x=s-c/(l-1)$).

5. [B] Prove Proposition 5. (Hint: Make the change of variable $x=\log(s)$).

6. [B] Prove Proposition 6. (Hint: Use Definitions 1, 2 and 3).

7. [C] Proposition 7 provides that from any invariant function one can derive a loop invariant. Can one say that any loop invariant can be derived from an invariant function?

8. [C] What can you say of the loop invariant derived from a strongest invariant function? (First hint: Before you answer, consider that **false** is a loop invariant for any while statement; second hint: Use Proposition 8).

9. [B] Let w = (**while** t **do** lb) be a while statement on space S = **boolean**. An invariant function f of w is characterized by

$$t(s) \Rightarrow f(s) = f([lb](s)).$$

A loop invariant p of w is characterized by

$$t(s) \wedge p(s) \wedge s{:}\mathbf{dom}([lb]) \Rightarrow p([lb](s)).$$

a) Prove that any invariant function is a loop invariant.
b) Prove that a loop invariant may fail to be an invariant function.
c) Assuming the ordering {(**false,true**), (**false,false**), (**true,true**)} on set **boolean**, explain why the name *increasng predicate* is more appropriate to describe loop invariants.

10. [B] Discuss the mathematics of changing variables (for the purpose of finding more strongest invariant functions).

11. [B] Prove that if f is stronger than f' and f is the strongest invariant function for statement w then f' is an invariant function for w.

Appendix C

The Self-Stabilizing Effect of While Statements

In this appendix we shed some light on one more aspect of while statements: their capability to smooth out damages done to their state.

1 Basic Configuration

Let F be an I-function on set S such that **dom**(F) = S and let w = (**while** t **do** lb) be a while statement on S. We assume that there exists a subset D of S such that

$$s{:}D \Rightarrow F(s) = [w](s), \qquad (0)$$

i.e. w computes function F over set D. We want to use w to compute function F over all of set S. We assume that there exists a SM-Pascal statement i (initialization) such that

$$\begin{align}
&\textbf{dom}([i]) = S, &(1)\\
&\textbf{rng}([i]) \subseteq D, &(2)\\
&F(s) = F([i](s)). &(3)
\end{align}$$

From equations (1), (2) and (3), it stems that

$$F = [i; \textbf{while } t \textbf{ do } lb].$$

EXAMPLE 1. We define the set S as:

$$\begin{align}
&S = \textbf{set}\\
&\textbf{crt}\\
&\quad a{:} \textbf{ array } [1..n] \textbf{ of real};\\
&\quad k{:} \textbf{ integer};\\
&\textbf{sub}\\
&\quad k \geqslant 1 \wedge k \leqslant n+1\\
&\textbf{end},
\end{align}$$

for some positive integer n. We define over S the I-function F by

$$F = [\textbf{true}, (std(a(s)),n+1)],$$

where std(a′) is the sorted permutation of array a′.

Let w be the while statement

while k≤n **do** insert,

where the loop body (insert) inserts a(s)[k(s)] in its proper place among a(s)[1] , a(s)[2] , . . . a(s)[k(s)] then increments k(s).

We define D as

```
D = set
crt
   a: array [1..n] of real;
   k: integer;
sub
   k≥1 ∧ k≤n+1 ∧ a[1]≤a[2]≤ ... ≤ a[k−1]
end.
```

Clearly, D is a subset of S; we leave it to the reader to verify that

$$s{:}D \Rightarrow F(s) = [w](s).$$

Let i be the statement

$$i = (k{:}=2).$$

It is left to the reader to verify that statement i satisfies all three equations (1), (2) and (3).

2 Defining Levels of Correctness

We consider the statement

f = **begin** i; L: **while** t **do** lb **end**,

where L is a label. We take the convention that label L is reached by the control of the program after each execution of lb, right before the test for t is executed (if we had wanted a label before the whole while statement, we would have written L:; **while** t **do** lb).

We consider the state of the program at label L after k iterations of lb; we wish to characterize the different levels of correctness (or, conversely, contamination) that this state can be in. It must be noted that the causes of errors that we consider in this study are those due to the supporting system on which statement f is executed: the SM-Pascal compiler, the underlying operating system, the hardware, etc . . . The correctness of statement f wrt function F is not questioned; this hypothesis is simplistic, but is nevertheless taken because it simplifies our discussions. How the errors of the supporting system are detected and how they are corrected are questions beyond the scope of this study. The context of our discussions is the following: upon the occurrence of an error, the cause of the error is diagnosed and removed and an error recovery routine is invoked and passed the current state which is potentially contaminated. If the contamination is not too extensive (to be defined later), the recovery routine is responsible for generating a correct state from the current contaminated state and returning the control to the program.

DEFINITION 1. State s at label L after k iterations is said to be *s-correct* (strictly correct) vis-a-vis the initial state s0 iff

$$s = ([lb]**k)(s0).$$

After k iterations, there exists only one s-correct state vis-a-vis s0: that obtained from s0 by k applications of lb . Inasmuch as the ultimate measure of success of a given execution of f is whether the execution has produced F(s0) upon termination, we must relax this definition of correctness.

DEFINITION 2. State s at label L after k iterations is said to be *l-correct* (loosely correct) vis-a-vis s0 iff

$$[w](s) = F(s0).$$

After k iterations, a state may fail to be s-correct, yet still be l-correct: Provided that continuation of execution will lead to the expected final result, no intervention is needed and the state may be considered loosely correct. Notice that the formula of l-correctness is independent of k: Hence we shall talk of l-correctness at label L. There may be, and generally is, many l-correct states at label L since [w] may be a many-to-one function.

DEFINITION 3. State s at label L after k iterations is said to be *recoverable* vis-a-vis s0 iff there exists a SM-Pascal statement r (recovery routine) such that:

$$[r]*[w](s) = F(s0).$$

Of course, statement r does not depend on s0 or s; it depends solely on F, D and w.

After k iterations, a state s may fail to be l-correct, yet be such that if we apply [r] to it we get a l-correct state. Notice here again that k does not appear in the formula of recoverability, hence we will talk about a state being recoverable at label L (without mention of k).

It is left to the reader to verify that if a state is s-correct then it is l-correct and if it is l-correct then it is recoverable.

DEFINITION 4. State s is said to be *unrecoverable* at label L iff it is not recoverable at label L.

3 Characterizing Levels of Correctness

In this section we use the formalism introduced in section 1 in order to give a workable characterization of the notions of l-correctness and recoverability, and, in the latter case we give specifications for the recovery routine.

PROPOSITION 1. State s is l-correct at label L vis-a-vis s0 if

$$s:D \ \wedge \ F(s) = F(s0).$$

Proof. If s:D then $F(s) = [w](s)$, by virtue of equation (0). We deduce

$$[w](s) = F(s0),$$

which is the result sought.

$$\text{QED}$$

This result is confirmed by a theorem given in [1] which proposes that

$$s:D \ \wedge \ F(s) = F(s0)$$

is a loop invariant for w.

PROPOSITION 2. State s is recoverable at label L vis-a-vis s0 if

$$F(s) = F(s0).$$

Proof. We must prove the existence of a statement r such that

$$[r]^*[w](s) \ = \ F(s0).$$

We consider statement i (introduced in section 1); by equations (1), (2) and (3), we have

$$[i]*[w](s) = F(s);$$

by hypothesis, we have

$$F(s) = F(s0); \text{ hence } [i]*[w](s) = F(s0).$$

QED

Some comments are in order here.

REMARK 1. Statement i is used to prove Proposition 2. The proof shows that i is a possible recovery routine; there are others (see Example 2).

REMARK 2. We assume that i is chosen as the recovery routine; this does *not* mean that the program is reset to its initial state when procedure i is called: the initial state is [i](s0) whereas the recovered state is [i](s), where s is the contaminated (but recoverable) state. See Example 2.

REMARK 3. Notice that if s is recoverable then [r](s) is l-correct: [r](s):D because **rng**([r]) ⊆ D and F([r](s)) = F(s0) because of equation (3).

REMARK 4. Predicate s:D is said to carry the *non-critical information* of the state at label L. This predicate may fail to hold without threatening the survival of the computation. Predicate F(s) = F(s0) is said to carry the *critical information* of the state at label L. This predicate is critical to the survival of the computation.

We now attempt to characterize recovery routines.

PROPOSITION 4. If statement r verifies the following equations

$$\mathbf{dom}([r]) = S,$$
$$\mathbf{rng}([r]) \subseteq D,$$
$$F(s) = F([r](s)),$$

then r is a possible recovery routine.

Proof. The proof is very similar to that of Proposition 2.

It is noteworthy that the initialization statement i, and the recovery routine r, are subject to the same equations. For a given program, they may be chosen

identical or distinct. The reasons for choosing them distinct is that their invo-
cation patterns may be very different (i is invoked every time f is invoked
whereas r is invoked upon occurrence of an error), hence they are subject to
different performance requirements.

EXAMPLE 2. We continue the study of the program introduced in example 1.
Proposition 1 provides that state s is l-correct vis-a-vis s0 if

$$s:D \ \wedge \ std(a(s)) = std(a(s0)) \ \wedge \ n+1 = n+1.$$

The first conjunct is equivalent to

$$a(s)[1] \leqslant a(s)[2] \leqslant \ ... \ \leqslant a(s)[k(s)-1].$$

We abbreviate this by the predicate:

$$psd(s),$$

to stand for: a(s) is partially sorted.

The second conjunct means: If we sort a(s) we find the same array as if we
sort a(s0). We abbreviate this by the predicate:

$$perm(s0,s)$$

to stand for: a(s) is a permutation of a(s0).

As for the third conjunct, it is **true** and can be deleted. Hence we are left with

$$psd(s) \ \wedge \ perm(s0,s).$$

Many states may fail to be s-correct, yet are still l-correct: After iteration 6, k
has been inadvertently set to 4 instead of 8; after iteration 6, k has been inadvertently set to 9 instead of 8 but a[8] happens to be greater than a[7]; during
iteration 6, a[10] and a[16] have been inadvertently swapped.

State s is recoverable vis-a-vis s0 if

$$perm(s0,s).$$

As long as a(s) remains a permutation of a(s0), there is hope that a l-correct
state can be generated: One can apply statement i (setting k to 2); notice that
invoking statement i would set k to its initial value (2) but would not set array

a to its initial value (which is not known anyway): Hence procedure i does not reinitialize the program. Alternatively, one can, e.g., set k to the largest value such that psd(s) holds and return the control back to the loop. Examples of recoverable states that are not necessarily l-correct: any value of k, any rearrangement of the cells of a, etc . . .

4 Exercises

1. [B] Following the pattern of Examples 1 and 2, discuss the recovery of the following statements.

$$S = \textbf{set}$$
$$\quad n, f, k: \textbf{natural}$$
$$\textbf{end},$$
$$Fc = [\textbf{true}, (n(s),n(s)!,n(s))],$$
$$w = \textbf{while } k<n \textbf{ do begin } k:=k+1; \ f:=f*k \ \textbf{end}.$$

2. [B] Same as 1.

$$S = \textbf{set}$$
$$\quad n, f: \textbf{natural}$$
$$\textbf{end},$$
$$Ft = [\textbf{true}, (0,n(s)!)],$$
$$w = \textbf{while } n>0 \textbf{ do begin } f:=f*n; \ n:=n-1 \ \textbf{end}.$$

3. [C] Following the pattern of Examples 1 and 2, design a linear search program and discuss its recovery.

5 Problems

1. [C] Consider a statement of the form

$$f = \textbf{begin } st1; \ L: st2 \ \textbf{end},$$

on some space S.
a) Characterize the different levels of correctness at label L.
b) Characterize recovery routines at label L.

6 Bibliography

1: Basu, K S and J Misra. Proving Loop Programs. IEEE-TSE 1(1) (March 1975), pp 76-86.

Index